Wrong Side of the Wall

The Life of Blackie Schwamb,
the Greatest Prison Baseball Player of All Time

Eric Stone

THE LYONS PRESS
Guilford, Connecticut
An imprint of The Globe Pequot Press

This book is dedicated to my mother, Elaine Stone. She
gave me the gift of curiosity about, and love for, the stories and
history of our hometown, Los Angeles, taught me to
love literature, and encouraged me to experience life in
a way that informs and stimulates my writing.

....

And also to my uncle, Fred Stone. Not only did he
introduce me to the story of Blackie Schwamb, but
his own story is an inspiration to those of us who are
crazy enough to pursue our dreams.

....

The Lyons Press is an imprint of The Globe Pequot Press.

10 9 8 7 6 5 4 3 2 1

Printed in the United States of America

Designed by Kirsten Livingston

ISBN 1-59228-439-6

Library of Congress Cataloging-in-Publication Data is available on file.

INTRODUCTION

BLACKIE SCHWAMB WOULDN'T TALK TO ME unless I showed up with a carton of unfiltered Pall Malls and at least a quart of Kessler. I threw in a case of Lucky Lager for good measure.

"I was a celebrity because in those days both San Quentin and Folsom had baseball. It was headlines. I was the first major league ballplayer to ever be convicted of murder and sentenced to life in prison. So when I got there, nothin' was too good [for me]."

I stopped for the supplies at a liquor store just off the Avenue L exit in Lancaster, in the high scrub desert at the northeast corner of Los Angeles County. It was a hellishly hot clear August day. Santa Ana winds, unseasonably early, were kicking up dust and pushing the smog out to sea. I was a freelance journalist on the prowl for a good story and I was nervous about the meeting. I'd first heard about Blackie Schwamb because my uncle Fred had recurring nightmares that featured him.

Growing up in Los Angeles in the 1940s, my father's younger brother had been a hotshot pitcher for both his high school and semipro baseball teams. Baseball was everything to him and my father. Then his world caved in. He injured his arm. The last game he ever pitched was against the scary, temperamental, flamethrowing Schwamb. He heard later that Blackie had been a gangster, as well as a major-league ballplayer, spent a lot of time in nightclubs and seedy bars, had killed a doctor, and gone on to become the greatest prison baseball player of all time.

Like my parents and uncle, I also grew up in Los Angeles. My father talked baseball, constantly. The Brooklyn Dodgers moved to L.A. when I was five. It was as if the skies had opened up, the clouds had parted, and sunny Southern California shone like never before. I had started tossing a ball around and fantasizing about being a baseball player from around the age of four.

At the same time my mother would load my sister and me into the car and we'd go for drives. The history of the city fascinated her and she'd take us around town, pointing out the sites, telling tales.

I was raised by both my parents on stories of the sprawling city that came into its own after the Second World War. The stories I liked best were of baseball and crime and the ebb and flow of life in the city's neighborhoods. I became a voracious reader and my books of choice often as not fell into one of three categories: baseball, crime, and history. I didn't know much about his life before I met him, but I had a hunch that Blackie Schwamb's story embodied all of that.

It was 1985 by the time I drove out to Lancaster to talk with the jailbird pitcher; thirty-nine years since my uncle had pitched his last game, twenty-five years since Blackie had got out of prison and tried to make a comeback. It had been surprisingly easy to find him.

A baseball encyclopedia gave me his full name. A friend who worked in the California Department of Motor Vehicles forwarded a letter from me to the address of the only Ralph Richard Schwamb with a California driver's license. He'd written back with a phone number on a piece of paper that looked like it had been torn off the bottom of a government form: "Yes, you have the right Ralph Schwamb. Give me a call. I'm home all day, disabled."

His voice on the phone was so deep and gravelly that I could barely understand it. He got mad when I asked him to repeat the directions to where he lived but calmed down quickly enough when I assured him I'd bring what he wanted.

He lived with a woman and her daughter in a dull green, metal-slab-sided house that looked like a double-wide trailer that had been permanently affixed to a dry brush and dirt lot. One small tree fought a losing battle to survive by the mailbox. A big-engined mid-1960s Dodge in so-so shape crouched out front. Drying laundry scooped up blowing dirt at the side.

A whip-thin tall man, whittled and darkened by the sun, came onto the front step to watch me get out of my car. "You bring the Kessler and smokes?"

I held up the liquor store bag.

"Good, then come on in. You can call me Mr. Schwamb." His lips turned up in something halfway between a sneer and a smile when he said that. He emitted a slow rolling basso profundo chortle, turned and went inside.

A lanky six foot five, ropy strong, a face etched by years of hard work and anger, a shock of still black hair falling over his forehead into his left eye; he looked intimidating. His arms were covered in long blurred jailhouse tattoos. Age, and whatever his disability was, hadn't hunched him over so much as pushed his upper torso aggressively forward.

He'd killed a man and pitched baseball in both the major leagues and two of the toughest prisons in the country. He was twenty-six years older than me and obviously in bad shape, shuffling in pain when he walked. But he looked like someone whose hard life had made him strong and who could still be dangerous. I was wary, but intrigued.

I followed him inside and got shoved at by a hurricane blast of warm air from a gunmetal gray industrial-sized fan in a corner. A television was blaring, competing with the roar of the blades. There was a small window with the curtain drawn. The only light was from the TV and the bright sun filtered through the dirty screen on the door. A young woman, a girl really, but prematurely developed in the way that teenage girls are constructed in Jim Thompson novels, lounged on a sofa in short, tight cutoff jeans and a very small T-shirt.

I was relieved that she was there, that I wasn't going to be alone with him.

Schwamb took the bag from me and set the case of beer on the coffee table next to the reclining girl. "Make yourself useful. Put this in the icebox and bring me a cold one." She snorted, but stretched herself off the couch and squeezed with the box of beer past the fan into another room.

Then I saw another side of him and I relaxed a little more.

His whole posture softened and he smiled as he watched her walk out of the room. The scary guy I'd just met disappeared for a moment while a proud and loving father took his place. "That's my daughter, Denise. She looks like trouble but she's a good kid. A helluva lot better than I was at that age." Schwamb motioned for me to sit on the sofa.

Denise came back with a cold beer for him, nothing for me. She coiled back up at the opposite end of the couch to continue watching her soap opera.

"Ah fuck it, let's go outside." Schwamb turned and headed back out the door with his beer. I followed with my tape recorder.

He didn't remember my uncle, or the game they'd played against each other. He must've pitched a thousand or more games in his life he figured. He'd been drunk for most of them, even a lot of them in prison, hungover for the rest.

No one had asked for the story of his life for a while, although he'd never been shy about spilling it over a few drinks at a bar. He wondered if there'd be something in it for him, in his talking to me. Maybe a magazine article could lead to a movie or something like that and he'd come into some cash. I didn't encourage that thought. I didn't discourage it either.

I spent a week with him, showing up every morning around ten, leaving not long after the beer and whisky struck him incoherent by the middle of the afternoon. The first day was easy. He was glib and articulate, by turns funny and poignant, sometimes maudlin, always, in an offbeat way, charming. I didn't have to ask any questions, just let him talk. He had me turn off my tape recorder a few times, but it was more when he didn't want to get caught with his emotions running away from him than for any details he wanted off the record.

As I drove away that first day I realized that I liked him, even if I couldn't figure out quite why. The story he told was horrible. He was the jocular, smart-ass hero of a lot of the specific incidents he recounted, but the overall effect was pathetic. He'd squandered a lot more talent and opportunities than most people ever have. He knew it, was honest about it, regretted it, but didn't seem at all remorseful about it. He was a man who seemed strangely comfortable lying in the really crappy bed that he'd made for himself.

Over the next few days I grew to like him even more. It was disconcerting. He told me terrible tales in a straightforward manner, pulling no punches. He'd left a long line of victims behind him, but other than the one man he killed he had done worse to fewer than he had done to himself.

I also caught glimpses of a man who had finally found some peace. When he talked about the woman he lived with and Denise, her daughter, his voice would choke and his eyes would tear. His time with them, he'd say, was the best thing that had ever happened to him.

He was a very strange man. Life had beaten him and tormented him and tortured him and almost always disappointed him and he had been its perversely willing accomplice. Yet most of the time he seemed almost cheerful recalling even the worst of the things that had happened. He was a masochist, that was certain, but the most oddly optimistic one I'd ever met.

Blackie Schwamb wasn't anybody's idea of an underdog and I knew it. But there was something about him that made me want to root for him as if he were. As I listened to his story and fell under its spell, it was all sort of confusing and fascinating. He had come out of the same world, amid similar circumstances and at the same time as my father and uncle. If anything, he had even greater advantages, greater natural talents than either of them. When he signed a major-league baseball contract he became what each of them had most wanted to become and never could. But Blackie's only real success came when he was locked away where it hardly mattered. My father went on to tremendous accomplishments as an entrepreneur. My uncle is one of the world's most successful painters.

I wanted to understand the differences between Blackie Schwamb and my father and uncle. How the same cultural and social experiences could create such thoroughly different people. How someone with so much right in his life, could go so utterly wrong. Besides, just as I had suspected, Blackie's story was all mixed up with baseball, crime, and the history of the city I grew up in and love.

On September 12, 1948, he had been the starting pitcher for the major-league St. Louis Browns, in front of a crowd of nearly fifty-six thousand screaming fans in a game against the Cleveland Indians and Bob Feller, the greatest pitcher of the decade. A year and a month later he killed a man, and it wasn't by mistake. A year after that major-league scouts were bringing ballplayers to San Quentin prison to play against him, to see how they would do. In ten years in prison, against surprisingly tough competition, he compiled an astounding record, by any standards, as a ballplayer.

His story was a real-life noir. It grabbed hold of me and like a fast-paced novel breathlessly raced me through Depression-era and World War II Los Angeles, into the postwar boom time. It involved gangsters and nightclubs and baseball from Mexico to Canada and mostly behind prison walls. There were girls and guns and gambling and booze and ball games. There were frozen hula dancers and a burning ballpark. Even though the thread that ran through all of it was Blackie constantly screwing up his own life, it was heady stuff.

In the 1940s Blackie Schwamb could have had it all. He should have had it easy. Smart and charming, alarmingly tall, thin and strong, he also had a vicious fastball and a brutal curve. He was one of the brightest baseball prospects ever, at a time when the game was in its heyday. He came of age in Southern California, ground zero at the beginning of the greatest economic boom in history. He had the opportunity to live large the fantasies of most American men and boys of his time.

But there was something wrong with him, something dark and terrible that festered and grew, nurtured by the very same events and culture that also produced good, hard-working solid citizens. The economic hardships of the Depression stimulated the kindness, generosity, and entrepreneurship in some people and at the same time encouraged the greed, cruelty, and scheming of others. The horrors of the Second World War brought out the bravery, compassion, and camaraderie in some, but gave vent to the cowardice, heartlessness, and selfishness of others. The American Dream has always had its nightmare side.

Blackie had spent the early part of the night of October 12, 1949, downing beer and shots at Jimmy's, a dark neighborhood workingman's bar at 81st and Vermont. It had been a hot day, over ninety. The temperature had plummeted almost thirty degrees by nine or so that night. Schwamb was out on bail for a robbery and was sticking close to home. He lived nearby, because he never drove drunk, "Never have and never will."

He was pretty well in the bag by the time Ted and Joyce Gardner, some old pals, showed up. Ted was a nattily dressed guy with romantic-lead good looks. He was a carpenter when he worked, which wasn't often, but he always seemed to have cash. He flaunted an oversized onyx ring and drove new cars. Joyce was a doll. To look at her you'd just know that the guys must've fallen all over her. She had dark, thick reddish hair, deep slow eyes, and full lips. Standing still she'd cock a hip in a way that made you think she was rotating, slowly. Schwamb said she was "built right in all the right places." She worked in a dime store.

The Gardners had a drunk doctor in tow. They'd picked the guy up at the Colony Club, a burlesque house down on Western in Gardena. He'd been with his wife at the Normandie, a poker palace across the street, told her he was taking a break to cash a check and see a couple of friends, and crossed over to catch a show.

"So they came and got me. Told me this doctor had been at Hollywood Park all day and made some money."

Blackie Schwamb and trouble were already well acquainted by then.

For four days his story poured out of him without much prodding. On the last day I decided to push him a little. He'd already told me two different versions of what happened on the night he murdered the doctor. I pestered him into telling me the story again.

The third time was not the charm. It was a little different from the other two. It wasn't any closer to the truth. But whatever was going on in his head while he spoke got to him in a way that it hadn't before. He broke down crying. It was the only time that I saw him feel sorry for himself. I paused the tape recorder, set my attention on my notepad, and waited.

After a couple of minutes he collected himself. We were sitting on folding, plastic lawn chairs in his front yard. He stood and loomed over me. I looked up at him and he looked angry, he was clenching his fists. "That's it," he growled. "Get the hell out of here before I fuck you up."

I got the hell out of there and never saw him again.

Wrong Side of the Wall

RALPH RICHARD "BLACKIE" SCHWAMB, nineteen years old, a bad conduct discharge stuffed into his shirt pocket, was mustering himself for the long bus ride home from the military prison near Chicago. Things were looking up. The war had ended the Depression, and the war itself had ended about a month before, while he sat in a cell for a variety of offenses. For the first time in nearly two years he was a free man. And he was anxious to take advantage of that. But the world was supposed to come to an end before he got back to Los Angeles.

Seven years before, God had spoken to the Reverend Charles Long of Pasadena, California, a small man with a neat bow tie and thick round glasses, and told him of the end of the world: 7:33 on Saturday morning September 21, 1945. Actually, God had said that the end would come at 5:33 P.M., but the Reverend figured he probably meant Jerusalem time. The news had been spread across the front pages of papers all over America and in a number of other countries.

Impending doom, however, didn't slow advance ticket sales for that Saturday evening's scheduled "Hit Parade of Stars" at the Hollywood Bowl, featuring Bob Hope, Bing Crosby, Artur Rubinstein, Bette Davis, Dinah Shore, Frank Sinatra, and others.

And it was nightlife as usual on what was supposed to be the final Friday. Max Baer, making hay from his one year as heavyweight champ ten

years before, was coaxing laughs out of the crowd at Slapsie Maxie's on
Beverly Boulevard. The Florentine Gardens on Hollywood Boulevard was
packing them in with its new "Parisian Nights, All-Girl Revue." Down on
Central Avenue, south of downtown, the jazz and rhythm and blues clubs
were swinging and honking and bebopping like there'd be no tomorrow.

Shirley Temple wasn't worried either. At least not about doomsday.
She'd been the number one box office attraction in American movies
from 1935 through 1938. But as the child star became a teenager, her
popularity slipped. The day before the planet's scheduled demise, the
then seventeen-year-old married twenty-four-year-old Army Sergeant
John Agar. The church, where five hundred guests attended the cere-
mony, was thronged by a mob estimated at around four thousand. As the
newlyweds began to leave the church, the crowd of fans broke through
police lines. The dashing groom whisked his bride back inside to safety.

There were at least some people concerned about the end of the
world. The L.A. *Times* reported that a Mr. Wallingsby of the London
Times had spent the considerable sum of $30 plus tax on two, three-
minute station-to-station phone calls to Pasadena to check out the
story. The night before the appointed date, churches throughout the
country were fuller than usual. In Mexico City, where for some reason
the prophecy was being taken more seriously than elsewhere, the
churches were downright crowded.

Around six on the appointed morning, a gang of reporters dutifully
gathered to await Armageddon in a cool drizzle on the lawn in front of
Rev. Long's Maple Street stucco bungalow. Newspapers across the
country splashed Shirley Temple's wedding on the front page.

At six thirty a radio reporter broadcast that he could smell bacon
frying from inside the house. "The family is apparently using up its red
points [food ration coupons] while it can," he announced. The Long
family ate their breakfast in peace. The world's date with destruction
came and went uneventfully, although some reporters hung around
until 5:33 that evening just in case.

Not long after, thirty-six miles south of Pasadena, Blackie Schwamb's
bus arrived in front of the Terminal Island Naval Prison in Los Angeles.

He had a sizable chip on his shoulder. "I had got drunk, missed a ship, hit an officer, and did two years. That terminated my Navy career. I was very bitter. It was the biggest point in me deciding that life was unfair, was goin' against me. I decided it was never goin' to happen again unless I caused it." He was, he said, not afraid of anything.

He stepped from the bus, showed his discharge paper to the guard at the gate, and walked out a free man into a rapidly changing world.

The war had ended abruptly. Most people had been ready for it to drag on for another bloody six months to a year. In America the war had been easier on people than in any other combatant country. Despite rationing and shortages, wartime full employment had brought economic stability back to the country. Now, with production likely to slow down to peacetime levels, people were afraid that the Depression might come back.

"Sudden peace scared the country," read an editorial in the October 1945 issue of *Fortune* magazine. "Unemployment of uncomfortable proportions seemed almost sure."

But, just like the end of the world, the second coming of the Depression didn't materialize. Rationing ended and scarce products began to come back onto the market.

There hadn't been much of anything to spend money on during the war, so people saved. By the time Blackie got back to Los Angeles it was estimated by the government that the reserve of cash waiting to roam free amounted to more than $1,000 for every man, woman, and child in the country. More than half of that had been saved by people who had been earning less than $5,000 per year. Businesses had about $75 billion in ready cash. This was at a time when a good family house could be bought for around $3,000.

Fortune summed it up: "There is a good deal of money for industrial expansion and lots of consumer buying power to justify and support it."

Besides all that pent-up money waiting to push the economy to greater heights than had ever been imagined, the war had also set into motion forces that would lead to tremendous social change.

During the war women had been hired to do work that until then had been thought of as exclusively "men's work." By 1944 more than three and a half million women were working alongside six million men on war material assembly lines. Single working women could relate to men on a more equal footing than ever before. For the first time massive numbers of women were bringing home their own paychecks. With their husbands in the military, many married women took over the role of "head of the household." Greater independence for women was a by-product of the war effort that would eventually lead to social, cultural, political, as well as economic, upheaval throughout the country.

The war was a transitional time for minorities as well. Japanese families, many of them in their second or even third generation as Americans, were dispossessed and herded into camps. Attacks on and lynchings of blacks continued to take place, primarily in the South, but also in other places. Rioting and street fighting between whites and blacks, with the blacks always getting the worst of it, broke out in 1943 in downtown Los Angeles, Detroit, Harlem, and several other cities. During the "Zoot Suit Riots" in L.A., roving gangs of white military men assaulted and publicly humiliated Mexican Americans.

But, though racism remained a reprehensible fact of daily life and the armed forces were segregated, minorities were accepted into the workforce to do jobs that had previously been closed to them. In June 1941 President Roosevelt issued Executive Order 8802 establishing the Committee on Fair Employment Practices, largely to protect the rights of black workers in the defense industry. At that time there were only four black production workers on aviation assembly lines in all of Southern California. By 1943 Lockheed Aviation alone employed about three thousand blacks. While minorities still faced terrible abuse in their working places, they were paid better than in the past, in many cases for the first time they were paid the same as their white counterparts.

During the war teenagers also entered into the economy in much greater numbers than ever. As men eighteen and over were drafted, sixteen- and seventeen-year-olds, male and female, stepped up to take over jobs. With almost all able-bodied adults at work, babysitting became a steady source of income for younger teenage girls. For the first time, teenagers became a market force to be reckoned with and catered to.

When the war ended most of the wartime workers lost their jobs, either immediately, as armaments factories shut down or cut way back, or over a period of six months to a year as the troops were mustered out and came home looking for work. Women and minority workers were, of course, the first to lose their jobs. But the social changes the war had brought on weren't so easily dismissed.

Hundreds of thousands of women, grown accustomed to the independence of their own paycheck, stayed at their jobs or found new ones in the fast-expanding peacetime economy. Minorities became more militantly active in asserting their rights and fighting segregation. Nonwhite soldiers came home from war and made use of the same generous GI Bill that white soldiers did. Youth ran wild, taking advantage of their newfound status as market makers. In 1948, as 45 rpm records became popular, jukeboxes took in more than five billion nickels.

The center of the economic whirlwind after the war was Los Angeles. It changed more, and faster, than almost any other city in the nation. When the fighting stopped, America was left with the only developed economy in the world that wasn't mostly in ruins. Factories, enormous numbers of them in Southern California, that had manufactured munitions, airplanes, ships, uniforms, processed food for the army, fuel, military vehicles and parts, an astounding range of goods for the war effort, quickly converted to products for civilian use.

Between 1940 and 1944, $800 million had been invested into building almost five thousand new industrial plants in Southern California. When the war ended the War Assets Administration was set up to sell off or lease out government-owned and government-financed factories. Throughout 1946 and 1947 full-page ads in *Fortune* and other business publications promoted the government's *Plant Finder,* a catalog of wartime assets now available for peacetime industry.

The two Los Angeles harbors, at San Pedro and Long Beach, adjacent to rich oilfields, had boomed to service the Navy in the Pacific. They quickly became the major export ports on the Pacific Rim.

It's hard to picture now, but even agriculture had played a large role in wartime L.A. Los Angeles, more than any other county in the country, had fed the troops. Some two hundred fifty thousand acres of commercial crops were grown within the city limits alone.

After the war a huge influx of newcomers increased the population in the area. Soldiers returning from overseas wanted the good, comfortable life. They wanted to be where jobs were easy to come by and where their children could play outdoors year-round. They wanted college educations paid for by the government and Southern California's colleges expanded to accommodate that. In 1947 more than 40 percent of UCLA's student body was made up of veterans on the GI Bill. At USC it was more than half. They wanted their own homes with a patch of yard, and flush with cheap government-backed loans, they could afford them.

Hundreds of thousands of soldiers returned in late 1945 and 1946, spent some time reacquainting themselves with the folks back home, then packed up and moved west. About eight hundred fifty thousand returning veterans settled in California immediately after the war and Southern California was by a long shot the destination of choice.

The population explosion caused a severe housing shortage. In L.A. retired streetcars were refurbished into small apartments and parked on vacant lots. With aircraft factories shutting or slowing down, airplane fuselages minus their wings were converted into trailerlike housing. Starting in the late 1940s vast acres of farmland were plowed under to make room for housing developments. It was to be the greatest residential construction boom in history.

In 1946 the entire country began easing slowly into the tremendous growth period of the late 1940s through the 1960s. Los Angeles was far out ahead of the curve.

Blackie Schwamb wanted his slice of that pie. But the first thing he wanted to do when he walked out onto the busy streets of Los Angeles was to straighten things out with his brother, Chester Jr. They had been estranged from one another for the past two years.

He could have walked. His brother lived about six miles from the front gate of the Terminal Island Naval Station and it had been two years since Blackie had walked much farther in one direction than the hundred or so feet a prison yard had allowed. It would have felt good to stretch his long legs. But he was in a hurry to get away from there, so he took the streetcar.

Chester lived in a second-floor apartment in a nice, 1920s Spanish-style building just a couple of blocks from where the brothers had grown up. Blackie walked up the stairs to his older brother's apartment and knocked on the door. It was early afternoon and Chester was already drunk, which wasn't unusual. He answered the door, looked into his brother's face for a few seconds, then slugged him in the nose and shoved him down the concrete steps. At least that's what Blackie said. That was the last time they ever saw each other.

They had a history of bad blood. While both of them had been drinking from a young age, unlike his younger brother, Chester Jr. was otherwise a sober, solid citizen, hardworking and conventional. Blackie's behavior often embarrassed him. There had also been something of a romantic rivalry. Despite their mother Janet's warning that it was a bad idea, Chester Jr. had married one of his brother's ex-girlfriends.

Picking himself up from the bottom of the stairs, Blackie needed a drink. He walked the couple of blocks over to Vermont Avenue and found several. He probably picked up a girl. It wouldn't have been hard, he had always had a way with women, and in 1945 there were a lot of single, widowed, lonely, and independent women to go around. The worst war in history was just over, it was heady times, everybody was hopped up on optimism and ripe with possibilities.

He'd served his sentence and been discharged. The navy was done with him. He needed work. He liked money and the good life it could buy. Two years in military prison hadn't rehabilitated him, but it had changed him. Blackie wasn't too particular about what sort of work he did, so long as it paid reasonably well. He found just what he was looking for providing muscle for Los Angeles's uniquely high-profile and "glamorous" gangsters.

CHAPTER 2

LIKE A LOT OF KIDS GROWING UP DURING THE DEPRESSION, Blackie had thrilled to the cinematic and newspaper exploits of gangsters. Everyone knew that they were supposed to be the bad guys, but they were exciting; they lived large, they got the sexiest girls, fastest cars, and fattest wads of dough. Blackie hated authority. He didn't like anyone telling him what to do. Bad guys, good guys, what did it matter to him? The gangster's life looked like the good life.

On his navy discharge paper, under the category of "job preference," he'd put "professional baseball player." He'd always loved playing ball and had a natural talent for it. Like most American men he dreamed of being a ballplayer, of striking out batters in Yankee Stadium, of the roar of the crowd. But, while he'd have never written it down on a legal form, "gangster" seemed like a pretty good job choice as well. There was nearly as much glamour, and certainly more money in crime. And that work was easier to get.

Crime was a growth industry. Los Angeles, especially after the war, was a cash cow for mobsters. Defense contracts, the entertainment industry, and even agriculture—Los Angeles County was the largest farming area in the country—had made a lot of people a lot of money. Like the fruit on the trees, those dollars were ripe for picking.

The Mafia was a relative latecomer to the West. A guy named Jack Dragna headed what there was of it before the late 1930s, but it was strictly small potatoes. He had set up the Italian Protective League, which sold protection from itself to Italian and other business owners. The police and city hall ran all the truly profitable enterprises: gambling, prostitution, drugs, and labor rackets.

In 1935 Benjamin "Bugsy" Siegel, one of the founders of Murder Incorporated, had been given California to run for the mob as a reward for his services in New York. Siegel had movie star good looks, oozed charm, and despite, or perhaps thanks to, being a brutal thug quickly made himself a fixture of L.A. high society. It was rumored that he had come to L.A. because he wanted to make it in pictures.

Hollywood didn't have many qualms about making movie stars out of former small-time crooks like gangster star and ex-bootlegger George Raft, who was closely associated with Owney Madden, the Irish mob boss of New York. But a slick contract killer with a rumored thirty to fifty notches on his gun butt was a bit much even for the town's amoral studio heads. So Bugsy just got invited to their parties, to their private boxes at the races and VIP rooms at ball games, onto their yachts, and into their bedrooms. Within a couple of weeks of moving to Los Angeles, Siegel was double-dating with Cary Grant and Betty Furness, dancing the night away to the rumba orchestra at the Trocadero with his girlfriend, socialite Countess Dorothy di Frasso. George Raft was one of his closest friends. Jean Harlow was godmother to one of his children.

Bugsy, with the support of the national syndicate bosses, pushed the resentful but compliant Dragna into a subordinate position and elevated the Mafia into L.A.'s criminal limelight. In short order he muscled into the well-established but still fast-growing rackets. He pioneered heroin smuggling routes up through Mexico. Somehow he retained his cozy relationship with Hollywood, despite extorting money out of the studios and taking over the extras union.

He even managed to accomplish his goals with very little gunplay. No one wanted a repeat of 1920s Chicago with gangs gunning each other down in the streets. So long as violence remained in check and drugs and prostitution were discreet, the public for the most part didn't seem to object to the gangsters in their midst. To some extent they romanticized, and even admired them.

People figured that gangsters were only a danger to each other. To the general public they provided a number of popular, if illegal, services. Their flashy clothes, cars, and behavior made them glamorous. In image-conscious Los Angeles, a high profile was good marketing.

While prohibition in the 1920s had made organized crime extremely profitable, the hard times of the Depression created a lot of individual criminals. According to a Justice Department estimate, by 1935 crooks outnumbered carpenters by four to one, grocers by six to one, and doctors by twenty to one.

At a time when people had lost much of their regard for established authority, antiheroes became popular. All across the country bankers were foreclosing on mortgages, putting farms, homes, and small businesses up for sale. Bank robbers didn't seem so bad.

In Los Angeles it was hard to tell the cops from the bad guys anyway. Both groups were tough and brutal, the main difference being that the police were more successful at running the local rackets and vice. One L.A. police chief liked to show off to reporters by having a marksman shoot a cigarette out from between his lips. In 1933 L.A. police officers shot and killed at least forty-three "offenders," a body count that was reminiscent of the gangland wars in 1920s Chicago.

Gangster movies were popular. And while the bad guys had to die in the end it was obvious to anyone watching that they had it pretty good in the meantime. Blackie loved the movies. He grew up thrilling to the antiestablishment antics of James Cagney, Edward G. Robinson, George Raft, and Humphrey Bogart. They fought the law and the law may have won, but they all went down over and over again in a blaze of glory. Throughout his life Blackie was known for his excellent Cagney and Bogie impressions.

He also followed the accounts in the tabloid press of the real-life exploits of 1930s gangsters like John Dillinger, who despite having killed at least ten people in his career, became a sort of Robin Hood figure when he broke out of a supposedly escape-proof jail with two hostages, then gave his captives four dollars each for car fare home when he got away.

Bonnie and Clyde were reviled by many of their fellow criminals for their excessive violence, but were rumored to leave bags of money for farmers to pay off the banks.

George "Machine Gun" Kelly could supposedly write his name on a barn door with bullets from his tommy gun. His pretty wife, Kate, passed out empty shell casings as much sought-after souvenirs.

The Depression made a lot of people think that things would get better if they only worked harder. But others simply dreamed of getting rich quick. Organized crime, having thoroughly established itself by catering to the nation's thirst in the 1920s, was well positioned to add to its coffers by pandering to people's delusions and greed during the 1930s.

Gambling, though illegal in most of the country, was commonplace everywhere. Many shops had one or more slot machines in their back rooms. Card parlors and floating card and craps games were easy to find in almost every part of every town. It was a rare barbershop where you couldn't bet on the races or play the numbers. Cockfights were held in backyards and vacant lots in many neighborhoods. In 1937 the reform movement in Los Angeles estimated that eighteen hundred bookies openly did business in the city, there were three hundred illegal gambling dens (as well as six hundred brothels), and twenty-three thousand illegal slot machines.

Gambling was just a fact of life for Blackie Schwamb and a lot of other people in the 1930s. He grew up surrounded by a family and a society that wagered as an almost daily matter of course. He started laying bets on everything from local pickup ball games to his skills at tossing quarters from an early age. It was a big part of what formed his attitudes toward money and work and what led him to take the path he did after the war.

Bugsy Siegel's biggest success was in gambling. He took large cuts of the action at Aqua Caliente Racetrack just across the border in Tijuana, the other racetracks in Southern California, the local numbers games, the illegal but well-known casino in the back room of the very swank Clover Club on Sunset Boulevard, a number of popular card clubs in Gardena and south central L.A., the dog track in Culver City, and at least 15 percent of the take from the gambling ships anchored in Santa Monica Bay.

Quasi-legal gambling ships had been operating off the coast of Los Angeles since 1928. They clustered just beyond the three-mile U.S. territorial limit. They were tolerated, and often patronized, by the well-paid-off authorities. Movie stars, sports heroes, musicians, socialites, and all manner of the beautiful people were often featured in the society pages of local newspapers, caught by photographers as they climbed in or out of the speedboats that taxied them to and from the floating casinos.

In May 1938, when Blackie Schwamb was just a few months shy of twelve years old and living about a half hour by trolley from the beach, Tony Cornero, a gangster or businessman depending on your point of view, anchored the SS *Rex* three miles and a bit out from Santa Monica. Full-page ads in local papers announced its very grand opening. It was the talk of the town.

The *Rex* was wildly successful from the first day, open around the clock and rarely with fewer than a couple thousand gamblers on board. Transportation to and from the ship was free, the food was high quality and cheap, and a swing orchestra featured some of the musical greats of the day.

Attracting crowds meant attracting attention and just a few months after it opened, at the order of California's ambitious attorney general Earl Warren, later governor of the state and finally chief justice of the U.S. Supreme Court, the *Rex* was shut down. At the first trial the state successfully argued that the true coastline followed a straight line between the headlands of the bay and so territorial waters extended three miles past that. On appeal, Cornero's lawyers claimed that the "bay" was actually a "bight"—a large coastal indentation, with the coastline at the beach—they won and the *Rex* reopened.

The trial was covered heavily on the front pages of all the Los Angeles papers. By its end there wasn't a man, woman, or child of school age in the city who hadn't heard of the *Rex* and who didn't know that its owner had taken on the state of California and won. Tony Cornero was a big, and admired, celebrity.

The business did so well that Cornero soon expanded. He bought three barges, fixed them up, and anchored the *Showboat,* the *Tango,* and the *Texas* beyond the law's reach. His personal monthly take from the floating casinos was reported at about a half million dollars, at a time when a U.S. congressman's annual salary was $8,663 and a steelworker made about $500 a year.

The high times at sea lasted just over a year until Attorney General Warren issued an order declaring the gambling ships a public nuisance.

On the morning of Tuesday August 1, 1939, there began what the *Los Angeles Examiner* called "a spectacular battle of wits and writs." A number of plainclothes officers accompanied by "expensively gowned women," took water taxis out to the *Showboat* and the *Tango,* anchored off of Long Beach. Not long after, a raiding task force of fifty officers sped up in a motor launch, boarded the vessels, and joining with the undercover cops already on the inside shut them down.

Then they sailed north and set upon the *Texas,* bobbing in the gentle swells off of Ocean Park. They closed it down without a fight and tossed the gambling equipment overboard. The Coast Guard later issued a warning to the officers as "the wholesale jettisoning of elaborate gambling devices created a menace to navigation."

By midafternoon the law enforcement armada had surrounded the *Rex* and was preparing to board it. Thus began the "Battle of Santa Monica Bay."

Cornero rallied his crew to seal off the gangway with a large steel plate. When the police and sheriff's deputies tried storming the boat they were fought off with fire hoses.

A standoff ensued that occupied the front pages of all the city's newspapers for the next ten days. The high drama of Hollywood had made its way out of the theaters and into everybody's homes. Like two battling bull elephants, Cornero and Earl Warren bellowed and fulminated against each other in two editions a day of the Los Angeles press.

Local bookies took bets on what was going to happen next. Large crowds lined the beaches, peering out to sea with binoculars and renting telescopes by the minute to watch what they could of the siege.

Blackie and his family, like almost all families in the city, read the latest exploits with glee. They talked about the days' events at breakfast and again at dinner. They sided with Tony Cornero. Handsome and nattily dressed in a tan soft felt hat and matching topcoat, accusing the government of attempted piracy, he was the hero of the story for a lot of people. It was almost as if he had stepped down out of a movie screen to fight back against capricious authority.

A widely reported exchange on the third day of the siege of the *Rex*, between a suave and comfortable-looking Cornero and a seasick and nauseated Captain George Contreras of the Sheriff's Department, was typical of the confrontation.

While Contreras's small boat rocked and rolled in the white-tipped swells, the captain managed a conversation with Tony via megaphone.

"Are you ready to give up?" yelled Contreras.

"I'm not going to surrender," answered Cornero. "The Coast Guard tells me I'm within my rights not to allow boarders on board my ship. I'm on the high seas, so keep your distance or take the consequences."

"Do you mean you'll use force to keep us off?"

"We're ready for action and we know how to handle pirates."

"But Tony, what are you going to do?"

"I'm gonna sit tight. What are you guys gonna do?"

It was tough-guy dialogue straight out of the movies. The smart, refined gangster hero who just wanted to be left alone to provide a service to his customers, was making fools out of the schlumpy cops. Blackie and his family and his friends cheered for the good guys. Or were they the bad guys? Who knew? It didn't really matter.

After holding out for ten days the well-groomed gambler had had enough. Photogenic, quotable, and unflappable as ever, Cornero stepped off the *Rex* onto a speedboat rented by *Examiner* reporters and explained, "The only thing I haven't got aboard the ship is a barber."

His seventy-five employees remained on board with orders to repel all boarders.

The reporters took Cornero to the sheriff's boat where the still queasy Contreras awaited him. "I surrender to you as a representative of the sheriff," said Tony. "I'm in a hurry to go ashore and get a haircut. I demand to be taken to the nearest magistrate."

It was the perfect Hollywood ending. Gambling, and even the gangsters who ran the business, seemed more glamorous than ever to the young Blackie Schwamb and his pals.

Cornero and many others had voluntarily, or not, formed partnerships with Bugsy Siegel and organized crime. But they weren't really his associates. Bugsy's closest comrade in arms, his bodyguard and chief of gambling operations, and later Blackie Schwamb's boss, was Meyer Harris "Mickey" Cohen.

Born in Brooklyn but having grown up in Boyle Heights, a then Russian Jewish neighborhood to the east of downtown Los Angeles, the scrappy five-foot-five Cohen had been a professional boxer before opting for a life of crime. Like his boss, Bugsy, he was a flamboyant high roller with a large appetite for publicity and the nightclub life. He was popular with the newspapers because he was always good for a quote or a picture with one or more tall, glamorous showgirls dwarfing him on each arm. By the mid-1940s he boasted that his gambling operations took in six hundred thousand dollars a day from the Hollywood film set alone.

Talking about Bugsy and Mickey, Clint Anderson, a Los Angeles police official of the time said, "No gangsters in criminal history ever had such open association with the big names of the town."

Blackie admired Mickey Cohen. He liked reading about him in the papers. The short mobster, with his expensive suits, beautiful women, and coterie of Hollywood pals was living the life that Blackie wanted for himself. He figured, there was a guy who just reached out and took what he wanted, and he envied that. A friend, possibly Ted Gardner, put the recently freed Blackie in touch with Mickey Cohen.

CHAPTER 3

RALPH RICHARD SCHWAMB WAS BORN IN LOS ANGELES on August 6, 1926. The oldest family photo in his collection comes from his mother's side of the family. It is of his maternal grandmother, Jennie Tarling, with her second or possibly third husband, not in any case Ralph's grandfather. Jennie was a hardy-looking woman, matronly and rounded by the time the picture was taken, but with an apparent tough edge and self-assured bearing. According to Ralph she ran a bar in a mining camp in Montana or Colorado. His mother, Jeanette, whom most people called Janet, grew up there, playing in, and then working in the bar.

Janet married Chester Hinton Schwamb in Detroit, Michigan in 1921. Chester was a dapper, smartly dressed tall man who smiled easily and lived, if not beyond his means, pretty much right up to the edge of them. Before long the family was well established in Los Angeles and comfortably middle class. A master builder and carpenter, Chester never lacked for work. Janet had a plain and pleasant look, but she liked nice clothes and often wore furs. By all accounts she was a loving, giving homemaker, sober and supportive of her husband and two sons. Their first son, Chester Jr., was born in 1923.

When Ralph came along his father was twenty-five, his mother twenty-three. Almost from the start his family called him Rich, or Richie. They brought him home from the hospital to a small house on a recently paved street at 1638 South Westmoreland, about three miles southwest of downtown and a block and a half from the Red Car tramline that ran to Venice by the Sea.

Southern California in the 1920s has been described by a historian as "one long drunken orgy, one protracted debauch."[1] Dreams of stardom filled the streets of fast-developing Hollywood with small-town beauty queens and handsome high school sports heroes. Musicians, artists, photographers, writers, and creative people of all sorts from all over the world flocked to what was being heavily promoted as the new Eden.

Even in the heady economic boom of the decade, life was hard in rural America. Whole farm families sold out, packed up, and drove west in search of city jobs in a place where the nights were warm and exotic palm trees swayed in cooling breezes.

Los Angeles grew at a ridiculous pace. Besides the lure of Hollywood's bright lights, it was also the Middle East of its time. As many oil derricks as palm trees sprouted from the landscape, pumping out enormous quantities of the world's supply of oil. Los Angeles's ports at San Pedro and Long Beach exploded in size to accommodate oil shipments and then the products made in all the new factories fueled by the region's oil wealth.

Civic boosters went wild advertising the attractions of Southern California (which was first insistently spelled with a capital letter *S* in advertisements of the time.) In 1923 a huge sign reading HOLLYWOOD-LAND (the "land" was removed in 1949) was erected in the hills above the movie capital of the world and became an instant landmark.

Tourism went berserk. Visitors were attracted by stories of frolicking in the snow-capped mountains in the morning, followed by an afternoon swim at the beach, and topped off with dinner and dancing on one of the world's largest and most extravagant amusement piers at night. And the stories weren't just public relations nonsense, it really was possible. You could even stop along the way to pick an orange or two for a snack from the many orchards along the route.

---

1 McWilliams, *Southern California*.

Between 1920 and 1930 L.A. County was the destination of choice for what was arguably the largest internal migration in the history of America. Between those years the county gained nearly 1.3 million people, while the city of Los Angeles added more than 650,000, its millionth resident showing up not long before Blackie Schwamb was born. By 1930 it was the fifth largest city in the United States, with a population pressing on 1.25 million.

All those new residents set a real estate boom in motion unlike anything that had ever been seen before. In 1923 more than sixty-two thousand building permits, valued at more than $200 million, were issued. The city sprawled as developers and speculators bought up land at its ever-expanding edges. But there were limits. As one historian put it, "Los Angeles had subdivided itself into a city of seven million people half a century before the realities of population caught up with the speculations of real estate investors."[2] By 1925 the rush to supply the market had outpaced the demand, so that almost six hundred thousand subdivided lots waited, empty.

The city, flush with tax dollars from the booming economy, went on a road-building and street-paving binge to accommodate all the new motorized arrivals. At the same time public transportation, mostly light rail, expanded rapidly, crisscrossing the whole area. It was widely admired as one of the most extensive, cheapest, and fastest systems in the world.

The neighborhood that Ralph was taken home to had been annexed by the city of Los Angeles in the 1890s. Until the early 1920s it had been a wealthy residential area. Many of the silent-era luminaries of Hollywood lived there in what was unusual, for the time, a racial and ethnic mix. Large Victorian-, Colonial Revival- and Craftsman-style houses were occupied by Busby Berkeley, Theda Bara, "Fatty" Arbuckle, Ethel Waters, Hattie McDaniel, Butterfly McQueen, and Leo Carrillo among others.

To the north and a bit west, Hollywood, the neighborhood not the industry, was just taking off in the 1920s. As late as 1928 there was an

---

2 Starr, *Material Dreams*.

orange grove at the intersection of Hollywood and Vine. More than a few people in the area kept horses and it wasn't all that rare to see riders mixing it up with drivers along the still not fully paved Hollywood Boulevard. Yet by the middle of the decade the movie people who could afford it had begun to move to the Hollywood Hills and to Beverly Hills and Bel Air farther to the west.

In the mid-1920s the neighborhood in which the Schwambs lived was solidly middle class and largely German, Greek, and Italian. The Pacific Electric Red Car tramline, which ran along nearby Venice Boulevard, provided easy and quick transportation to the beach or downtown from where riders could connect to trains going pretty much anywhere.

In 1928 the 454-foot-tall Los Angeles City Hall opened. It was one of the tallest buildings west of the Mississippi River and the tallest building in L.A. until the 1960s. That same year daily commercial flights began between L.A. and San Francisco. In early October the next year groundbreaking ceremonies were held in downtown for the new home of the Pacific Stock Exchange. One week later the stock market crashed and the depression that had started a year or two earlier in rural areas, crushed the boom in the cities.

While Chester Sr. had work all through the Depression, and Ralph recalled the family as always having had meat on the table for supper, like most working people the family had to cut costs. The family moved south along the route of the Pacific Electric Blue Line to 69th Street near Vermont Avenue. It was another, though slightly lower-working-class neighborhood settled by German and other northern European families and beginning to attract Eastern European Jews moving out of Boyle Heights to the east of downtown. The area was not densely populated and housing was cheaper than in the old neighborhood. There were a lot of open spaces, empty lots, and huge fields of strawberries.

Ralph went to the 68th Street Grade School, just a couple of blocks from home. Jim Muhe, a childhood friend, remembers that one day they went to a Saturday matinee. It was a Western and the bad guys all wore black. Ralph thought that was pretty cool so he started wearing black Frisko Jeans and black pullover shirts to school. The other kids soon nicknamed him "Blackie."

He had prominent ears, a family trait that got him teased and into a lot of fights. By his own account, and those of others who knew the family, he was an active, bright, happy, and other than bouts with the mumps and measles, healthy kid.

He also had the best throwing arm in the neighborhood. Muhe remembered a fort that he, Ralph, and some other friends had dug into the dirt of a vacant lot next to a glass factory. One time the guys bet Ralph that he couldn't throw a rock and break one of the big panes of glass that was being taken out of the factory on trucks. He did, from more than a hundred feet away.

"We all just stood there for a moment watching the glass rain down on the pavement," said Muhe. "Then we ran like hell, laughing all the way. We didn't get caught."

Ralph's brother and he could be good students when a subject caught their attention. He skipped fifth grade and after that mostly hung out with older kids. He was about average height until he turned eleven or twelve when a growth spurt pushed him up more than a foot over the course of the year. After that, long and lean, his childhood awkwardness having given way to a natural grace, he excelled at every sport, but most especially baseball.

Baseball was wildly popular in the 1930s and '40s. Admission prices to games were low, almost every town in the country had a ballpark, and though it remained exclusively Caucasian in the major leagues, it was something of a melting pot for the sons of European immigrants. It would have been very tough to find a man or boy who didn't harbor fantasies of playing major-league ball.

It was played everywhere in the country and in Southern California it was played year-round. Some of the game's biggest stars, such as Joe DiMaggio, Ted Williams, and Lefty Grove came from California. After school during the week and all day long on weekends, city parks, school yards, vacant lots, and streets without much traffic cracked with the sound of balls hitting bats and smacking into mitts.

When he was a young boy, Ralph and his pals played on a rough baseball diamond that his and Jim Muhe's fathers built for them on a vacant lot near their houses.

The baseball being played in Ralph's neighborhood was especially high-quality. When he got to be a teenager he started hanging around Manchester and Harbor playgrounds, about halfway between downtown and the harbor. There he played with Gene Mauch, Al Zarilla, George Metkovich and his brother Johnny, and a lot of other guys who went on to careers in the major and minor leagues. The home park for the Ironworkers was at 60th and Western, not far away. They, along with the Rosabell Plumbers were regularly in contention for the title of the best Los Angeles semipro team. That meant a lot more then than it means now. Until the late 1960s many major-league players and prospects played for semipro teams in the off-season.

Saturday was the big day on Manchester playground's four baseball diamonds. The playground director would provide each game with one new ball and one old bat. In the off-season major leaguers whose families lived in the area would play in some of the games. Big league scouts would mingle with the spectators, looking for their next hot prospect.

Los Angeles didn't have a major-league baseball team until 1958 when the Dodgers moved from Brooklyn, but before that minor-league and semipro ball were popular. The first known team in the city, in 1870, was made up of high school girls. In 1886 professional teams from back East began coming to Los Angeles in the spring for training. Sixth Street Park, which is now Pershing Square in the city's financial district, was their playing field. In 1892 the city entered its first team in the California State Baseball League and won 101 of its 175 games.

Baseball really took off in Los Angeles in the 1920s. After 1926 there were two Pacific Coast League (PCL) teams in the city, the Angels and the Hollywood Stars. The PCL was a triple-A minor league that produced a number of baseball's greatest players. Baseball as played in the PCL was so good that it was often called the third major league. A number of players even turned down offers to play for American and National League teams because they were paid more in the PCL. In

1952, it was classified as an AAAA league and its players were protected from the major-league draft.

Chewing-gum baron William Wrigley Jr. owned the Angels. He had
bought the major-league Chicago Cubs in 1919 and also purchased
Santa Catalina Island, "26 miles across the sea" from the Port of Los
Angeles, for the team to use for spring training. The Angels were the
Cub's primary farm club, the only PCL team with a direct connection
to a major-league team. Wrigley built a namesake ballpark in south central Los Angeles to give the Angels a home.

Wrigley Field opened on September 29, 1925. It cost $1.1 million to
build, had seats for 22,457 fans, and was designed in a modern Spanish
style with a red tile roof and white stucco facade. It was distinguished by
a twelve-story office tower with a large clock at the entrance to the park
and was easily accessible from all over the city by streetcar. A bit less than
six years after it was completed lights were installed. After that all weekday games were played at night to give working people a chance to at-
tend. Four years later the first night game was played in the major leagues.

The Angels' big rivals were the Hollywood Stars. The two teams
shared Wrigley Field from 1926, when the Stars moved to Los Angeles
from Salt Lake City, through the 1935 season. Pacific Coast League ball
was so popular that in 1930 the two teams drew more than eight hundred fifty thousand in combined attendance—more than the St. Louis
Cardinals, who were in the World Series that year, and the St. Louis
Browns, two major-league teams that were sharing their much bigger
stadium. At the end of the 1935 season the Wrigley Corporation doubled the rent, to $10,000. The Stars couldn't afford it so they moved
south to San Diego where they became the Padres.

Two years later baseball returned to Hollywood. In 1938 the San
Francisco Mission Reds, who had once been the Vernon, then Venice,
then Vernon again (all in what is now Los Angeles) Tigers, moved back
south and changed their name to the Hollywood Stars. They were
bought by Robert Cobb (the Cobb salad is named after him) who
owned the Brown Derby café, one of the very few places in town that
the high-society swells from Pasadena and Hancock Park mixed with

the Hollywood crowd. A number of Cobb's celebrity customers—Gary Cooper, Bing Crosby, Gene Autry, William Powell, George Raft, Barbara Stanwyk, Robert Taylor, George Burns, Gracie Allen, Harry Warner, and Cecil B. DeMille—also had stakes in the ball club. (George Raft borrowed the money for his stake from his pal Bugsy Siegel.)

The Stars played the 1938 season at Gilmore Stadium, which was otherwise used for midget auto racing, boxing, football, rodeos, wrestling, dog shows, the occasional political rally, and even a cricket match. The stadium had opened in 1934, built by the A. F. Gilmore Company. The founder of the business had been a dairy farmer who owned Rancho La Brea, a large part of which is now L.A.'s Fairfax district. Drilling for water on his land, Arthur Gilmore struck oil instead. By the mid-1920s the company had become the largest independent oil distributor in the western United States.

The Gilmore Oil Company, run by Earl Gilmore, grandson of the founder, opened the world's first self-serve gas station, called Gas-A-Teria. It advertised heavily with its slogan: Give your car a kick in the gas. Earl has a place in auto racing history having started the sport of midget auto racing, which evolved into the type of race held at the Indianapolis 500. He also promoted Gilmore Economy Runs, an ancestor of today's stock-car race.

The area where the Gilmores made their fortune was heavily agricultural into the late 1920s. When nearby Fairfax High School was opened in 1924 it offered classes in agronomy and forestry. The Farmer's Market, which still exists, started up in 1934 when local farmers began to set up stands on a part of the Gilmore property.

In 1928 a synagogue had been built in the area and large numbers of Jews began moving out of Boyle Heights to the newer and more affluent neighborhood just south and a little west of Hollywood. By the late 1930s the Fairfax district was predominately Jewish, suburban, and beginning to attract a variety of urban-type businesses such as restaurants and nightclubs.

A year after the Stars came back to Hollywood (or, more accurately, to Fairfax), on May 2, 1939, their own Art Deco-style Gilmore Field opened next to the Farmer's Market, on the site of what is now CBS Television City. That was conveniently close to Hollywood and the swank residential districts to the north and west where the movie stars and moguls lived. Gilmore Field, with its VIP boxes that were popular with movie stars, politicians, and mobsters, rapidly became known as a place for stargazing as much as watching baseball.

Blackie lived about three and a half miles from the less glamorous Wrigley Field, in a mostly white working-class neighborhood. General admission to ball games cost fifty cents, but that was more than most kids could scrape together in the 1930s. He and Muhe would take the streetcar or ride their bikes to the ballpark. They'd get there early to stand just outside the left field fence, waiting for baseballs that were hit out of the park during batting practice. Once Ralph snagged four balls in one day. "We used those babies for about six months in our sandlot games," recalled Muhe. If they hung around until the second or third inning of a weekday game, often as not a gatekeeper would just wave them inside for free. Throughout the 1930s Blackie and Jim went to a lot of games and saw a team that dominated its league. Their favorite player was Jigger Statz.

The 1933 Angels were spearheaded by their center fielder Statz. Arguably one of the greatest outfielders of all time, he turned down offers to move back East and play for major-league teams. He made more money and liked the weather better in Southern California. The rest of the team was also impressive and resoundingly won the pennant with a record of 114 wins to 73 losses.

That same year future Hall of Famer Joe DiMaggio became a regular with the San Francisco Seals and established a still unbroken professional baseball record of hitting safely in sixty-one straight games. (Eight years later he set the also still standing major-league mark of fifty-six straight games.)

The 1934 Angels were better yet. They won 137 games and lost only 50. They were almost certainly the greatest minor-league team of all time. They finished 30 games ahead of the second-place Seals. Since the Angels had won both halves of the season, and the winners of each

half were supposed to play for the championship, the league put together an all-star team to play them instead. The Angels beat the best
of the rest of the league 4 games to 2. Baseball provided good, cheap
entertainment during the often grim '30s.

The Depression had a powerful psychological impact on the country. It instilled in the national character a split personality that endures
to this day. At the same time that a great deal of the country was on the
skids, it entertained, and to some extent taunted itself with the carryings
on of what was known as Café Society. In 1935, when a six-room house
with a two-car garage in Detroit sold for less than $3,000, Brenda Fra-
zier had a clothing allowance of $5,400 per year. She was fourteen years
old. Three years later she had her "debut" and was named the "Glamour Girl of 1938." Her comings and goings, dates with movie stars and
others of the rich and famous were breathlessly reported on the pages of
much-read newspapers. Alfred Vanderbilt was her male equivalent, almost daily reported nightclubbing with glamour girls and starlets. They
were envied for their excesses rather than despised for them.

Still, it was not uncommon that people reading those very society
pages while waiting in long soup kitchen lines on the east side of
Broadway in downtown Los Angeles, would jeer at the better-off folk
waiting in line to get into the theaters, nightclubs, and restaurants on
the west side of the street.

For many the Depression created a challenge that could only be
overcome by concentrated, hard labor. It reinforced the solid values of
family, work, and conformity that seemed to have been on the wane
during the boom years of the 1920s. Only in America and Britain did
the Depression not lead to mass movements that seriously threatened
the established order.

But to others, a large minority made up of nonwhites and Jews who
had long been discriminated against by the mainstream, disenfranchised
workers at the lower rungs of the economic ladder, nonconformists, intellectuals and artists, the Depression was, if not exactly liberating, at
least stimulating. It was a time of tremendous intellectual and artistic
ferment and restlessness. It was a time when previously unpopular ideas

gained stronger voices. Communists and socialists developed a degree of respectability and made inroads into labor unions. Black jazz and blues and poor white hillbilly music crashed through the barriers into popular culture. Outlaws and gangsters became folk heroes, celebrated in song and film.

Baseball during the Depression seems to have been zanier, attracting more eccentric players than at any time since. In the major leagues the antics of Dizzy Dean and the St. Louis Cardinals (known as the Gashouse Gang) were legendary. "Da Bums" (Dodgers) of Brooklyn played their own wacky brand of baseball. Despite segregation, Negro League ball was in its heyday and attracting large, often integrated crowds of fans. William C. Tuttle, the president of the PCL, said that when fights broke out on the field they shouldn't be broken up. They simply added to what brought in the crowds. Throughout the sport players were admired for their scrappy, brawling, aggressive style of play.

Today's sports heroes are expected to be exemplary citizens, nicely groomed role models for the nation's youth. But the ballplayers of the 1930s were another matter. They were warily admired outcasts, fondly regarded for their ability to booze it up all night in the company of "dames" and "shady characters," and then still get the job done on the field the next day. It wasn't unusual for athletes to endorse cigarettes or alcohol. Through the '30s a lot of baseball cards came packaged with chewing tobacco or cigarettes. Few respectable parents wanted their kids to grow up to be ballplayers.

What kids were going to do when they grew up was a matter of some concern during the late 1930s and through the war. The Depression and poverty had torn up a lot of families. It had lessened respect for authority at all levels, from the government on down to mom and dad. The rebelliousness of teenagers, a perennial popular topic in the media, was more widely written about than ever before. And this generation of teens was bigger than most that had come before it; the high times of the 1920s had led to an urban baby boom.

CHAPTER 4

"I ALWAYS HAD AN ANGLE," BLACKIE SAID. "Things were too easy for me. It seemed that whatever I decided to undertake I could make work." He wasn't alone. More teenagers than ever were looking to cut themselves in on the action.

In 1940 nearly two million young people graduated or left high school and tried to find work. They joined another two million or so who were just a year or two older and also unemployed. They had more spare time on their hands than teenagers had ever had before and not a lot of constructive courses into which to channel their energies.

The country as a whole was entering an unsettled, transitional period. The Depression wasn't really over, but it seemed like it might be. The hit song of 1940 was "When You Wish upon a Star." The most popular radio shows were all comedies—Amos & Andy, Fibber McGee & Molly, The Edgar Bergen/Charlie McCarthy Show, Red Skelton, Bob Hope, and Jack Benny battled each other for listeners in the early evening. Later at night Ellington, Basie, Benny Goodman, Artie Shaw, and Glen Miller filled the airwaves live from the glittering ballrooms of New York and Los Angeles.

Screwball comedies and fantasies were all the rage in movie theaters. *Pinocchio* and *Fantasia* played to big crowds in 1940 and *My Little Chickadee* with W. C. Fields and Mae West continued strong after

having been released late in the previous year. Charlie Chaplin had his
first big flop with *The Great Dictator,* a political satire of Hitler that nobody wanted to see. Teenagers, in time-honored tradition, wore fashions
that their parents didn't like and danced the jitterbug, a wild, individu-
alistic dance that the Nazis in Germany had banned as subversive.

Meanwhile Europe and Asia were at war. Horrific news reports
were regularly broadcast into American homes and terrible scenes were
shown in movie theater newsreels. Refugees from Europe were arriving
in droves. Eastern European intellectuals, artists, and Jews fleeing per-
secution had already had a significant impact on the country's culture
and arts.

Though America was at peace, the overseas wars were beginning to
affect life in the United States. In mid-September 1940 Congress passed
the Selective Service Act that established the first peacetime draft in the
country's history. In November President Franklin Roosevelt was re-
elected on a promise to keep the country out of foreign wars. He did,
however, know an opportunity when he saw one. A week before Christmas Roosevelt announced that the United States needed to build fifty
thousand airplanes and numerous warships in the next year. He proposed the Lend-Lease Act, which was passed by Congress in March
1941 and appropriated fifty billion dollars to produce military equipment to sell, lend, or lease to countries fighting the Axis powers of
Germany, Italy, and Japan. Aircraft factories and shipyards, many of
them in Southern California, geared up to meet the demand.

California was a long way away from Europe. In San Francisco the
Nazi consul-general, a dashing charmer, was invited to all the best parties. And as for Japan, during the first half of 1940 the cruise lines were
heavily advertising trips to see the many festivals and events that were
being celebrated in the country to commemorate the twenty-six-hun-
dredth anniversary of the reign of the first emperor. The port at Long
Beach was piled high with scrap metal and crowded with oil tankers
and freighters loading up with materials destined for Japan. The Japanese consulate in Los Angeles was known for throwing parties to which
high society coveted invitations.

Intervention in foreign affairs was not a popular idea. In June 1941 some thirty thousand people rallied at the Hollywood Bowl against the United States getting involved in "Europe's war." The speakers included aviator-hero Charles Lindbergh and movie star Lilian Gish.

It almost seemed as if good times were finally around the next corner. A lot of Americans were laughing and dancing, maybe just a little too hard, while the rest of the world caught fire.

Blackie Schwamb entered Washington High School, at 108th Street and Denker Avenue, just west of Watts in 1940. Like all Los Angeles public high schools at the time, the student body was integrated even if the faculty wasn't. Because of the greater pool of talent from which L.A. high school coaches had to pick, the level of athletic competition in the schools was very high. Because of the weather sports could be played year-round. A disproportionate number of professional athletes came out of Los Angeles's high schools, but Washington led them all. Blackie excelled in all sports, but he played only sporadically, preferring to hang out in the stands with older boys, smoking cigarettes, drinking beer when they could get it, and yelling at the guys on the field.

Unlike today, high school athletes weren't expected to be strait-laced, sober good students. They were often as not the wild boys of their schools. Blackie fit right in. From the time he was twelve or thirteen he began to get into trouble—smoking, drinking, gambling, and coming home late. He'd known Ted Gardner, who became his "crime partner," since grade school, and when he wasn't playing or watching sports, he and Ted were often out looking for trouble.

In those days pinball machines paid off in nickels, rather than free games. Blackie, sometimes with Ted, sometimes alone, would break into malt shops after hours, usually through the skylights that were a common feature of shops built before the Second World War. He'd pop the glass off the top of a pinball machine, tape the tilt mechanism in place, prop it up so that it was flat and quickly run through two to three hundred games a night to collect the coins. Ten to fifteen dollars was a good piece of change in the early 1940s and he'd spend it on his friends, taking them downtown to Clifton's Cafeteria on Broadway to impress them by paying for meals.

"I was also," he said, "the champion quarter lagger of the neighborhood. I could make twenty dollars a day just tossing quarters." With money always in his pocket and his success on the playing field, Blackie was popular, especially with the girls. A pretrial court-ordered psychiatric report in 1949 described him as "sexually promiscuous since the age of thirteen or fourteen."

Later in life he would claim that he had been an excellent student. He said that his wealthy aunt, who was married to his father's brother, Herbert, who was a vice president with JC Penny, offered to pay his way through Dartmouth. But that seems unlikely. Making decent money from petty crime and a little extra playing semipro baseball, Blackie quit high school at sixteen, just after finishing the tenth grade.

That was also about the time that he started drinking heavily, beer mostly, but whiskey with a beer chaser when he could afford it. Despite being well underage, he started hanging out in bars and pool halls. He continued playing sports, but like some of the players he admired he'd play drunk or hungover. His mother disapproved but couldn't do anything about it. His father had mixed emotions, after all his youngest son was just taking after himself.

Blackie came from a long line of drunks. The 1949 psychiatric report states that his father and two maternal uncles "drink alcohol to excess." His father drank heavily much of the time he was at home. His elder brother, Chester Jr., and several other family members also battled the bottle.

Ralph began to acquire the taste at a young age. One evening when he was four, his parents had some friends over. Ralph knocked back two whole bottles of beer. "It became a feat," he recalled, "something my dad told over and over again." He fondly remembered his first taste of whiskey at about the same time. And while he didn't think of himself as having a problem with it, all the times he got into trouble, or at least caught, booze was along for the ride.

One Friday night when he was sixteen, he was in the garage drinking a beer with his father. He told his father he was going to Tijuana, Mexico, for the weekend with a friend and his father said no.

"I say, 'I'm going,' and he hit me. I knocked him down. Worst day of my life. I went to Tijuana and things were real chilly for about a week around the house, but then they settled down and he didn't put any pressure on me anymore. That ended the discipline. It broke his heart. He hit me right in the chin and all it did was just back me up a little. I hit him and flattened him."

Blackie denied that his father ever physically abused him as a child, just the usual spankings and corporal punishment that were common at the time. But his father was known as a mean drunk and Blackie was known to get into a lot of fights. That and the chillingly matter-of-fact "and he hit me. I knocked him down," seem to indicate that physical violence of some sort or other was not unknown in the Schwamb household.

Gene Mauch, who played nine seasons in the majors and managed for another twenty-seven, played ball with Ralph when they were teenagers; they grew up together. "When sober, Blackie was one great kid," he said. "With alcohol he actually pursued daring and trouble."

The late '30s and early '40s were unsettled times. Trouble of one sort or another seemed to fill the air. During the first year of the war the country was particularly on edge. In Los Angeles frayed nerves led to events that were as surrealistic as they were tragic.

On Sunday afternoon, December 7, 1941, following the attack on Pearl Harbor, Los Angeles's sociable Japanese consul-general opened his house to the press, saying that he was "quite sorry" about the attack and that "all this is very hard to believe." At the same time there was a squadron of eight Japanese submarines in the vicinity. Two days before Christmas the submarine *I-17* sank a U.S. tanker off the coast of Oregon.

On February 15, 1942, soldiers raided the Japanese-American fishing community that had peacefully existed on Terminal Island, in L.A.'s harbor, for many years. They forced nearly five hundred families from their homes and impounded their boats. Two days later several thousand Japanese Americans attended a rally in downtown's Little Tokyo district to express their loyalty to the United States.

Five nights later *I-17* was just barely submerged in the waters off of Santa Barbara. Following orders from Tokyo, rather than acting on its commander's impulse to shoot at the lights of downtown, the sub fired twenty-five five-inch shells at an oil storage depot seven miles north of the city. Two days later Los Angeles had its first blackout, from about 2:30 A.M. until dawn. There were rumors of enemy airplanes approaching the city.

Early the next morning, at 3:12 A.M. on Thursday, February 26, all hell broke loose in the skies above Los Angeles. The Japanese attack was on, or so thought the 37th Coast Artillery Brigade stationed near the port of Long Beach. Over the next one hour and two minutes the city's defenders fired 1,430 shells into the air. Five civilians died during the blitz, three from traffic accidents and two from heart attacks. Clyde Lane of Long Beach was the only direct casualty of the artillery barrage; he was injured by falling shrapnel as he stood on the street. The Schwamb family lived about six miles north of the gun emplacements. Nobody got much sleep that night.

The next day's papers trumpeted the city's valiant defense of the country. Los Angeles, it was headlined, had fought off the murderous invaders. Articles claimed that Japanese Americans had guided the planes from the ground. Editorials screamed for the removal of Japanese people from all coastal regions.

There was a problem though. There hadn't really been an attack. It was all imaginary. There had never been any enemy airplanes. There were just young men with big guns and a bad case of jitters.

Less than a month later President Roosevelt issued Executive Order 9102 and within four months one hundred ten thousand Japanese, most of them American citizens, had been dispossessed and locked into camps.

Without the Japanese to worry about, people in Los Angeles began to turn their fear on Mexican Americans to the extent that Nazi propaganda singled out the city as an example that Americans didn't even trust their own allies. In 1943 sixteen Los Angeles Mexican Americans and one Anglo who lived in a Mexican neighborhood, were put on trial for homicide. The "Sleepy Lagoon Trial," as it was known, was the largest mass trial for murder in U.S. history. It was a sensation in the press. All seventeen defendants were convicted and sent to prison.

But just like the Japanese invasion the previous year, it was all imaginary. There might not even have been a murder, nobody knew. There was no real evidence; the charges were entirely fabricated. Two years later the defendants were all released.

In June 1943 the "Zoot Suit Riots" broke out. Large gangs of Mexican Americans dressed in zoot suits were reported to be massing to attack sailors and soldiers on leave. A group of two hundred sailors were said by radio news broadcasters and over police radios to be under attack in a Mexican neighborhood just east of downtown. For several days the newspapers blared big headlines about the terrible rioting taking place.

But it was also, for the most part, imaginary. There may have been a few scattered fights here and there around the city between men in uniform and men in zoot suits, but there never were any organized mass attacks other than by soldiers and sailors against almost entirely innocent young Mexican American men who knew better than to fight back against overwhelming odds.

Mauricio Mazon, historian and psychoanalyst, has characterized wartime Los Angeles as being in a state of near "delusional paranoia."

In late 1942 Ralph ran away from home with some friends. They stopped off in Tucson where one of them knew somebody and the group broke into some resort cabins in the nearby hills. "We didn't steal anything, just drank up the booze and ate some food." He got caught when one of his friends' mother turned them all in. After two days in jail the judge gave him probation so long as he agreed to join the service on his seventeenth birthday and sent him back to L.A.

More than a few teenage boys entered the military that way. During the war when fathers were absent and mothers were working long hours there was a tremendous surge in juvenile delinquency. While the war gave some people a new sense of purpose and resolve, a sense of fatalism came over others, especially young, fit males who faced an uncertain future.

Young women too had their lives and hopes disrupted. The phenomenon of "V-girls" titillated newspaper readers on a regular basis. They were white, middle-class rebellious teenage girls who were widely reputed to be sexually promiscuous. Venereal disease rates skyrocketed, a fact that struck many as proof that traditional virtues were no longer in force.

The Depression and the war had an enormous impact on the psychology of the country. Adversity brought out the best in a lot of people.

But the hard times brought out the worst in other people. Throughout the 1930s and 1940s people were frightened and insecure. They faced the all too real possibilities of dire poverty and then death in combat. Some rose to the occasion, most just hunkered down and tried to get by, others lashed out or got greedy. Crime, especially violent crime, was very much a growth industry. The Mafia, which could have been virtually bankrupted by the end of prohibition, found new sources of wealth in gambling and then profiteering on the black market during the war.

Interracial and ethnic violence, in factories and on the streets, became more commonplace than ever before as different groups of people found themselves working side by side for the first time.

War brutalizes and hardens its participants, no matter how honorable the cause. There were numerous deadly internal incidents within America's armed forces, on military bases at home and abroad, on streets at home and in foreign cities, and even on the battlefields.

In cities like Los Angeles where large numbers of servicemen spent their leave time, as many as fifty thousand on any given weekend during the war, there were frequent outbreaks of violence. Sometimes soldiers, sailors, and marines fought each other. Sometimes, pumped up on a bad mix of envy and resentment they fought with civilians. In one two-week period in mid-May 1943 there were eighteen serious confrontations between servicemen and civilians in Southern California; seven people were killed.

CHAPTER 5

O N HIS BIRTHDAY IN 1943, two months after the Zoot Suit Riots, Blackie Schwamb joined the navy. He figured that he was less likely to see action at sea, than he would on land. In the Pacific the battle of Midway had taken place a little more than a year before and the Japanese were thought to be in retreat across the Pacific. In November the previous year, the U.S. Navy had suffered horrendous losses during the battles around Guadalcanal, but the Japanese had finally been driven from the island in early December. By the time Blackie joined up, the U.S. Navy was successfully supporting the marines' tough drive north through the Solomon Islands toward New Guinea and hadn't suffered any significant losses since December.

That August, the navy engaged in two battles in the Pacific. The battle of Vella Gulf took place on the sixth and seventh. Japan lost three ships and more than twelve hundred men. The U.S. forces didn't lose any ships and suffered no casualties. On August 18, during a battle off the island of Horaniu, United States ships sank a couple of empty Japanese barges and once again the United States suffered no losses. The marines and army were getting the worst of the fighting for the Solomons. The First and Fourth Raider Battalions were slogging through the jungles and swamps of New Georgia, just to the north and west of Guadalcanal.

Blackie's own account of his naval career was heroic, sad, and as illusory as the attack on Los Angeles and the rioting zoot suiters had been. His story was that he was on a destroyer headed for the Pacific front that was torpedoed and went down fast. He was one of fewer than twenty who survived. He was sent back to Hawaii and was supposed to get leave to go home for thirty days, but instead he was reassigned to a ship that was headed back out in a day or two. The officer who delivered the news wasn't very nice about it, so he and a friend, another survivor of the ship that had sunk, flipped a coin to see who was going to slug the officer. Schwamb won, saluted the flag, turned around and decked the officer. He was arrested, dragged to the brig, and sentenced to a naval prison.

The story ended there when he told it to friends. But according to Bea Franklin,[3] with whom he lived for the last seventeen years of his life, the story continued and provided an explanation for Ralph's estrangement from his big brother, Chester Jr. Arriving at the brig in handcuffs, Blackie discovered that his brother, who had also joined the navy, was in charge. Without saying a word and without removing the handcuffs, Chester Jr. hauled him into a room, locked the door, and beat him up.

The story as told in his navy personnel records, however, is much more complete and very different.

On September 1, Schwamb went straight into training at the naval Station in San Diego. His pay was fifty bucks a month. His rate (what the navy calls a rank) was AS (apprentice seaman)-V-6, the lowest rank at which someone could enter the navy. At 168 pounds he was rail thin. "Distinguishing marks" were listed as a tattoo of a ship on his upper right forearm, a half-inch scar on his left front torso, a one-inch-by-half-inch birthmark on his left lower abdomen, a one-inch scar on the back of his left hand, and a tattoo of a bird on his right upper arm. He designated his father as his beneficiary.

Three days later he had completed gas mask instruction in the gas chamber, a large battery of physical and mental tests, had signed his

---

3 Her family name has been changed to protect her privacy.

copy of the rules and regulations, and submitted his form for life insurance. He'd been rated a "swimmer—third class."

The military needed men quickly at that time but they still required
several months of training. Blackie was finally assigned to active duty,
with Squadron Flight Air Wing 14 at San Diego Naval Air Station on
January 8, 1944. His rate was upgraded to S2c (seaman second class)-
V-6 and he was given a conduct mark of 4.0, which is about average. He
was also rated a 3.6 in seamanship, 3.6 in mechanical ability, and 3.6 in
"ability as leader of men." Unless a sailor stood out from the crowd, rat-
ings were a perfunctory business; nobody expected them to mean much.

True to form, he began to get into trouble. On February 1 he was
declared a "straggler." He'd been missing from base, "absent without
leave," since 7:30 in the morning on January 29. He finally brought
himself back to the base on February 6. At what is called a "deck
court" on March 9 he pleaded guilty and was sentenced to twenty days
of confinement and docked $36 of his pay.

On April 3 they let him out and assigned him to the USS *Prince
William,* a small aircraft carrier that had been launched just a year and
a half before. The ship had been operating between San Diego and the
Pacific Islands since July 1943. On April 4, one day after he reported
for duty, the *Prince William* put out to sea. It was a short trip to ferry
some planes and supplies to other ships and ports.

By April 12 Ralph was back in San Diego and was transferred to
the USS *San Jacinto,* another light aircraft carrier that was scheduled to
head into the thick of the fighting in the Pacific. One of the young pilots on the ship was future president George H. W. Bush. Navy pilots
and lowly seamen didn't fraternize much, so it is unlikely that they
would have crossed paths.

The *San Jacinto* left San Diego, headed for the fighting, at seven in
the morning on April 14. Blackie wasn't on board. An hour later, having missed the ship, he was officially declared a deserter, with the nota-
tion, "intentions unknown."

A couple of hours later he woke up with a hangover in a cheap hotel.
He wasn't sure of his intentions either. Navy discipline didn't sit well with

him. Bored on a boat, surrounded by a bunch of other scared young guys, headed to god knows where to get shot at by god knows who wasn't nearly as inviting as the highlife at home. He caught the train back to L.A.

A week later the shore patrol caught up with him around Central Avenue in L.A., put him in handcuffs and delivered him to the brig at the navy base in nearby San Pedro.

Ralph was brought before a summary court-martial, a step up from a deck court, on May 17. He pleaded guilty. There wasn't much else he could do. On May 30 he had his pay docked $27 per month for five months and was sentenced to thirty days of solitary confinement at Terminal Island Naval prison. He got bread and water, with a full food ration every third day.

They let him out on June 30, restored him to full duty the next day, and sent him to San Pedro to await reassignment. At 11:30 on the night of July 10 a couple of marine guards found him just outside the fence of the base. Lights out had been a half hour earlier. They threw him back in the brig.

He'd been absent without leave for only thirty minutes, but brought up once again before a summary court-martial he was sentenced to a pay loss of $23.80 per month for six months and another thirty days in solitary on bread and water and a full ration every third day.

Blackie hadn't known his own intentions that time either. He'd just been restless, got up to walk around, and found himself where he wasn't supposed to be. He knew the rules but it seemed unfair, thirty days for thirty minutes; that made him mad.

Cigarettes and matches were hard to come by in Terminal Island. He found the smokes, but had to improvise to light up. On July 28 he was cited for possession of contraband and "endangering the lives of co-prisoners by inserting a graphite pencil in the light socket to create sparks to light cigarettes." At the summary court-martial for that offense they added twenty days to his confinement and took another $36 out of his pay.

In Europe the Allied invasion was pressing east. In the Pacific the fleet was battling its way north toward Japan. Both fronts needed a lot of troops. On September 8 Ralph was released and once more sent to San Pedro to await assignment.

But once again he wouldn't stay put. Just two days later, around 11:30 on another of those restless nights, he vanished again. He was either unlucky, or more likely just drunk and careless, but the shore patrol nabbed him hanging around his old haunts three days later. This time he was recommended for a general court-martial, the most serious judicial proceeding in the military.

Blackie was an uncooperative prisoner. While awaiting trial he received several warnings for his conduct, though they were mostly for minor infractions. One was for removing a red armband from his shirt.

On October 3 he was found guilty of "Absence from station and duty without leave." He was demoted to the rating of apprentice seaman and sentenced to two years in Terminal Island prison at the end of which he was to be dishonorably discharged from the navy, and to "suffer all other accessories of said sentence."

The military was, however, desperate for sailors. So a few days later his sentence was reduced to fifteen months of confinement with the possibility of being restored to full duty after eight months if he behaved himself. The dishonorable discharge was softened to a "bad conduct discharge," a less grievous separation from the service that would make his transition to civilian life easier.

On October 16, 1944, Ralph was transferred to the Naval Disciplinary Barracks on Terminal Island in the Los Angeles harbor. On the same day the secretary of the navy, acting on a recommendation from the chief of navy personnel, cut another month off of the initial part of his sentence. He could be back on duty in seven months if he was a good prisoner.

He wasn't. On December 5 he was cited for a violation of prison regulations and thrown into solitary confinement on a diet of bread and water for five days. On December 22, while being transferred somewhere, he escaped. He went home for Christmas and stayed drunk through New Year's Eve. Blackie turned himself in at a little after eight in the evening on New Year's Day 1945.

The next morning he woke up angry in his cell and shredded his prison uniform. That earned him five days in solitary on bread and water for destruction of government property. All his "good time" and the possibility of getting out after only seven months were canceled.

Finally he settled down. He began to cooperate, figuring it was the only way he was ever going to get out. On June 1 he was transferred to the prison at Great Lakes Naval Training Center in Chicago. Two months and sixteen days of his good conduct allowance was restored.

The navy kicked him out not too long after Emperor Hirohito of Japan had announced his country's surrender. He was given a bad conduct discharge, civilian clothing "not to exceed $30 in value," and $25 in cash. On his mustering-out form he listed his main civilian occupation as "carpenter's helper" and his job preference as "professional baseball player." The navy offered him a bus ride home. He couldn't get back to L.A. fast enough.

CHAPTER 6

JUST AFTER THE WAR WAS THE PERFECT TIME for Blackie to hook up with Mickey Cohen's crew. Bugsy Siegel broke ground for the Flamingo Hotel and Casino in Las Vegas in December 1945. Distracted by his grand vision for the desert town, he had turned over his lucrative gambling, loan sharking, and other rackets in L.A. to Cohen. Mickey went on an expansion binge.

Blackie's new boss was a short blocky guy, given to wearing impeccably tailored double-breasted suits, always with perfectly starched white shirts, silk ties, a white handkerchief in his breast pocket, a well-blocked matching fedora, and shoes buffed to a bright gleam. His legal fronts included a haberdashery on the Sunset Strip, a few dry cleaners, and several nightclubs. One of his several offices was in a barbershop in a nice working-class Jewish neighborhood.

Mickey was born in Brooklyn. His mother, a widowed Ukrainian Jewish immigrant, brought the family out to Boyle Heights, just east of downtown L.A. in 1915 or 1916 when he was two or three years old. At that time the neighborhood was a ghetto shared by Mexicans who were the original inhabitants, Italians, and Russian Jews. By the time he was eight Cohen was working in a drugstore owned by his brothers, who were also running an illegal gin still behind the store.

Mickey was feisty and got into a lot of fights. He became a boxer and went to Chicago, Detroit, and then New York where he started doing favors for gangsters. By the time he came back to Los Angeles he was well connected to the Mafia, although still independent. He had been "asked" to hook up with Bugsy Siegel who had recently been sent out to take over the rackets in the West.

Busy celebrating his homecoming with his family and old friends, Cohen didn't bother calling on Siegel. Before long he got together his own crew and started robbing fellow crooks, knocking over card games and bookie parlors.

"We never even gave a fuck about Benny [Siegel]," Cohen wrote in his autobiography. "We were just rooting, just taking off scores. I was out with ten different broads every night and I was in every cabaret that they could possibly have in the town. When we needed money we always had two, three scores in advance. We always had tipsters waiting for us to get together with them."

It wasn't long before Cohen and his guys held up the wrong bookie joint. Jack Dragna, whom Siegel was trying to keep on his good side, ran it. Bugsy called Mickey on the carpet and told him to make restitution, but he admired the little mobster's moxie and they ended up pals.

After the war Boyle Heights was in transition. Mexican Americans had originally settled the hilly area in the late 1800s. Then the Italians came in the early 1900s. By the 1920s it was mostly Jewish, Russian, and poor. By 1940, with an estimated Jewish population of nearly one hundred forty thousand, Boyle Heights was the Los Angeles equivalent of New York's Lower East Side. Synagogues, kosher butchers, bakers, and delis had all but completely crowded out the few remaining taquerias, bodegas, and Italian groceries. But that didn't last long.

The end of the Depression brought quick change to a lot of L.A. neighborhoods. When jobs became available and people once more had money, they began to move. The Jews moved west, some to the German and Italian neighborhoods of South Central, but most to the newly developing Beverly-Fairfax district just slightly to the south and west of Hollywood. Mexican Americans in search of cheap housing near the industrial parts of town east of the Los Angeles River began to move back into Boyle Heights. Returning veterans, easily able to finance houses that their families couldn't have afforded just a few years before, accelerated the process. By the late 1940s Boyle Heights was once again mostly a Mexican American neighborhood.

When Mickey Cohen came back to L.A. he lived in the Beverly-Fairfax area before making it big. Then he moved farther west, to very swank Brentwood where he lived among movie stars and other members of the city's new elite. But he was still in charge of the rackets in Boyle Heights. His old friends Joe and Freddy Sica ran the neighborhood for him.

The Sica brothers were inseparable from Cohen. They were Italian, and the Jewish gangster relied on them as his liaison to the Italian mob. In his memoir, writing about another mobster who was murdered, Cohen says, "He had a run-in with Fred Sica, which is naturally the exact same thing as having a run-in with me." The Sicas had been with Mickey when he robbed Jack Dragna's betting parlor.

In the fall of 1945 Blackie Schwamb was introduced to Mickey Cohen. They chatted for a little while, then Mickey sent him to see the Sica brothers. They could use a tall strong young man who was good with his fists, liked money, and didn't seem to be infected with too many scruples. Blackie quickly found work as a "leg-breaker," collecting debts for bookies and loan sharks.

He didn't work in Boyle Heights for long. His old neighborhood around Manchester and Vermont, Wrigley Field, Hollywood Park Racetrack, and Central Avenue with its dozens of nightclubs, gambling parlors, and brothels provided greater opportunities. By early 1946 he was breaking legs closer to home. He liked the work.

> They didn't care if you worked as a carpenter, or if you were a pool shark. If you owe some money, Friday night you'd better have it. I had run-ins with a couple of movie stars—happily so. I kicked their ass and got their money; but they were in big, like thirty-five or forty thousand dollars and they deserved it. I never

got any satisfaction from hitting a workingman for a couple of hundred bucks. But he's causing it. I didn't cause it.

To get worked up I'd eat four or five whites [amphetamine tablets] and start drinking black coffee. I could be in a blind rage by the time I got where I was going. I've always hated four-flushers and welshers. The pay depended on how far you wanted to go, how bad they wanted them, how much you had to hurt them.

I was in it for money, clothes, lunch at the Derby or Lucia's, dinner at the Zephyr Room. Everyday you'd pat your pocket. I've still got that habit. When I wake up in the morning and put on my pants, first thing I do is pat my pocket to see if I've got any money in there. It was wonderful at the time, the high was fantastic when you woke up in the morning and hit your pocket and hey, you've got it.

L.A. was an especially great place to be flush in the late 1940s. Hollywood was living up to its glitzy reputation. Swank restaurants and nightclubs were packed almost every night of the week. Klieg lights criss-crossed the night skies, drawing attention to the latest event rather than searching for enemy aircraft. Gambling dens and brothels, from sleazy to high-toned, were operating almost openly and were easy to find throughout the city. Glamorous clubs were popping up all over. The Cotton Club, the self-proclaimed "largest dancehall in the world," with a fittingly big chorus line and top acts brought the crowds to Culver City. The ornate La Monica pulsed with big-name bands on the Santa Monica Pier. Duke Ellington played to sardine-can audiences at the Trianon Ballroom down on Firestone Boulevard, more than halfway out to the harbor.

But the real heart and soul of Los Angeles nightlife, what gave it its distinctive flavor and brought it international recognition, was to be found along Central Avenue stretching south from downtown to Watts. It was in that area that Blackie found more work, bodyguarding and running errands for some of the singers and musicians who were making Los Angeles one of the music capitals of the world.

In its heyday, which lasted from the 1920s through the early 1950s, Central Avenue was as famous as Bourbon Street in New Orleans, Beale Street in Memphis, or the jazz districts in Kansas City and Harlem. It had its own sound, a rhythm and blues, honking and driving jazz beat that was immediately recognizable to aficionados.

The street kicked into high gear after 1917 when wartime puritans shut down New Orleans's legendary red-light district, Storyville. A lot of musicians moved west looking for work. Jelly Roll Morton showed up in town and before long was playing piano and pimping at the Cadillac Café on Central between Fifth and Sixth streets. Kid Ory, one of the most famous New Orleans bandleaders, arrived in L.A. in 1919 and put together a new band. He also played at the Cadillac.

In 1921 San Francisco's Barbary Coast was the next victim of American puritanism and a lot of musicians headed south, where the climate was warmer in every respect.

At the south end of Central Avenue Watts was an independent city in the early 1920s. Clubs opened there to pull in the crowds after L.A.'s midnight curfew. When the Cadillac Café closed, Jelly Roll Morton would take a cab down the street to keep playing. Rudolph Valentino was well known for dancing in Watts. Charlie Chaplin would show up frequently with groups of his Hollywood pals.

In 1926 it looked like Watts was about to elect a black mayor and city council. The local racists weren't going to stand still for that. A lobbying effort, largely led by the Ku Klux Klan, resulted in the city of Los Angeles annexing the city of Watts. The after-hours clubs, however, remained and more opened north along the avenue. They were illegal but for the most part tolerated so long as they stayed in the black part of town. That brought in even more crowds.

In 1928 the Dunbar Hotel, originally called the Somerville, opened on Central at 41st Street just in time to house delegates to that year's convention of the NAACP. It was, according to its guests, who included such luminaries as W. E. B. DuBois and Louis Armstrong, the biggest and best black-owned and -operated hotel in the country.

Next door to the Dunbar was Club Apex, which in September 1931 changed its name to Club Alabam. It reigned until the early 1950s as the most famous nightclub in the area. The club featured mostly black entertainers who played to the first integrated crowds in the city. Count Basie, Billie Holiday, and Duke Ellington were regular headliners. The chorus line had as many as fifty dancers. In the early 1930s, at the greatest depths of the Great Depression, the club employed about one hundred black people. The Alabam was popular with movie stars; among its regulars were Mae West, Cary Grant, Clark Gable, and Jean Harlow. Stepin Fetchit, the black comedian, would park his long cream-colored Packard in front of the club, leaving his pet lion in the backseat.

Despite the hard times, Central Avenue and the surrounding area boomed through the 1930s. On March 10, 1933, Prohibition officially ended and people came from all over town to drink up the free beer and wine that flowed from the celebrating clubs up and down the avenue.

More than two-thirds of the city's black population lived along the narrow corridor centered on the avenue and while not affluent, the neighborhood was reasonably prosperous. More than a third of the black families in the area owned their own homes, the highest proportion in the country for a big city with a large black population. Though most of the nightclubs in the area were white owned, blacks usually ran them and a large number of other businesses were owned and run by people who lived in the community.

In 1940 the state of California passed a law banning the sale of alcohol after 2 A.M. On Central Avenue that just increased the market for after-hours clubs and brought yet more people to the area late at night. During the war, clubs that didn't serve food had to close early so a lot of places quickly became "cafés" with music and bootleg sales of booze on the side.

The nightlife scene expanded north into what had been Little Tokyo. Shepp's Playhouse at First Street and Los Angeles Avenue had been a Japanese restaurant before the war. The new owners bought it cheap from the Japanese owners who were in a hurry to sell before they were shipped off to a detention camp. It became a popular cocktail lounge and jazz venue. Coleman Hawkins regularly played there.

Barely having slowed down during the war, Central Avenue had built up a powerful head of steam by the time Blackie Schwamb became a regular. *The California Eagle,* a black newspaper, referred to the "Furious Forties of the Brown Broadway," meaning Central Avenue between 40th and 50th streets.

In the last half of the 1940s, those ten blocks were home to many of the greatest musicians and clubs of the time. The Dunbar Hotel held big dances with name acts in its Golding Room. In the Turban Room, the Dunbar's cocktail lounge, Art Tatum would play piano after hours but only when someone would bring him a bottle of VO and a case of Pabst Blue Ribbon beer to wash it down.

All through 1946 the Johnny Otis Big Band tore up the house at the Alabam while across the street at the Downbeat, which was owned by Mickey Cohen, the Stars of Swing featuring Charles Mingus, Buddy Collette, and Teddy Edwards—one of the greatest jazz groups ever— were their rivals. The Breakfast Club was above the Alabam. It opened at 2 A.M. for drinks, gambling, and fried chicken and was usually busy until just past sunrise.

Also across from the Dunbar was the Memo, known for its elegant furnishings. The Elk's Auditorium, which had terrible acoustics but booked great bands at cheap admission prices, was just down the block. The Last Word, the Last Roundup, the Hi-De-Ho Club, the Big Apple, and Leer's Café were all rocking full tilt in that short stretch of Central.

A stretch of street some ninety blocks long was riotous with nightlife. Jack's Basket Room at 33rd and Central got going after 2 A.M. It sold baskets of chicken and french fries with setups (mixers and ice). A guy in the corner sold half-pints of whisky. Its Monday night jam sessions were legendary and radio shows were often broadcast from there. A rhythm section was always busy on the small bandstand and musicians would show up to jam. Charlie Parker was a regular.

Dynamite Jackson's at 55th was elite and expensive. Club Araby at 54th had big bands. The 54th Street Drugstore, open all night, sold setups at the lunch counter and had slot machines in the back. The Cabin Inn was at 23rd, across from the Lincoln Theater, Black and Gold at 12th and Lovejoy's at Vernon. Honey Murphy's at 93rd had an after-hours upstairs called Ivie's Chicken Shack. Ivie Anderson, the longtime singer with Duke Ellington's band, ran it.

Billie Holiday sang often at the Savoy at 103rd Street. The Plantation Club, a barnlike place with sawdust on the floor, featured the biggest of the big bands. Blainell's looked like a big old office building but was a multistory jazz club. The Brown sisters owned Little Harlem, off Imperial. They brought T-Bone Walker out from Oklahoma to headline on guitar and it was rumored that they shared him as a lover.

Brother's, down an alley and up a rickety flight of stairs, didn't open until 1 A.M. and you had to know someone to get in. The guy who ran it wore long robes, there were pillows rather than chairs, incense, low lights, and a warren of little rooms where anything anyone wanted—booze, gambling, drugs, girls or boys—was available.

Heading west, San Pedro Avenue also had clubs. Elihu "Black Dot" McGhee, a gambler and hustler who owned a lot of clubs, had his best-known after-hours on 23rd. Down the street on 27th was Café Society, scandalous and very popular as an interracial pickup joint. The Casbah on Figueroa regularly featured Sarah Vaughn and Dizzy Gillespie. Ebb's on Vermont was a well-known lesbian hot spot that featured all-women jazz bands. The Oasis on Western presented Nat King Cole, Al Hibbler, Billie Holiday, and Louis Armstrong when he was in town.

Farther south toward the harbor the town of Gardena had legal card clubs such as the Normandie. They were large and swank, open around the clock, and had special rooms for high rollers. Nightclubs and burlesque houses, the two most famous being the Bal Tabarin and the Colony Club, featured scores of chorus girls and risqué acts.

Blackie was twenty. He dressed sharp but not flashy in nicely cut loose jackets and sharply creased pleated trousers. The pleats were a bit of an extravagance, a sign of prosperity. During the war pants had to be made with flat fronts to save cloth for the armed forces.

His turf was close to home but he cut a wide swathe through L.A.'s raucous nightlife. He'd do his rounds, making collections, bodyguarding or driving for the occasional celebrity, delivering messages, and occasionally hauling some poor slob who owed money to the wrong sort of people into an alley or out to a dark vacant lot to make his point.

He liked to drink. And though he had a quick, mean temper when he was drunk, if you didn't rile him up he was usually friendly, loquacious, and charming. He was a big flirt and a big enough tipper that he was popular with waitresses, cocktail servers, and cigarette and chorus girls.

Money in his pocket, plenty of women, free-flowing booze, glamorous nightclubs, fine dining, hobnobbing with musicians and movie stars and sometimes getting to beat them up, Blackie Schwamb was living out his dreams.

CHAPTER 7

W HEN HE WAS YOUNG BLACKIE SELDOM SUFFERED from hangovers. He'd sleep late and awake with no more than a slightly queasy malaise. Coffee, a few beers, and by early afternoon he'd be back in high spirits.

Saturday afternoons, like a lot of people in his neighborhood, he would go to the park, usually Manchester Playground, and hang out with friends. Evo Pusich was the recreation supervisor at Manchester and clearly remembered when he first met Ralph: "We were having problems with someone breaking into the cars of the ballplayers. One day I noticed this big guy sitting up in the stands with a couple other crumb-bums, drinking and smoking. You weren't supposed to drink alcohol in a city park.

"Everyone was just giving these guys a wide berth. I figured the worst they could do was shoot me, so I went up to the big guy. Always take the big guy out first. So I tell him to put away the bottle and I ask him if he knew anything about cars being broken into. I told him the ballplayers didn't have the time or money to put up with that kind of crap. He just laughed."

After Blackie's friends left, he changed his tune. Pusich was surprised when the tall guy with the cigarette came up to him and politely asked if he could join one of the semipro baseball teams that played in the park.

The teams were already set for the season but the thirty-nine-year-old Pusich, who had recently started scouting for the New York (now San Francisco) Giants, looked over the tall, lanky, strong nineteen-year-old and thought he had the right build for a pitcher. A couple of days later Blackie was back and Pusich began to work out with him, tutoring him in some of the finer points of baseball.

"I found out he was an awfully nice kid," recalled Pusich. "He came from a pretty good background, was intelligent, and had good manners. Oh, he was a renegade and all that, but when I was working with him he was quiet and polite. After a few days I told him he had a chance to make something of himself in baseball but he had to steer clear of those bums he was hanging around with. He didn't listen. We'd finish at the park and he'd walk out the gate and go right back to those guys."

In spite of Blackie's unsavory pals, Pusich was impressed enough with his abilities to seriously consider signing him to a contract with the Giants. Years later, retired after forty-five years spent scouting, during which he signed dozens of future major leaguers including several very big stars, he said, "Ralph Schwamb was the best pitching prospect I ever saw.

"But then I find out that he's been in prison, had gone over the hill in the service, and all kinds of bad stuff. I knew the Giants would fire me in a minute if I signed a hoodlum like that."

Late one Saturday morning in early 1946 Blackie's childhood friend Jim Muhe dropped by to visit just about the time he was contemplating his first beer of the day. Muhe was playing for a semipro team that was loosely connected with the major-league St. Louis Browns. He asked if Blackie wanted to come along and watch the game.

It was one of those lovely Southern California winter days, just warm enough to be comfortable in short sleeves. There wasn't much of a breeze so there was no telling what had pushed the smog away, but the snow-covered San Gabriel Mountains were easily visible to the east. It was a good day for watching a ball game and sucking back some brews. Blackie didn't need to be anywhere until the evening. If the game went long he could just walk over to Central and hop on the U-line trolley north.

"So they were getting their butts kicked and I started complainin'," Blackie recalled. "I had had about six or seven beers by then and was yellin' that I could do better than that. The guy who was runnin' the club was a Brown's bird dog [unpaid] scout name of Pete Peterson. He came up and told me to 'shut up or show 'em.' I took off my coat and tie, went out there and walked six and struck out eleven. After that I played for 'em some and then they got the big scouts out from St. Louis after me."

The American League Browns were a terrible team. They were perennial losers. Between 1901 and 1944 they had finished in the top three (out of eight) of their league only six times, and never in first place. Year after year it was said about St. Louis that the city was "First in booze, first in shoes and last in the American League."

The team's attendance was usually so low (a mere thirty-four fans showed up to watch them lose one game in 1933) that in some years the only reason they didn't go broke was that they leased out their stadium, Sportsman's Park, to the Cardinals, St. Louis's National League baseball club. Because of the constant play the outfield grass almost never got a chance to recover between games. By midseason there were plenty of neighborhood baseball diamonds that looked more lush and inviting. Among the many ads that adorned the outfield walls, five were for local breweries, and cheap beer attracted as many fans to the Browns' games as the baseball they played.

The association with beer had a long tradition. St. Louis, with its large German population, was home to a great many breweries. Back in the 1880s the original St. Louis Browns had been very successful, winning four American Association championships during the decade. The team was owned by Chris Von der Ahe, a German immigrant who ran a grocery with a popular saloon in back and who had a knack for smart real estate deals. Von der Ahe was one of the founders of the American Association.

At the time baseball was seen as an unsavory pastime. Ballplayers were largely regarded as lazy, boozy ne'er-do-wells who were just trying to avoid real work. The existing National League had been struggling for respectability and a family audience. The American Association rose to compete with it on the strength of two great ideas that at the time seemed scandalous and were banned by the National League: Sunday games, and most important, beer sales at the ballpark. American Association owners, led by Von der Ahe who had agreed to finance the St. Louis team in return for the beer concession, kept admission prices low. They figured, rightly as it turned out, that fans would spend the money they had saved on tickets on cold mugs of highly profitable brew.

Von der Ahe treated his team's fans well, providing a variety of carnival-like amusements at the ballpark and going so far as to pay all the expenses of a large group of them to travel to New York for the 1888 championship games against the Giants. The use of the word "fan" to mean something other than a tool or machine for pushing air around has been attributed to Von der Ahe, who referred to his supporters as "fanatics." Sportswriters shortened the word.

Unfortunately the American Association lasted only ten years before a player revolt, other disputes between players and owners, and possibly illegal competitive practices by the National League killed it off. The Browns were absorbed into the National League.

In 1899 Von der Ahe was forced to sell the team because of lawsuits arising from a fire in the grandstands during a game the year before. There wasn't much of the team left to sell anyway, and what there was merged with the Cleveland Spiders who moved to St. Louis. A year later they became the Cardinals. In 1901 the Milwaukee Brewers moved to St. Louis and became the Browns of the newly formed American League. There they languished, poor cousins to the more popular and successful Cardinals, incessant losers of games and dollars.

In 1941 the Browns had finally made a deal to get out of St. Louis, to a big city that didn't have a major-league baseball team. The financing was in place, a ballpark had been arranged, and the other teams had given their assurances that they would vote in favor of the move at the next baseball meeting. The Browns were going to move to Los Angeles.

But the deal fell through. The late fall meeting of major-league baseball was cut short and nobody felt secure enough to vote in favor of any change to the status quo. It was held on the morning of December 8, less than twenty-four hours after the Japanese had attacked Pearl Harbor.

The war decimated baseball. Men between the ages of twenty (eventually reduced to eighteen) and forty-five were eligible for the draft. Single men without children were the first to go, married men with children and a job that contributed to the war effort were the last. Occupations were prioritized according to wartime necessity. Bartenders, astrologers, dance instructors, men working in Turkish baths or for social-escort services were among those singled out in a list of twenty-nine occupations and thirty-six types of business that were definitely not essential work. Aircraft technicians, chemists, and farmers were among those who got deferments, as did large numbers of people working in the movie industry and musicians over the age of twenty-nine. Baseball team owners argued that the sport was as important for morale as movies and so their players should be exempt from the draft, but they lost the argument.

In all of major-league baseball there were only ten players who didn't qualify for the draft. The major leagues considered closing down for the duration, but President Roosevelt asked them not to for the sake of home front morale. During the 1943 season more than half of the total major leaguers from the year before were in the military. The New York Yankees had lost every single one of their 1942 World Series champion starting players to the armed forces. By the start of the 1944 season 85 percent of major-league ballplayers were in the service, along with more than three thousand minor leaguers. There had been forty-three minor leagues in 1941, by 1943 and for the duration of the war there were only nine.

The quality of play during the war was for the most part abysmal. Older players came out of retirement for a last hurrah. Players who never would have otherwise made it to the majors found themselves in starting positions. Joe Nuxhall, a fifteen-year-old, came in one day in 1944 to pitch for the Cincinnati Reds. Pete Gray, a one-armed outfielder, played for the Browns in 1945.

It could only have happened during the war. But in the fall of 1944 while Blackie Schwamb sat bored stiff in his cell on Terminal Island, the St. Louis Browns won the American League pennant. He was able to listen to the unlikely World Series on the radio.

The Browns had an advantage that year. They were accustomed to playing in adverse conditions with a team of ill-paid, second-rate, on-the-verge-of-retirement misfits. Fielding the oldest, and some said the drunkest team in baseball, the Browns didn't lose any players of repute to the draft between the 1943 and '44 seasons. In 1944 they also led the major leagues in one of wartime baseball's most important categories: the number of players with 4-F, "medically unfit," draft classifications. Every other team in baseball lost most of their starting players. While the other teams were desperately trying to figure out how to cope with the unusual circumstances, it was business as usual for the Browns.

The opposing team in the World Series was their tenant, the St. Louis Cardinals. The Cardinals beat the Browns four games to two.

The next year the United States was fighting on two fronts, and a lot of pro athletes who had previously been exempt were reexamined, reclassified, and drafted. With baseball in tatters the Browns finished a respectable third. But it had been the worst season in the history of the game. One sportswriter trying to pick the victor between the Chicago Cubs and the Detroit Tigers, the two teams that were to play in the World Series, wrote that he was pretty sure neither team could win.

At the end of the 1945 season the Browns were sold. Because of having played in the '44 World Series and because attendance had been up during the past three years they actually had some money in the bank. The new owner used up all the cash buying Sportsman's Park and making some improvements. There wasn't a dime left for player development and it quickly showed.

In 1946 things returned to normal. There had been 384 major-league players in the service in 1945; by the next season only twenty-two remained in military uniform. The Browns returned to their rightful place near the bottom of the standings. By the middle of the season the new owner was selling off their few star players to make ends meet. They finished in seventh.

When the war ended people were hungry for life to get back to business as usual. The surrender of Japan came too late in the year to have had much of an impact on the 1945 season, but by early 1946 the minor leagues were starting up again, major leaguers were out of military uniform and getting in shape, and fans were planning to go to games in record numbers. In late 1945 a lot of returning major-league stars started playing exhibition games to get in some practice and to make up for some of the money they'd lost by not playing for three or four years.

In the fall of 1945 Blackie went to a couple of exhibition games in Los Angeles. Two teams, one led by Bob Feller, the greatest pitcher of the white major leagues, and the other by Satchel Paige, the greatest pitcher of the Negro Leagues, played two games against each other in November to record crowds in L.A.'s Wrigley Field. Paige outpitched Feller in the first game; Feller bested Paige in the second. Blackie was busy for a week collecting on the gambling debts that had resulted.

In early 1946 he was holding down two jobs. He was pitching, and sometimes playing shortstop, for the baseball team that his friend had introduced him to. They played around Los Angeles, more often than not in city parks. Sometimes they'd travel a little farther afield, to San Bernardino or San Diego. They'd take the trolley or train or maybe a teammate would have a car and they could catch a ride. Blackie would make two or three bucks for a game, which was about the same as doing it for free. He liked playing baseball but he also liked the good times that money could buy. He made a lot more money, an actual living, working for Mickey Cohen.

For the first few months after his release he had been living with his parents. His father helped him land a job with a glass company at $45 per week. It wasn't enough money for him and he either quit or was fired after a couple of weeks.

Things were tense around his parents' house and he didn't spend much time there. His father, Chester, who was working at Northrup Aviation, had gotten his secretary, Edith, pregnant and his parents were getting divorced after nearly twenty-five years of marriage. Edith was just a few years older than Ralph and his father planned to marry her as soon as the divorce was final. But then, Edith was married too.

"She was a stone fox," recalled Blackie. "He told me the whole scam, ran it down to me, never even mentioned it to my brother. We were in a bar across the street from Northrup and in walks this guy just looking around the room. My dad's back was to him and I was staring at him and he didn't go sit at the bar or nothing, he just stood there. He was about six feet, one hundred ninety pounds. I asked my dad, 'you know that guy?' My dad turned around. He says, 'That's Edith's husband.' I say, 'I can't help you.' He says, 'OK.' So he got up and the guy took him out in the parking lot and beat the shit out of him. But that's the last that ever happened over that. He gave Edith a divorce. I didn't cause that problem. I had no business getting in that. My dad always said it was worth it. They were together until he died. None of that stuff changed my attitude about life or made me a worse person or a better person."

While his parents, Chester and Janet, were getting divorced, Ralph was getting married to Nell.

Nellie Ann was born to Helen Paul,[4] a seventeen-year-old whose occupation is listed as "domestic" on the birth certificate, and Clarence Cross, a twenty-five-year-old salesman in Ironton, Minnesota, on September 7, 1926. Clarence apparently didn't remain on the scene for long. Nell's birth certificate states, "child also known as Nellie A. Eisen," and cites an affidavit from her stepfather Walter. Nell, adopted by Walter, was the oldest of the four children that he and Helen raised.

Ironton is tiny. Its population in 1990 was 498. It never was big but that was down considerably from 1926 when Nell was born. In the 1990 U.S. official census map it appears to be the smallest of all possible dots, floating in the waters of an unnamed lake.

Nell went to Crosby-Ironton High School where she was one of the class beauties. She looked a lot like Linda Darnell, a hot screen siren of

---

[4] Nell's maiden name and the surnames of Nell's family have been changed in accordance with the wishes of her surviving family members.

the day. She was a tall brunette, with a perfect creamy complexion, sculpted cheekbones, and piercing icy-blue eyes. She was smart and outgoing, well liked, and quite the catch.

About six months before her graduation Nell's parents packed up and moved with her two sisters and brother to a logging camp called White Horse in the High Sierras of California's northeasternmost county. The family had relatives there and the promise of better work, even an ownership stake in a timber company. Nell stayed behind to finish high school. Then she succumbed to the lure of the big city.

Nell moved to Los Angeles in late 1943 or early 1944. She got a job as a clerk with the OPA (the Office of Price Administration, which oversaw price fixing and rationing during the war.) One of her coworkers was Ralph's mother, Janet, who wanted to fix the pretty young woman up with her son.

It isn't clear whether or not Nell met Ralph before he was sent to the naval prison. It's possible that Janet introduced them when he was on leave, or during one of the several times he was "absent without leave." It's also possible that they met through the mail when he was in prison, exchanging letters and pictures.

However they met, the two hit it off right away. Nell thought Ralph was good looking. She was naive about his drinking and troubled past, figuring that whatever scrapes he'd gotten into, he'd snap out of it before long. The war was on and Ralph was a man in uniform, never mind how he got there. He was charming, flirtatious, had a nice easy manner and a good sense of humor. He was young but he knew his way around Los Angeles. He knew where the movie stars went to eat and drink, where the good music could be found. Out of uniform he was a sharp dresser and he almost always had, or at least had access to a car. He must have been pretty impressive to a girl from Ironton, Minnesota, even one who was heartachingly beautiful.

Ralph's family also impressed Nell. She came from a very traditional background, the kind of family in which, according to her sister, "the men brought home the bacon and the women cooked it." Not long after she met Ralph, Nell went to dinner at his parent's house. She wrote to her family in northern California about it, commenting on how different it was that Chester, Ralph's father, had cooked the meal.

Sometime in 1944 or '45 Ralph sent her a photo of him in uniform, very young and goofy looking with a broad smile, his arms crossed, and his curly hair held into waves by pomade. It's inscribed: "To Nellie—the most wonderful girl in the world—all my love—Rich." It's written in tidy block letters with a few slight flourishes that look as if it wouldn't take much of a shove for them to skid out of control.

They were married by Harry C. Nissen, a "Christian Minister" in Los Angeles on March 8, 1946, a little less than six months after Schwamb was released from naval prison. They were both nineteen. On the wedding certificate Ralph's occupation is listed as "carpenter" and his address is the same as his parents' on New Hampshire Avenue near 82nd Street. Nell lived a mile and a half away on Denker Avenue. Just about the time his father moved out, Ralph and Nell moved in with Ralph's mother.

There were problems almost from the start. Nell, homesick, by now all too aware of Ralph's drinking and tendency to get into trouble, and having got over some of her initial starry-eyed reaction to the big city, wanted them to move up north to White Horse, in Modoc County in the far northeast woods and mountains of California. According to Ralph she talked him into it. She convinced him that logging was a good business and with her family connections and a dozen or so years of hard work they could be rich, or at least well off. She wanted a family and figured that a small town was a better place to raise kids than Los Angeles. Not long after getting married they moved.

White Horse was a company town built by the McCloud River Lumber Company, known as Mother McCloud to its employees. The town, which got its name from a legendary wild white stallion that couldn't be caught, was moved from place to place as the big trees were cut. In 1929 White Horse had been moved from its site at Ham Bone (the early settlers had hung a ham bone in the trees to mark the trail to the settlement) to a new, still densely forested spot about twenty-five miles farther along the rail line.

Mother McCloud was what economists would call "vertically inte-grated." The company felled its own timber, built its own towns to serve the logging camps, and moved the logs on its own railroad to its sawmill at McCloud, California.

When it came time to move to a new location, the company's car-penters would dismantle the buildings. The houses and other buildings had been constructed out of wood in whole sections on skids, so that the structures could be easily taken apart, moved, and fitted together again. The company towns were built along the company railway, so it was a simple and quick matter to take down the buildings, skid them to the track, put them on flatcars, and move them on down the line.

By the time that Ralph and Nell arrived in White Horse the town had a population of around three hundred people, housed in thirty-five to forty L- or H-shaped, three- or four-section family homes and bunkhouses and cabins for about two hundred single men. There was a company store from which employees were required to buy all of their supplies, a large cookhouse where the single men ate, a post office, a union hall, and a single-room school. There was no electricity, just oil, gas, and wood and the town was buried deep in snow five months of the year.

It was remote. The nearest paved road was thirty miles away down a rutted, muddy lane. Five years before, when the new schoolteacher came to town, her directions on how to get there involved finding her way to "Roaring George's Roadhouse" near the Lookout Junction then to follow the beer bottles along the dirt road to White Horse.

The road to White Horse may have been lined with beer bottles, but there wasn't a lot of entertainment to be found in the area. On Satur-day nights when the weather was good, the community of Day, a five-mile slog over the hills, held dances and a midnight potluck supper. The fiddle and guitar groups that played didn't have much appeal for Blackie, who was accustomed to big-city big bands.

Ralph never was a country-living sort of guy and he couldn't change his ways. "[Nell] wanted me to work in the woods," he said. "There wasn't a neon sign within fifty miles. I got so tired of scamming those loggers' pay and then having to fight them. It was hard work. I couldn't handle it.

"I made a couple of phone calls and the Browns said they'd sign me. My wife didn't want anything to do with it. She hated baseball. She wanted me to stay up there. I told her, 'Forget that.' So she served me an ultimatum, either baseball or me. I came down to L.A. and signed with the Browns."

Pete Peterson, the scout who ran the team in Gardena, asked Jack Fournier, the Browns head scout, to take a look at his great prospect. Fournier's report said, "He's a screwball, but he can pitch," and recommended signing the young right-hander.

They signed the contract on the fender of a car in the parking lot at Manchester Playground. He was the Brown's best pitching prospect, better than the three other young pitchers the team signed around the same time—Ned Garver, Don Larsen, and Bob Turley, who all went on to good, if not great, careers.[5]

Because of his build and speed Blackie reminded the scouts of Ewell Blackwell, the fearsome Cincinnati Reds' flamethrowing sidearm right-hander. Two different catchers, Cliff Dapper, later with the Dodgers, who had caught Blackie in semipro games in Los Angeles, and Tom Jordan who was to play with him in winter ball and on the Browns, said that they guessed he threw the ball as hard as Bob Feller, which was as fast as anyone had ever seen a baseball thrown.

"I used to work out in the winter at Manchester playground along with a lot of the major leaguers from the area," recalled Dapper. "One day the supervisor at the playground asked me to go down to the bull pen and warm up some tall drink of water.

---

[5] Garver played in the major leagues for fourteen years and in 1951 miraculously won twenty games pitching for the worst team in baseball. Larsen also played fourteen years in the majors, appeared in ten World Series games and is the only pitcher to have ever thrown a perfect game in the World Series. Turley was in the majors twelve years, a three-time All-Star, appeared in fifteen World Series games and in 1958 won both the Cy Young Award, baseball's highest honor for pitching, and the World Series Most Valuable Player.

"He just had on jeans and a T-shirt. He threw a couple and then cut loose and Christ that ball just exploded. I said, 'Wait a fucking minute here,' and went back to put on my chest protector, mask, and shin guards. I went back to the bull pen and this guy is just laughing at me. I tell him, 'OK, I'm ready for you now, you big motherfucker. Go ahead and throw.'

"Man, could he throw that ball. I had no idea who the hell he was. Turns out that he was Blackie Schwamb and he had just signed with the Browns. Nobody knew who the guy was; he just came out of nowhere. Might as well have been from the moon."

The Browns gave Blackie a meager signing bonus of $600. "I wasn't shopping around, I didn't know that I could play," he said. "I didn't know that this scout for Cleveland, Johnny Angel, was really bird-doggin' me. He's a little unobtrusive guy who never sat in the first row or anything, never talked to the manager. He confirmed, two days after I signed with the Browns, that Cleveland was going to give me $37,500."

In 1946 baseball was in transition and in turmoil. Before the war most minor-league teams had been independent and baseball scouts traveled far and wide looking for talent. Once they found a major-league prospect it rarely took long, or much money, to sign him to a contract. Among the big league teams, only the St. Louis Cardinals had put much effort into creating a system of "farm clubs" in which they could raise their own stock of players. The Cardinals built a very successful and profitable franchise on the basis of their minor-league system. Still, the other teams didn't follow their example until after the war when they tried to catch up in a hurry.

Economic competition in baseball really heated up. Minor league teams, most of them still independent, came back with a vengeance. With the Depression over and having lost three or four years of their careers to the military, major league players came back wanting higher salaries than before. By the 1946 season most baseball people with even modest foresight realized that the long-standing racial barrier was about to come down and that within the next few years black stars would begin to play in the previously white-only leagues. (The Brooklyn Dodgers signed Jackie Robinson to play for their Montreal minor-league team in 1946.) And across the border the Mexican Professional Baseball League was trying to outbid the major leagues for some of their players.

The first big-name big leaguer to head south was Luis Olmo, a fast, hard-hitting outfielder for the Dodgers. He signed a three-year contract with Veracruz for $10,000 per year and expenses for himself and his wife. The Mexican league also signed Danny Gardella, an outfielder and first baseman with the New York Giants. Gardella had turned down the Giants' offer of $5,000 for the year. Several big-name stars, including George Stirnweiss, who led the American League in batting the previous year, and Pete Reiser, who before the war had been a bright new superstar, were holding out for better contracts. Their arguments were strengthened by Mexican offers.

When spring training began in March 1946, forty-five players, not including those who had already jumped to the Mexican league, were holding out for more money. On March 7 the Associated Press reported that the Mexicans were offering Bob Feller, the best pitcher in baseball, $300,000 for a three-year contract. The Cleveland Indians were paying Feller a reported $40,000 to $50,000 per season.

Jorge Pasquel, president of the Mexican league, further terrified the U.S. big leagues saying, "That is nothing." He went on to announce that he was in touch with Hank Greenberg and Ted Williams, two of the other greatest players of the day, and hoped to get them to join his league for the 1947 season. He also showed off plans for a "baseball city" that he intended to open in Mexico City by 1948. It was going to cost two million dollars to build and would seat fifty-two thousand fans in cushioned comfort.

On March 8 Feller denied that he had been made an offer by the Mexican league and said that he wouldn't consider it if he had. But, he said, "International competition is just around the corner. It wouldn't surprise me if a city like Mexico City was in some major league some time."

Three days later Happy Chandler, the commissioner of baseball, announced that any player who had signed with a Mexican team who wasn't back with his major-league team by opening day of the 1946 season would be suspended for at least five years from the U.S. leagues.

All the turmoil rapidly upped the money stakes in baseball. Back in 1935 Cleveland had signed Bob Feller off his family farm in Van Meter, Iowa, for one dollar and an autographed ball. Just a couple of years after Blackie was signed, the Pittsburgh Pirates signed Paul Pettit, who had pitched around the same parks in Los Angeles as Blackie, for a reported $100,000 signing bonus. Petit went on to appear in only thirteen major-league games.

In September 1946 the Browns came to terms with Blackie Schwamb. They assigned him to the Aberdeen, South Dakota, Pheasants, a Class C Northern League farm club. The season was almost over by then so he was told to report to the team the next year.

He cashed his check and convinced Nell, who was pregnant, to move down to Los Angeles. They settled in with Janet, into the small, second-floor apartment in a solidly built Spanish-style brick and stucco four-unit building on New Hampshire Avenue. He was back in his old neighborhood, hanging out with his old buddies, and soon, with nearly six months until his first Browns paycheck and his $600 signing bonus a fast-fading memory, he was back at work for Mickey Cohen's bookies and loan sharks.

"It would have been a million percent different if I had waited and signed with Cleveland," he said. "They had a [good] baseball team. No doubt it would have taken me a lot longer to break in, but I would have. I was a lousy gangster, but I was a great pitcher."

CHAPTER 8

I N ST. LOUIS THE CARDINALS HAD JUST BEAT the Boston Red Sox four games to three in the World Series. The first six games hadn't been anything special but the seventh game had thrilled baseball fans all over the country. Blackie had listened to it on the radio and studied the pictures in the paper of Sportsman's Park, where the Browns also played.

He wasn't delusional. He knew that with the Browns he didn't stand a chance of getting into a championship game. He was more than just a little bitter, and mad about the screwup that led him to sign with St. Louis rather than Cleveland. Blackie felt cheated by himself, by his ball club, and by the way that life always seemed to stack up against him.

All through the fall and winter of 1946 to '47 he kept in shape pitching with semipro teams around Los Angeles. He pitched in several off-season exhibition games between his team of major- and minor-league Browns and opposing teams of the best semipro players. He was usually drunk when he played, or working off the last night's drinks with beer between innings. People who played against him said that he was scary, very fast, loose, and lacking control. But he felt fine when he was pitching. He knew he was good; he was cocky and confident on the pitcher's mound.

Blackie was less sure of himself at home. He and Nell were lucky to have a place to live at all. With so many returning veterans and others moving to Southern California there was a severe housing shortage. The apartment they shared with his mother was almost luxurious by some standards, but it wasn't all that cheap.

Richard Page, their son, was born on December 2, 1946. Ralph wanted a son sooner or later, but this was a lot sooner than he had counted on. Despite the rumblings of the economic boom, straight jobs weren't that easy to come by for a guy who had dropped out of high school and had a bad conduct discharge from the navy. But Blackie wasn't too particular about how he made his money. Los Angeles was in the midst of a crime wave and he made himself comfortable in the thick of it.

By late 1946 and throughout the next year the city was averaging a new murder every two to three days. They'd become so common that unless they were as spectacular as the dismemberment of Elizabeth Short, the "Black Dahlia," they were buried in the back pages of the local papers.

The police, as usual, weren't much better than the other thugs in town. They were known nationwide for their artistry with rubber hoses in beating confessions out of suspects. (Rubber hoses don't leave marks.) By many accounts the meanest, most brutal cop in town was hard-drinking detective lieutenant Harry Fremont of the vice squad. He was said to have shot down one captive in cold blood—took off his cuffs, told him to start running, then plugged him in the back. Word had it that wasn't the only one.

The city offered vices for all tastes. Down near the harbor the low end of nightlife was at the foot of Liberty Hill in San Pedro. For many years sailors on leave had flocked to the area as soon as they got off their ships. In 1923 it was the scene of mass demonstrations as the Marine Transport Workers Industrial Union, affiliated with the far left Industrial Workers of the World, had gone on strike, shutting down ninety ships in the harbor. During one demonstration the author Upton Sinclair was arrested for reading to the crowd from the Bill of Rights.

Along Beacon Street, one block in from the waterfront, bars, whorehouses, pawnshops, tattoo parlors, thinly disguised bookie joints, and bail bond offices lined the sidewalk. On weekends, starting during the war and continuing for several years after, as many as one hundred thousand shipyard workers, sailors, and soldiers converged on the area in a teeming horde, pumped up on adrenaline and testosterone.

Nat King Cole had his first regular headlining job at the Club Del Rio, one of the few semirespectable places on Beacon. The Bank Café was, appropriately, the place to find loan sharks. The Silver Dollar was famous for its exotic oriental murals and equally exotic Asian waitresses and bartenders. The roughest bar on the street was Shanghai Red's at the corner of Fifth and Beacon, just about the spot where Sinclair had been arrested. It featured round-the-clock gambling in a back room that was bigger than its front room. Two lesbian bouncers, "Big and Little Stormy," manned the door.

To the north, Central Avenue, fully recovered from the war years, was rocking and hopping and jiving as ever. New nightclubs, burlesque houses, and gambling parlors were opening all over Gardena, near enough to Hollywood Park Racetrack to service the crowds who wanted more after they spent the day betting on the horses. The Bal Tabarin Café was famous for its huge chorus line of "hot colored dancing girls." The Colony Club had "burlesque as you like it" on tap and chicken dinners for a buck. The Normandie Card Club was more posh than anything that Las Vegas had yet to offer. An estimated ten thousand bookies were at work all over Southern California, and Mickey Cohen, by now a local celebrity who was regularly stopped on the street by autograph seekers, was raking in more money than he knew what to do with.

L.A.'s nightlife scene was moving west. In Hollywood the Florentine Gardens had dinner, dancing, cocktails, three floor shows nightly and regular "girl revues." The Seven Seas featured a Hawaiian orchestra, showgirls in grass skirts and an "Island atmosphere, complete with rain on the roof." The Earl Carroll Theater offered two acts with thirty principals and a "60-girl revue." The new branch of the Brown Derby Café, on Vine, was big with movie stars, especially on Friday nights after the prize fights at the nearby American Legion Hall.

The Garden of Allah, the Drake, and the Roosevelt hotels were swank and popular places to drink and dance. If someone needed a nice room for just an hour or two, the Town House Hotel on the east end of Wilshire's "Miracle Mile" was accommodating. If they wanted someone to bring up to that room they had only to make a quick stop by the hotel's Zebra Room cocktail lounge.

Slapsie Maxie's on Beverly near Gilmore Field was as popular as ever and one of the few nightclubs where the Hollywood wild bunch mingled with the city's old money, high society. The Trouville Club at Beverly and Fairfax regularly headlined Billie Holiday and Big Joe Turner. It was owned by Billy Berg whose jazz club in Hollywood was one of the first places off of Central Avenue to cater to an integrated audience.

Farther west, the Sunset Strip, an unincorporated slice of L.A. County run by corrupt deputies of the Sheriff's Department in cahoots with the mob, was becoming the place to go. The Trocadero had been packing in movie stars, gangsters, and other fun lovers since 1934. Just down the street was Mickey Cohen's Men's Wear, the haberdashery where he had his headquarters. Cohen kept a large supply of neckties and pocket handkerchiefs on hand to give away to potential customers that the store clerks had standing orders to get rid of. Actually selling something could cause bookkeeping headaches. Nearby were the popular Bublichki Russian Café and the Little Gypsy, both of which were famous for dining, dancing, and mostly their bars. In the same area Ciro's, the Player's Club, and the Mocambo had opened in the early 1940s and by the beginning of 1947 were *the* places to see and be seen.

Blackie's working territory was mostly around Central Avenue, Hollywood Park, and Gardena. He'd make a percentage on debts he collected and take in fees for the brutal lessons he'd teach four-flushers and welshers. In a good week he'd easily rake in more than the measly six hundred bucks the Browns had paid him and after rent and food he'd quickly burn through all the money on drinks, nightclubs, gambling, and a compulsive largesse around attractive women.

Every now and then to make it look good he'd take a job pouring concrete or working construction, but he never lasted more than a week

or two. Why bother, he figured, making fifty bucks a week or less bust-
ing his back just for the sake of appearances. But for the most part he
was happy. He loved baseball as much as he loved the high life and for
the time being at least he had both.

Life at home though was tense. Nell may or may not have known
how he was supporting the family, but she certainly had her suspicions
and didn't approve. He was out too many nights and spent plenty of
time with willing other women, something that Nell was all too aware
of. Sometimes she'd go out to movie theaters or nightclubs looking to
find him. She knew for sure of one girlfriend, Janine, but wasn't quite
sure what she'd do if she found him with her. A husband who, when he
came home at all, stumbled home drunk and wafting trails of strange
perfume wasn't what she had hoped for.

In January 1947 Blackie was arrested on suspicion of burglary. The
circumstances were unclear and he was drunk enough that it could well
have been an honest mistake. He was known to occasionally blunder
into the wrong place. In any case the charges were dropped "due to his
high state of inebriation" at the time of the crime.

It is likely, however, that the arrest had something to do with the
Black Dahlia murder that was on the front page of the local newspapers
every day during the last half of that month.

Sometime between 10 P.M. on Friday, January 10 when she was last
seen, and 10:30 A.M. on Wednesday, January 15, when her body was
discovered, twenty-two-year-old Elizabeth Short was horribly murdered. She'd been tied up and tortured for two or three days before having her throat slit. She choked to death on her own blood. After death
her body was disfigured, then carefully cut in half at the waist. The
blood was completely and deliberately drained from both halves. Her
hair was thoroughly washed and then dyed bright red. Her severed
corpse was scrubbed clean before being dumped in a lot about six miles
to the northwest of where Blackie lived.

The police were under intense pressure to quickly solve the gruesome case. They blanketed the streets in the areas where Blackie regularly hung out, bracing everybody they could for information and

especially concentrating on anyone who came close to fitting the descriptions of possible suspects.

One of the prime suspects in the case was described as very tall, about six foot five or six, thin, strong, and with dark hair. He was said to hang out in many of the same bars and nightclubs as Blackie. It would not have been unusual for the cops to have picked up Ralph on bogus charges and then rough him up, hoping to sweat "it" or beat "it" out of him. In any event no charges of any sort ever held up. As for the Black Dahlia case, it remains unsolved.

Spring training began for the Browns in March. The major leaguers reported to the team in balmy and pleasant Miami, Florida, the minor leaguers to a rather more rudimentary camp in Pine Bluff, Arkansas, where the March temperatures average in the mid-50s. The Aberdeen team was going to pay Blackie $250 per month. That wasn't much but it was enough to support Nell and the four-month-old Rich in an apartment in South Dakota. He left them in Los Angeles.

He told Nell that he might be moving around from team to team, would certainly be on the road much of the time, and that they'd be better off staying put, where they had family and friends nearby. All of that was true enough but the twenty-year-old Blackie didn't bother to add that a family was sure to cramp his style.

"Baseball was another door to the things I liked, to the bright lights," he said. "The girls are the same if you play in a D League or an A League. Just come out about eleven o'clock at night after you've showered and everything, and take your pick of the town belles. Just take your pick. It's easier to get a tab at a local restaurant or get a suit at the local shops. 'Oh I'll pay you when I can.' 'Can we put in the paper that you bought your suit here?' 'Why certainly.'"

Pine Bluff was a thriving little industrial town, forty-five miles south of Little Rock. It's a railhead and port on the Arkansas River, which is navigable into Oklahoma to the northwest and seventy-five or so miles to the east where it flows into the Mississippi about six hundred miles north of New Orleans. The city's major industries have long been paper and forestry products. In 1942 the government opened one of the country's two major chemical warfare plants at the Pine Bluff Arsenal on the outskirts of town. A lot of anthrax bombs were made there, then stockpiled when they weren't used. Nearby is the site of the first concrete highway in America. It was laid in 1913 and is twenty-four miles long.

In 1947 colleges and other schools throughout the country were swelling with veterans. Housing construction was going through the roof. Pine Bluff's paper mills and sawmills were working overtime.

Spring training was held at an old naval air training station on the edge of town. The playing fields were laid out between abandoned runways and war veterans shared the creaky old wooden barracks with the ballplayers. The Browns' minor-league pitching coach was known for working his players hard. Every day he'd run them through the very soft plowed dirt in the fields nearby until some of them dropped from exhaustion.

Blackie was the tallest of about three hundred minor leaguers who showed up in Pine Bluff for spring training camp. He must have been among the least experienced. Jim Muhe recalled Ralph telling him that when he got to Pine Bluff he didn't even know how to put his uniform on. He'd always played ball in jeans and T-shirts and was confused by such exotica as "sanitaries," a specialized type of baseball sock that looks like a sort of jock strap for the foot.

Roy Sievers, an outfielder who was also in camp that year, recalled that players were given a number when they arrived. "Every day after breakfast you'd go over to a big board and find out where you were supposed to work out that day, or if you'd been cut [from the team] overnight or if maybe you were going to play in a game that night." He remembered it as a lot of hard, tiring work and good camaraderie among the players. Blackie was known for being something of a cutup. "One time he looked up the chimney of a fireplace," recalled Sievers, "turned around grinning and told us that he'd see us all on the twenty-fifth."

Despite the long days and communal living, Blackie kept to at least some of his usual habits. Pine Bluff is the county seat of Jefferson County. While to this day about half of Arkansas' counties are dry, Jefferson isn't one of them. Though hardly regarded as a honky-tonk town, with its industrial base, the arsenal, and a lot of rail- and ship workers passing through, the city has always had plenty of customers for its bars, liquor stores, a few nightclubs, and brothels. Sneaking out of camp or disappearing on nights he wasn't pitching, Blackie got to know his way around town.

By day though he pitched well enough, and began to develop a good curveball, so that when the team packed up for the move north to South Dakota for the regular season he was one of their starting pitchers.

It was a little more than eleven hundred miles by rickety bus on small roads and rough highways through a largely featureless landscape to Aberdeen, an attractive little town in the Glacial Lakes Region of northeast South Dakota. It's a popular area for lake sport fishing, very near the Sand Lake National Wildlife Refuge that several times a year is overrun with birds migrating south or north for the season.

Throughout the year the town is smack in the middle of the major habitat of the Chinese ringneck pheasant. The bird makes mighty fine eating. Hunters come from far and wide to flush it from cover and blast it out of the sky with their preferred twelve-gauge shotguns loaded with small four-to-six-size shot. During hunting season the days are regularly punctuated with small booms from the fields.

The Ward Hotel, just a block from the rail depot, is a fine old late 1800s vintage brick edifice. It was once an example of Midwest elegance. It advertises that it will happily accommodate hunting dogs. The ballplayers couldn't afford to stay there, but in the late 1940s it was one of the few places in town that a drinking man could quench his thirst.

Blackie's first month with the team was spent largely on the road. The Aberdeen Pheasants played a circuit that took them around the northern Midwest agricultural depots. They traveled on their beat-up old bus over crummy highways to Fargo, Duluth, Eau Claire, St. Cloud, and other towns throughout the Dakotas, Wisconsin, and Minnesota. Early in the season they'd play in fierce cold, the balls and bats making their hands ring with pain. By summer they played on parched fields that were more dirt than grass, or on others where they were worn down by the heat and humidity. During night games they'd try to keep moving because when they stood still swarms of mosquitoes were intent on draining them of blood.

Still, one of Ralph's teammates, Don Lenhardt, recalled playing for Aberdeen as a pretty good time. "It was a great little town. The people treated us well, they were very good and we drew a lot of fans. We ate pheasant every way imaginable; they'd even pickle it in a jar. A lot of the ballplayers rented rooms in somebody's house. The only bad part was the bus trips. They were brutal. We'd ride all night after a game, eventually getting to the next town just in time for the next game."

Don Heffner drove the bus. He was also the team's manager. He'd fired the bus driver and split the savings with the underpaid ballplayers. The thirty-six-year-old had played eleven years in the big leagues as an infielder, mostly with the Yankees and the Browns. He'd been on two Yankees World Champion teams. He was plainspoken and well liked. Sometimes, when players were getting rowdy on the bus, he'd yank the bus over to the side of the road and walk down the center aisle until the guys quieted down. He'd pull off his Yankee ring and watch, have the players pass them around and say, "You can have these or you can collect tin ones in the C leagues all your life. Take your choice."

Heffner wasn't a teetotaler but he didn't much care for Blackie's alcoholic excesses. The young pitcher had a nasty habit of disappearing for all the days in between the games in which he appeared, then showing up scruffy and hungover to play. Heffner told him that he was good enough to make it to the majors, but that he was a bad influence on the team. If Blackie didn't straighten up he'd get rid of him, whether he was winning or not. From the start though, he was winning.

The first minor-league game Blackie Schwamb pitched was in early May 1947. He beat Fargo-Moorhead six to one and gave up only three hits. He continued to pitch well for a month. By June first he'd won five, lost none, struck out more than his fair share of batters, and had a great earned-run average of 1.62. In one game against St. Cloud he struck out fourteen batters. Maybe he was a bad influence but he was happy, convivial, and had a well-appreciated quirky sense of humor. Lenhardt remembered him as "a very eccentric and outgoing person who got along with most everybody." Then he stepped in a hole.

The ball fields in the C leagues were never much good and they were worse in the Northern League than in most. They were unkempt, scraggly looking, and mined with potholes of all shapes and sizes. Blackie was on the field working out, took a wrong step, and tore up the ligaments in his right ankle. He was put on the disabled list and sat out the games for the next month and a half.

In early July, while he was taking up room on the bench, baseball held its annual All-Star Game. Bob Feller, the highest-paid pitcher in baseball, with an annual salary of $75,000, started the game for the American League. Big, mean Ewell Blackwell, a six-foot-five fireballing pitcher, who was paid about $10,000 a year, started the game for the National League.

Scouts had been favorably comparing Blackie with Blackwell since they first took notice of him. Pitching coaches had been trying to get Ralph to copy the major leaguer's scary sidearm, almost underhand, pitching delivery. But Ralph naturally threw the ball straight overhand, or occasionally at a three-quarters' angle. Throwing sidearm felt awkward to him; sometimes it even hurt. It was one of the reasons he never got along very well with his coaches and managers.

There wasn't much he wanted to do during those six weeks on the disabled list, other than drink. "I finally got run out of town for drinkin'," he said.

But there was more to it than that. Sometime during his stay in Aberdeen he met Pat Bertelsman[6] and fell for her. They started an affair and weren't too secretive about it. But for two things, that would have been perfectly acceptable, even expected in baseball circles where ballplayers, even married ones, often had girls in every town. It was a very small town and Pat was a high school senior, just sixteen or seventeen years old. She also had two older, protective brothers.

---

6 The family name has been changed to protect the privacy of her family.

Between his uncontrollable drinking and involvement in a simmering scandal that was threatening to boil over and possibly even turn violent, Heffner finally asked the Browns to take his best pitcher off of his hands. On July 16 the team released Blackie from Aberdeen and assigned him to the Class C Globe-Miami Browns of the Arizona-Texas League.

"The league was the burial ground for all the lushes who couldn't make it," Schwamb said. "I got on the train and went home."

CHAPTER 8

GLOBE-MIAMI WAS EVEN HARDER TO FIND on the map than Aberdeen. Blackie figured it was a dead end for his baseball career.

Highway 60 slithers east from Phoenix up through the Pinal Mountains of Arizona's Tonto National Forest, past BHP's Pinto Valley open-pit mine, and the Phelps Dodge Oxhide and Bluebird leach dumps, about sixty-five miles to the small town of Miami. Wedged into what was once a steep, red rock canyon—before intensive mining tore down the canyon walls—at about thirty-four hundred feet, Miami was founded in the late 1800s by copper miner Black Jack Newman, who it is said named it after his fiancée Mima Tune.

Seven miles farther up the road, through a moonscape of slag heaps and bulldozed hills, is the somewhat larger town of Globe. It was established by silver miners in 1876, three years after General Crook finished his brutal suppression of the San Carlos Apaches, who were the original inhabitants. Before long the silver mines played out, but copper ore was discovered and that's the reason the town is still there.

Stories of Globe figure prominently in tales of the Wild West. The phrase "he died with his boots on" may have originated there. In August 1882 Lafayette Grimes was hung from a tree in downtown for having robbed the Globe stagecoach. Before walking up to the noose

Grimes sat down in the middle of the street and took off his boots. "Damned if I'll die with my boots on," he said.

The town had a reputation for its hangings, and seemingly for the pithy last words of the condemned. Tom Kerr was hung on Christmas Day in 1882. His last words were reported to be: "Well, here goes Tom Kerr's Christmas present to the devil."

One of the town's most famous criminals was Pearl Hart. The twenty-nine-year-old Globe resident, known for her good looks and sharp wit, robbed the stage with a partner in May 1899. They got $421 and a watch but gave back a dollar to each of the passengers so that they "could get something to eat." Pearl was arrested soon after.

While in jail in Tucson she became something of a feminist cause célèbre, maintaining that she "would never consent to be tried under a law she or her sex had no voice in making, or to which a woman had no power under the law to give her consent." On October 12, fifty years to the day before Blackie Schwamb committed the murder that got him sent to prison, Pearl, assisted by a petty thief who had become sweet on her, escaped from jail. She didn't get far before being caught and brought back to stand trial. Sentenced to five years Pearl got out after three. She was pregnant and neither the warden nor the governor thought that the scandal of how she got that way in prison would do them much good.

Not too many years later the bandit Butch Cassidy, having survived the shootout in Bolivia made famous by the movie *Butch Cassidy and the Sundance Kid,* moved to town under the name William T. Phillips. Or so say a number of historians. It is a matter of some controversy.

Globe remained a rough-and-tumble place through the first half of the twentieth century. The town boomed during the two world wars and the Roaring Twenties when copper was in great demand. The mines were still working overtime in July and August 1947 when Ralph was supposed to report to his new team. So was the weather, which it always does that time of year when the daily high temperature hunkers down around a hundred in the shade and the monsoons blowing up from the southwest call out a stupefying humidity.

It was also hot in L.A. and smoggy. "I stayed home a few weeks, fretting," said Blackie. And drinking, and disappearing from home for days at a time, picking up some extra cash from his gangster pals and building up a heady froth of resentment and anger.

While Ralph stewed in his bitter juices the world was getting back to normal all around him. The newspapers weren't full of doom and gloom and war for a change. Princess Elizabeth of Great Britain got engaged to Prince Philip of Greece. The Dow Jones average was up for the eighth, then the ninth week in a row and investors were hailing the new bull market. *The Age of Reason* by the French existentialist philosopher Jean-Paul Sartre was published in the United States and in *Time* magazine someone wrote: "What is existentialism? As far as most Americans are concerned, it is the latest incomprehensible fashion from France."

Whether French philosophy made any sense or not, Americans were once again wanting to travel there. Air France advertised its sleeper plane service from New York to Paris five days a week on the new, fast, high-flying Constellation 749. And flying saucers had been spotted over the eastern United States and England almost every night since July 14.

Blackie was figuring, so what if baseball didn't want him anymore, it was a whole new world; there were a lot of things he could do.

But Lloyd "Gimpy" Brown, the ex-pitcher for the Washington Senators and Cleveland Indians who was managing the Globe-Miami team, tracked him down. His team was in fourth place and he needed a pitcher. Somehow he soothed Ralph's rumpled ego and got him to agree to join the team.

Blackie rode the bus into Globe from Phoenix on July 29. It was hot, 104 in the shade, humid, and he was in a bad mood. The bus wasn't air-conditioned, the mostly dirt road had curves in all the wrong places, and he'd spent most of the overnight train ride from L.A. drinking. The town looked like a dump to him. But it was rowdy with bars and brothels. Miners need somewhere to blow off steam. Blackie quickly felt right at home.

The team, the whole league for that matter, was a mixed bag of old guys on their way out; guys who had got into ball during the war and were still trying to hold onto it even though they didn't have a hope in hell of getting back to the big leagues; some young guys from around the Southwest who might or might not make it; and guys like Blackie, disciplinary problems, mostly drunks, who the teams that had signed them were hoping would straighten up.

No one was expecting him to dry out. In those days ballplayers drank. It was all a part of being one of the boys. A lot of managers were suspicious of players who didn't drink. They just wanted them to keep it under control, to leave it behind them at home or at the hotel.

"'Never trust a man who doesn't drink,' was the motto for a lot of guys back then," said Ryne Duren, who until he drank himself out of the game was a great relief pitcher for the Yankees and a few other teams. Duren, who now lectures at high schools and runs a charitable organization dedicated to training athletes, including teaching them about the dangers of alcohol and other drugs, first came into professional baseball with the Browns organization in 1949. "Alcoholism was fairly common in those days. You didn't think anything of it; it was just a way of life. We were glorified juvenile delinquents without social skills. We were put on a pedestal from a young age. It really screwed us up pretty good."

As always in the minor leagues, the team traveled in a beat-up old bus. The distances weren't as great as they had been with Aberdeen, but it was still nearly three hundred fifty hot, dusty, bumpy, and boring miles southeast to El Paso and Juarez and a bit over two hundred south to Bisbee. With the manager on the bus it was hard to sneak a drink and no matter how hot it got, stopping along the way for a cold beer was not part of the program. Mostly the players would try to sleep, but it wasn't easy on those roads.

Despite the headaches of the road Blackie loved being with the team. The circuit they traveled—Phoenix, Mesa, Tucson, Bisbee, El Paso, and Juarez—was a world away from the straitlaced, staid Midwestern, church-infested towns of Aberdeen's league. The towns of the Southwest were more his kind of place, loose and rugged with plenty on tap to keep him busy at night after the games.

His teammates and the guys on the other clubs around the league were a convivial lot. He was always outgoing, sociable, and for at least the first few drinks, friendly. Drinking buddies were not hard to come by. Girls were always available, waiting in every town they played. It may have only been the low minor leagues, but it provided plenty of what he wanted.

When the team played Phoenix he met and became pals with Billy Martin, later the fiery and often fired and rehired manager of the New York Yankees. They remained friends for life, although rarely spending much time together, until they died within a few days of each other.

The Globe-Miami Browns were a weak team and Blackie pitched merely okay ball. He won three games, lost three, and had a mediocre 4.15 earned run average. But with his hard fastball and rapidly improving curve he struck out sixty-six batters in sixty-five innings, continuing to impress his manager, coaches, and the Browns' scouts. Not that it is considered awfully important for a pitcher, but he also hit well. Blackie had always liked coming to bat and his batting average was an excellent .323.

In the seven-team league the top four got into the playoffs. The Browns narrowly squeaked by in fourth place. In the first game of the playoff round, against the league's powerhouse Phoenix team, Blackie showed up for a game roaring drunk. He was so obviously wasted that he was barred from entering the ballpark. That made him mad as well as drunk, a bad combination. Spotting the flagpole just behind the centerfield fence he stumbled over to it and somehow managed to shimmy his way up. From his perch he hurled abuse at the players on the field and the fans in the stands. Finally the police came, dragged him down, and tossed him in jail. His manager, Brown, suspended him indefinitely.

Wild games were not unusual in the Arizona-Texas League. At Globe, in the second game of the best-of-three playoff, the score was tied four to four in the tenth inning. A Phoenix batter got a double and Billy Martin scored. As he crossed home plate a Globe fan yelled something insulting and before long Martin and the fan were fighting on the field. Then a bunch of fans got into it and soon everyone was throwing punches. The police tried to stop the fracas, and finally resorted to tossing a tear gas bomb into the middle of the melee on the infield. After the smoke and the players' and umpires' eyes all cleared enough that they could see, play resumed. Blackie was an honored guest in the town jail at the time. He would have enjoyed the scene if he'd been there.

Globe-Miami went on to surprise everybody and beat Phoenix, moving into the finals against Tucson for the league championship. Lloyd Brown still lacked pitchers and he knew that if he could somehow keep him focused and at least a little sober, Blackie had the stuff he needed. He offered to post bail and reinstate Schwamb if he would apologize to his teammates and get himself together for the championship series.

Ned Garver stopped off in Globe the next year on his way from the Brown's spring training camp in San Bernardino to the big leagues in St. Louis. "They definitely remembered Ralph," he recalled. "That was a tough little town, but Ralph was a tough guy. The only way they kept him sober for the championship series was that every night after the games, they would take him back to jail and lock him up until the morning."

Blackie did make his act of contrition and in the best-of-five series he won two games and saved the winning third game in relief. In his nineteen innings of pitching he struck out twenty-three batters. That was good enough to get him a contract offer from the Ciudad Obregón Yaquis, named after the local Indian tribe, of the Mexican Winter League.

Ballplayers had been heading south for the winter since the 1930s. The big leagues only had a conflict with the Mexican league that had been established to compete during the regular season and that was trying to poach major-league talent. Winter league teams in Mexico offered ballplayers a way to earn a living and to stay in shape in the off-season. And the level of competition was high. Major leaguers, some of the best minor leaguers, and Negro League players all played on Mexican teams from October through January.

After years of revolutionary upheaval Mexico was relatively calm and stable throughout the 1940s. Under a business-friendly, though

horribly corrupt, government it was industrializing and putting together
the infrastructure that would eventually lead to its becoming America's
leading source of agricultural imports.

Ciudad Obregón, named after a popular revolutionary general and
president, is eight hundred fifty miles southeast of Los Angeles and
thirty-five miles inland from the Gulf of California. In 1947 it was just
another little desert town that Blackie hadn't ever heard of until some
of his teammates helped him hook up with its ball team. It was a dusty
and achingly slow two-and-a-half-day train ride to get there.

That year two events took place that were to eventually prove mo-
mentous for Ciudad Obregón. Construction was begun in the fall on a
dam across the nearby Yaqui River. When the Alvaro Obregón dam
was inaugurated in 1952 it allowed the transformation of more than a
half million acres of mesquite and chaparral into some of the world's
richest farmland.

Also in 1947, Norman Borlaug came to town. The Iowa-born
agronomist, who won the Nobel Peace Prize in 1970 for his work in developing "the Green [agricultural] Revolution," was sent to Mexico by
the Rockefeller Foundation to help set up technological and agricultural research programs. Today Ciudad Obregón is a midsized industrial and agricultural city with one of the highest per capita incomes in
the country.

When Blackie Schwamb showed up it was a thriving place. Technicians from the United States and workers from all over the region had
come to clear the land for the dam and the other developments that accompanied it. Fleets of earthmovers and diggers rumbled through the
dusty streets. At night the local cantinas were rollicking with parched
laborers, flush with cash. Mixed drinks cost a quarter or less, a glass of
beer was a dime, available women were all over the place and usually
free or at a deep discount for ballplayers. Once more Blackie had
landed in his kind of town.

There were several other American players on the team. The manager was Rollie Hemsley, a five-time All-Star catcher who had played
with the Browns, the Cleveland Indians, and the New York Yankees.

The shortstop was Jack Conway, who had played with Cleveland. Bill Curly and Jim Basso, good, solid minor leaguers were on the team.

Tom Jordan, the catcher for the team, who had previously played for the Chicago White Sox and the Cleveland Indians and who was to play for the Browns in 1948, recalled that Blackie soon became known as "Cuba libre doble" (a double mixed-rum drink) to his teammates. "We all drank more than we should have," said Jordan. "They said don't drink the water so we drank a lot of beer. But I guess Schwamb drank a lot more. He was dead drunk most of the time."

There was plenty of money to spend on booze. The American players got a thousand dollars a month; four times what Blackie had been paid in the minor leagues, plus all their expenses. They were put up in as good a hotel as could be found, which was at least as nice as any in the small towns he'd played north of the border. When they traveled to play in places like Guadalajara, Culiacán, Hermosillo, Guaymas, Los Mochis, and Mazatlán it was by train, with sleeper cars for overnights, just like in the major leagues. It was such a good deal that he managed to talk Nell into coming down to Mexico to be with him. She left Rich back in L.A. with his grandmother, Janet.

Nell hated it.

"I guess she was figuring Mexico City or Guadalajara or somewhere like that," Ralph said. "At Obregón [we stayed in a] nice little hotel but there were dirt streets, a butcher in the outdoors market, a lot of flies. She didn't dig that." Nell stuck it out for about a week before packing up and heading home. Tom Jordan and his other teammates never did figure out what a nice, pretty young woman like her was doing with a drunk like him.

Once Nell left Blackie really began to indulge himself. It was a rough and rowdy place and he fit right in. The league lived up to most of the stereotypes of lawless Mexico. Cece Carlucci, later to become one of the most famous umpires in baseball history, got his start in the Mexican Winter League in late 1945. He was in the dressing room before his first game, at Guaymas, and he watched in horror as the head umpire, who was from Cuba, strapped on a shoulder holster over his chest protector and armed himself with a 9 mm pistol under his coat. The other umpire just shrugged and told him, "You've got to be prepared, rookie."

At home in Obregón the team would get good crowds for games, at least a couple of thousand. "They were always sold out," recalled Carlucci. "There were a lot of tequila bottles. It was very noisy, like a big celebration, everyone was always jacked up." Before long the crowds would get drunk and then nasty. Fights in the stands and on the field and even between players and fans were not uncommon.

Jordan remembered that there weren't many, if any, restrooms either. "If someone in the crowd needed to pee they'd just stand up right where they were and whip it out. It seemed like Obregón was the worst town of the bunch."

Blackie was known as a loudmouth. His teammates thought he was fairly funny, at least until he took that one drink too many and turned uncontrollable and mean. But his antics did provide the occasional amusement. One night after a game and more than just a few cocktails he stole a taxi and drove it in fast, tight circles around the statue of President Obregón in the town's main plaza. It took most of the town's police force to stop him and throw him in jail.

The next day several of his teammates managed to talk the police into letting him go. They needed him. The team wasn't doing very well and he was one of their brightest stars. Besides being their best pitcher, he was an excellent infielder and batter. Halfway through the season the Yaquis lost their shortstop. Blackie offered to take over. In his first game at short he committed a horrible error that led to two runs scoring, but his two-run homer made it up. After that he pitched only on occasion and only in relief.

Despite Blackie's performance on the mound, the team finished out of contention for the league championship. In January 1948 he returned to L.A., moving back in with Nell, Rich, and his mom. Spring training for the Browns that year was going to be held in San Bernardino, just seventy miles east of home. For the first time he was invited to join the major-league camp.

CHAPTER 10

PLAYING BALL IN MEXICO, Blackie had been paid in muscular Yankee dollars and his basic expenses had been picked up by the team. It was less than he'd made working for gangsters, but a lot more than he'd ever made in baseball. He came home about six weeks before spring training, flush with cash.

By 1948 the economic boom in the country was screaming along. It was, of course impossible to forget the war but it was beginning to seem like it had happened a long time ago and far away. Things were picking up all over.

Once the military campaigns finished, the U.S. dollar began to conquer the world. Usually when a currency gets too strong it bites into a country's exports; other countries can't afford to buy them with their own weak money. But in 1948 the rest of the world had very little choice. The United States was one of the only places left that could make the products other countries needed. When they couldn't afford the Made in America label, the U.S. government stepped in to loan them the money with which to come shopping. In such manner much of the postwar world was rebuilt and at the same time some of the seeds of modern-day problems were planted.

In France the mighty dollar bought 200 percent more than it used to. A two-week holiday cost a little less than a hundred bucks. A good room in the best Paris hotel might set a visitor back three dollars a day. The finest restaurants offered dinner, including wine and brandy, at a little under three dollars. Parisian nightclubs were, as always, more expensive than anything—two people could spend an evening in the best of them for around eight dollars. American Express also offered tours to even-cheaper Germany.

Los Angeles was on the verge of becoming the country's third largest metropolitan region. Southern California as a whole was making its move to become the nation's economic powerhouse. In Los Angeles County there were 1,720,253 registered motor vehicles, gas was once again plentiful and cheap, and the suburbs were growing like weeds after a heavy spring rain.

Nell was working at Sears, Janet in the mailroom of an insurance company, Ralph had sent some of his thousand-dollar monthly paychecks home. The family was living comfortably in the second-floor apartment that Janet and Chester had lived in before Ralph's father left. The two women kept a tidy house. Whoever got home first from work would cook dinner, though Nell sometimes worked evenings. There was meat on the table at just about every meal, which was good because Nell didn't much care for vegetables.

Blackie soon hooked back up with the Sica brothers and started making the rounds of old haunts. The nightlife scene was in transition. Central Avenue was still abuzz with almost constant activity, drawing crowds, especially on the weekends from all over town. But it wasn't destined to last for many more years.

Between 1942 and 1945 more than two hundred thousand black people had moved to L.A. Restrictive housing covenants had boxed them into the crowded areas around Central Avenue. After the war, in search of the good life and jobs, black veterans moved to L.A. by the tens of thousands. Having fought for their country in a segregated army, they had come home from the war and quickly got fed up with their second-class status in a racist society. In 1947 Jackie Robinson had become the first black player in the majors. Even for black people who weren't sports fans that had a galvanizing effect on their expectations and helped push the movement for equal rights.

But society wasn't about to change all that fast. When the war ended, the ranks of the L.A.P.D. had swollen with new recruits, almost all of them white and many of them from southern states. The police department was thoroughly corrupt and racist, and nightclubs, gambling parlors, and brothels in a predominately minority district were easy pickings. A lot of the new, southern officers especially didn't like what they saw around the popular mixed-race clubs like Café Society on San Pedro Avenue. By 1948 police harassment was driving some customers away from the Central Avenue area.

The scene started moving west to Western Avenue and south from there to the card clubs and burlesque houses of Gardena and to the neighborhood around Hollywood Park Racetrack. Patrons, gamblers in particular, came from all over town, a lot came from the fast-expanding working-class communities of San Pedro, Redondo, Torrance, and Long Beach around the port and the oil fields.

Business was very good for L.A.'s gangsters. During the war they had thrived because of all the loose cash and afterward their business expanded along with the rest of the economy. A lot of people were placing their bets with Mickey Cohen's bookies and borrowing from his loan sharks. In January and February of 1948 some of them had the misfortune to be on the wrong end of a visit from Blackie Schwamb.

He got in a lot of fights. Sometimes he even got beaten. Blackie liked to tell a story about one of his defeats. One of the people he told it to was Evo Pusich, the supervisor from Manchester Playground.

"Ralph is in a bar drinking," Pusich recalled being told. "He gets pushed from behind and he turns around and it's this little old guy. So he turns back to the bar and it happens again. This time Ralph turns around ready to throw a punch and all of a sudden he's on the floor. So he jumps up, and down he goes again. This happens a couple more times before Ralph just decides he better stay on the deck. The bartender is laughing and finally says to Ralph, 'That's Fidel LaBarba, a world champ.'"

LaBarba had been the flyweight boxing champion of the world in 1927. He was forty-two in early 1948, five feet three and a good fifty pounds lighter than Blackie, who always got a good laugh out of telling the story. "I'm not so tough," he'd say. "I got knocked out by a little old man who weighed one hundred twenty pounds."

Fighting wasn't the only thing that kept him in shape. Having pitched well in Mexico he stayed in good condition by pitching whenever he could with some of the local semipro teams and in major- and minor-league exhibition games. At one game in Brookside Park in Pasadena there were so many major leaguers and top-notch minor leaguers that he just sat on the bench and watched. One of the pitchers in that game was Ewell Blackwell, whom the scouts and coaches often compared him with. It was a drizzly, overcast day and Blackie watched with great interest as the Cincinnati strikeout king, who was also known for hitting batters, loaded up a spitball. (It is an illegal pitch that is notoriously difficult to hit and is often fouled off by batters in strange and unpredictable ways.)

"[The batter] swung at it, hit it right down at the plate, it bounced up and shattered his jaw," recalled Blackie. "It had stopped drizzling but everybody in our dugout headed for the clubhouse. Blackwell was out there trying to gunk this ball up and he was mean. It was a game then, you had to be on your goddamn toes."

Between ball games and going out most nights, Ralph wasn't home much. When he did come home he'd eat, start drinking, and then want to go out again. Sometimes he'd take Nell out to the movies or dinner. He tried to be attentive but he spent most of their evenings out flirting with waitresses or slouched deep in his seat in a dark quiet theater.

The Browns' players were expected to report to spring training on February 29. The team didn't pay for transportation unless a player could get himself to St. Louis in time to make the train chartered for the ride out to California. Players who already lived out West traveled on their own dime. Tom Jordan drove from his home in New Mexico. Blackie talked a friend with a car into giving him a ride; it was only about an hour-and-a-half drive.

San Bernardino was a lively little city of slightly more than forty thousand people. It was the main transportation and commercial hub for one of the country's largest citrus-fruit-producing regions. The biggest employer in town was the Santa Fe Railway and not too far west out Route 66 were the steel mills of Fontana. In 1948 a large number of the houses and buildings in the business district still dated from the late 1800s. The streets were well shaded, lined with old California oaks and newer, nonnative palms.

Every March, when the average high temperature is around sixty-five and blossoms are on the fruit trees, San Bernardino puts on its party attire and throws the National Orange Show. It used to be a very big deal. The whole town looked like it had been painted orange. Streets, storefronts, shop windows, streetcars, buses, and more than a few private homes were festooned with orange banners and other decorations. A grand parade through downtown to the fairgrounds opened the event. Big-name bands played every night and the city took on a festive air. It all added to the special feeling that the rookie ballplayers had at their first spring training.

Unless a player lived with his family right around the spring training camp, he was put up at the California Hotel in the middle of the business district along Route 66. The hotel, a beautiful Spanish-style building with arcade-surrounded, palm-lined, tiled courtyards, was the swankest place in town, and among the most active. Opened in 1927, it had a highly touted "blind pig" (a not-so-secret bar, gambling parlor, and nightclub) through the end of Prohibition. In the late 1940s it was known for its excellent dining room, congenial cocktail lounge, and live dance bands on the weekends. During the orange show and spring training it was hopping crazy.

Even Blackie was infected with enthusiasm. He'd made good money in Mexico, spent a lucrative month and a half at home, and here he was, on the verge of breaking into the big leagues.

He checked into the hotel on the evening of the twenty-ninth at about the same time the Freedom Train was pulling in at the station. The train, carrying an exhibit of American historical documents, was touring the country and drawing big crowds wherever it stopped. For a small city San Bernardino must have seemed awfully busy.

Tom Jordan, Blackie's catcher from Obregón, arrived at about the same time. The first practice was at 10:30 the next morning.

There was a lot of opportunity for rookies to make the team. Only thirteen of the 1947 St. Louis Browns had returned, including just six of the eleven or twelve pitchers the ball club usually carried on its regular season roster. There were only four players in camp more than thirty years old. Blackie and Jordan had high hopes.

The team worked out at Perris Hill Park in the northeast part of town. There were a couple of open fields and a monstrosity of a ballpark with a high, ratty, peeling-green-paint wood fence all around it. Beyond the park there were vineyards, fields of grapes stretched as far as the eye could see toward the mountains in the north and out to the west. It had been raining and cool for most of the past month and the ground was mushy and muddy.

The first day the team got fitted for uniforms. Ralph got number fourteen. Once suited up they did loosening-up exercises, stretching, wind sprints, and calisthenics. Despite his boozing and two to three packs a day of smokes, he was in pretty good shape. A lot of the other guys hadn't played much ball over the winter, but he had. The workout was only four hours, after which the bus took everybody back to the hotel.

He'd usually start off with a few beers in the hotel bar along with his teammates. When he began to feel the buzz he'd head out to take a look around town. There were always bars and girls to be found. If he didn't already know where to go it was easy to find out, just ask any cab driver or hotel bellhop. There was plenty to do and plenty of time to do it in before he needed to be back in his room for the midnight curfew.

The second day the pitchers started throwing the ball around, just taking it easy, getting their arms limber. The other players took their first batting practice the second day and Tom Jordan just crushed the ball. He knocked six home runs over that ugly, tall green fence and out of the park.

By the end of the first week the Browns' manager, Zack Taylor, and coaches were seeing what the scouts had already seen in Blackie. He could throw hard, as hard as anyone they'd ever seen, and he had a very good curveball. He lacked control and self-discipline but a lot of young pitchers have that problem. They figured that with some seasoning and the right coaching he had the makings of a star.

Once again, though, Blackie and his coaches were at odds over how he should throw the ball. They looked at him, saw Ewell Blackwell, and wanted a sidearm pitcher. He was a lot more comfortable throwing overhand and knew that he was better that way. Tom Jordan, his catcher, knew it too. In Mexico the team had left him alone to pitch however he wanted just so long as he kept winning games and striking out batters, which is what he did—overhand.

In practice, with the coaches breathing down his neck, Blackie pitched the way they wanted. He'd go back to the hotel afterward and rub his sore arm with liniment and let the water from the shower pound him in the upper back where he ached. It was going to be different when they put him into a game, he told himself. If he threw well and got batters out why should they care how he did it?

A week after training started he pitched his first game. It was for the Browns' "B Squad" against the Sacramento Solons, a strong Pacific Coast League team that was also in spring training. He pitched well, striking out five batters in five innings and giving up only a couple of runs. Tom Jordan won the game for the team with a two-run double in the eighth inning. The coaches continued to be impressed by Blackie but were disturbed that he wasn't throwing sidearm. He had a reputation for being difficult with coaches and management that he was living up to. He was not making friends with management.

He didn't have many friends on the team either. After the first few drinks, "He was a mean drunk, not a funny drunk," said Jordan. "He would brag about all the fights he had, and it seemed like he was always getting into trouble."

A lot of the other ballplayers respected his abilities but kept their distance. Most of them spent their evenings bending elbows in the hotel bar but few ever accompanied Ralph on his forays out on the town. They only wanted a few drinks; they weren't looking for trouble.

Chuck Stevens, the Browns' first baseman who had already spent a couple of years in the majors, thought Blackie was "spooky. I guess I'd consider him a street kid and I think everybody else on the club felt the same way. I don't think anybody warmed up to him. There was just something that backed everybody off. This guy listened to a different drummer. We didn't trust him. You're not going to volunteer for cancer."

Ralph had plenty of friends back in L.A., some from childhood, some from baseball, and too many from the underworld, but who were friends nonetheless. When he wasn't lonely he was often congenial, outgoing, even charming. He was a lousy husband and not home often enough to be much of a father but there was something about the proximity of home and family that calmed him down, at least a little.

Back in his neighborhood for an exhibition game against the Chicago Cubs at Wrigley Field, Blackie pitched a strong three innings in relief. He gave up just one hit, but it was the wrong one and he was the losing pitcher in the eleventh inning. His coaches still liked the way he looked, although the *San Bernardino Daily Sun* hadn't quite taken note—the paper mistakenly referred to him as "Johnny" Schwamb.

The paper finally got his name right when it interviewed the Browns' manager Zack Taylor a couple of days later. Toward the end of the column, it read: "Pitcher Ralph Schwamb, a rookie hurler, has impressed Manager Taylor during the regular workouts and particularly by his three-inning stint in which he held the Chicago Cubs to one hit Wednesday at Los Angeles." A second paragraph described Ralph's career so far and mentioned that he lived in Los Angeles.

A few days later he was back at Wrigley pitching against the Cubs again. A group of friends came out to see him. It was a Saturday but Nell didn't show up. She didn't like baseball and held it, along with booze, responsible for what had gone wrong in their marriage.

It was a crummy day in any event. Ralph and the Browns' starting pitcher Clem Dreiswerd got hammered for seven runs before the game was stopped because of rain after only four innings.

Since the teams were going to play at Wrigley again the next day, weather permitting, most of the players just stayed in L.A. overnight. Ralph must have done so but it is unlikely that he spent the night at home. Glamor attached itself to ballplayers who played with big-league or PCL teams and there were plenty of bars and clubs around the ballpark where Blackie could take advantage of his newfound status.

On March 17 the Browns announced that they had sold their triple-A minor-league team in Toledo, Ohio, to the Detroit Tigers. That put extra pressure on the rookie players to make it into the big league. Everyone knew that the Browns were cheap, that they would cut costs wherever they could. The Tigers weren't going to take possession of the Toledo team until the following season. It was a sure bet that in 1948 the Browns weren't going to put any money or much effort into a team they'd already sold.

The next day Blackie was the starting pitcher against the New York Giants. The Giants had been the hardest-hitting National League team of 1947 and the odds were that they were going to be just as tough in 1948. This was his chance to show that he was capable of pitching in the big leagues.

With a slight case of jitters and fighting a hangover, he got off to a shaky start. He gave up three hits and two runs in the first inning, two hits and a run in the second, but then he settled down. For the next four innings Blackie held the Giants hitless. He struck out Walker Cooper, the Giants' catcher whose batting average had been in the top ten the previous year. He also struck out Johnny Mize, the National League's home-run and runs-batted-in king who did not strike out very often. He walked five batters, but when he threw strikes, his hard-sinking fastball, his big sweeping curve and slider that just touched the outside of the plate against right-handed batters, and his mixing up of pitches had both teams talking about the tall kid nobody'd ever heard of.

"I was catching him," said Tom Jordan, "and those Giants didn't know where the hell that guy came from. He really shut 'em down. He was unhittable. I knew what Ralph was capable of, but for everyone else it was a real shock. This big tall rube out of some bush league setting a major-league team on their ears, those things weren't supposed to happen. That's one reason the Browns tried to stick with him over the next two years, they knew he could be good, maybe even great."

The next day's paper got his name right again and called him "a Los Angeles youth who now has become a most promising rookie pitcher for the Brownies." Blackie celebrated in his usual manner. It was looking like he was going to make the team.

But then something, as it so often did, went wrong. He came into a game in relief and had no control. He started a game against the Cleveland Indians and got clobbered. He could barely throw a strike. And when he did get a ball over the plate, it was just where the Cleveland hitters wanted it.

Depressed and frustrated, feeling let down after his initial success and now attacked by failure, Blackie did what he always did—made matters worse by drinking and falling into a funk. Meanwhile Ned Garver, the Browns' other bright young pitching prospect, came on strong in the last week of training. Up until then it had looked like Blackie was destined for the big leagues and Garver was headed back to the minors.

Something else happened. Blackie had a fight with management over money. The major-league minimum salary at the time was five thousand dollars a year. That was something of an improvement over just a few years back when Tom Jordan had played for the Chicago White Sox for four hundred dollars a month. Blackie figured that he'd be making at least the minimum. He'd shown that he could pitch against major leaguers, he was on his way to the Browns and that's what they'd told him his pay would be.

They offered him less if he didn't make the big-league team. Bill DeWitt, the Browns' general manager, was a bean counter and nothing if he wasn't cheap. Blackie argued, and when he lost his temper he could get pretty unpleasant. It didn't win him any points with the organization and it sealed his fate.

They told him to pack up and head to Toledo, take it or leave it.

CHAPTER 11

AVING JOINED UP WITH THE MUD HENS during an exhibition game in Texas, Blackie arrived on the train at "Toledo's oldest joke." Union Station was a huge High Victorian Gothic building that had once been called "the handsomest thing of its kind between New York and Chicago." By 1930 the old station had fallen far. It caught fire and crowds cheered as it burned. When Blackie arrived it was still in use, though condemned and half burned. Two years later it was torn down. In the parade celebrating the opening of the new Art Deco–style Union Station, the most popular float recreated the burning of the old building.

Not long after the team pulled in he called Nell and convinced her to bring Rich and come out to stay. He'd stumbled into a very sweet setup and was sure that she'd like it. He and two of the other pitchers on the team, Chesty "Chet" Johnson and Jim Wilson, had met a realtor who was a baseball nut. The realtor and his wife owned three beautiful bungalows on the shore of Lake Erie about twenty-five miles outside of Toledo. The bungalows shared a dock and the use of a twenty-eight-foot boat. The realtor was happy to rent to baseball players, cheap. Johnson, his wife, and their two kids took one. Wilson and his wife took one. And Blackie's family was all set to move into the third.

Like a lot of minor league towns, Toledo had a colorful history. Nobody knows the origin of the expression "Holy Toledo!" It's possible that it comes from Toledo in Spain, but most theories suggest the United States. Since the city was founded, saloons have outnumbered churches. That's probably true of most cities, but in the 1800s and early 1900s it was something that people took often sarcastic note of.

Vaudeville troupes didn't much care for playing Toledo. Holy Week, the week leading up to Easter Sunday, was always lousy for attendance and touring vaudevillians were known to complain, "every week is like Holy Week in Toledo."

In the 1920s the Toledo police department let it be known that crooks, especially from neighboring Michigan, were welcome to take refuge in the city so long as they kept their noses clean while in town. Detroit's infamous Purple Gang regularly went on the lam sixty miles south to Toledo when things got too hot for them at home. The sanctuary was undoubtedly holy to gangsters on the run, though it must have been profane to others.

Michigan and Ohio have long been rivals. Once upon a time they fought a war over which state owned Toledo, a valuable prize. It is at the northernmost part of Ohio along the shore of Lake Erie and at the mouth of the Maumee River, the largest river that flows into the Great Lakes. It is an important railhead, river port and lake port.

In 1835, as part of its application for statehood, the Territory of Michigan needed to draw up firm borders. Inaccurate surveys had left a strip of densely forested swamp between Michigan and Ohio in dispute. The land in question was known as the Toledo Strip, as that was the only city of any size within it. The territory and the state needed to agree on a common border but Robert Lucas, the governor of Ohio, made his move first. He carved out counties in the strip and appointed bureaucrats to run their county governments.

Michigan's territorial governor was Stevens T. Mason, an effete, hotheaded nineteen-year-old who had been appointed to the post by President Andrew Jackson, who was something of a notorious hothead himself. Mason wasn't about to stand for Lucas's "outrageous provocation," so in April he ordered his army, the state militia, to march south and engage the enemy in battle for the Toledo Strip.

The Ohio governor sent his militia north to repel the invaders and everyone girded themselves for bloodshed. Luckily both sides got lost. For a week. In the swamp. They never found each other. They finally found their ways home, weary, muddied, and unbloodied.

The Michigan militia then spent the next few months ineffectually chasing Ohio county officials around the area, occasionally arresting them and their families. The only casualty of the war was Sheriff Joseph Wood of Michigan who was stabbed in the thigh, suffering only a slight wound, by Two Stickney (the younger brother of One), the son of Major Benjamin Franklin Stickney of the Ohio Militia. The unlucky Sheriff Wood had arrested members of Major Stickney's family. Finally, at the end of August, President Jackson removed Mason from his post as Michigan's territorial governor.

But Mason wasn't about to go quietly. The bill that had created the Ohio county that included Toledo required that the Ohio Court of Common Pleas be opened in the city on September 7. Holding court would prove Ohio's jurisdiction over the area. Mason decided to put a stop to that. He led his troops to the outskirts of Toledo on September 6. They camped that night, resting up for the next day's battle.

Governor Lucas of Ohio outfoxed him. Figuring that a new day begins at midnight he had the court open at three in the morning. By the time Mason's army had woken up, breakfasted, and marched into town itching for a fight, court had already been held and adjourned, the judge had gone home to get some sleep and there weren't any Ohio soldiers to be found. Mason slunk off back home. A number of the Michigan soldiers stuck around Toledo for three days of drunken riot before disbanding. They made a real mess of Major Stickney's vegetable garden.

One hundred and thirteen years later Toledo was nearing a population of three hundred thousand and like everywhere else was booming after the war. It was a transportation and industrial hub, famous for its glass factories and as the manufacturing home of Jeeps. With the postwar housing boom and massive increase in automobile production, the city's windows, construction materials, and windshields companies were all working overtime. Jeeps added improved shock absorbers and springs, cushioned seats, front and rear tops, and an optional heater and were sold to civilians, especially farmers. In 1947 the company built 119,723 peacetime Jeeps.

Like Los Angeles, the city had also long been known for its streetcars. But by 1948 there was only one left—the old 838, the Long Belt Line. The others had all been replaced with buses. It trundled straight up Monroe Street through the business district, passing numerous bars, restaurants, and small glassworks out to the West End and its block after block of Victorian houses, to Swayne Field, home of the "Hens."

The Mud Hens had played at the big ballpark with the factory brick and steel-framed-windows facade since it had been built in 1909. The team had been called the Mud Hens since 1896, before which they were known as the Swamp Angels. A mud hen is a marsh bird with short wings and long legs that lives in swamps or marshes. There were a lot of them in northwest Ohio's Black Swamp until it was drained and turned into farmland and later into some of Toledo's suburbs.

The baseball Hens were desperate for pitching. All the sportswriters who cared had picked the Mud Hens to come in last in their league. There wasn't much optimism among their fans either for the coming season. When the Browns assigned Blackie to the minor-league team there was some relief expressed in the sports pages of the local newspapers, even if his reputation had preceded him.

In his column, under the subheading "Pitching Situation Eased," the *Toledo Blade*'s sports editor, Bob French, wrote: "Schwamb is a huge right-hander, 6 feet 5 inches tall, and according to reports he has a wild and carefree idea of how a baseball player should conduct himself. But he has so much speed they say that he can throw an egg through a burglar-proof safe."

In his first game with the team, an exhibition game in Houston, Texas, he got off to an impressive start. He struck out four of the first six batters to face him and got the other two out on meager ground balls that were hit right back at him. Then he got hammered. He gave up two hard hits in the seventh inning, then four in the eighth. Houston scored three runs and he was the losing pitcher.

The team lost its exhibition game the next night as well and then packed up for the train ride north to start the season.

About a week after he got to Toledo, Blackie picked up Nell and Rich at the train station, in a borrowed car. Nell's first impression of Toledo—the half-burned train station, a rundown downtown, and a lot of factories—couldn't have been all that heartening to a small-town girl who longed for a quiet house in the woods, but as they drove out of town and along the lakeshore things began to look up.

Blackie wasn't happy to be in Toledo with a lame-duck minor-league team. He wasn't happy to be making less money than he thought he was due. But for a change he was happy to have his family with him and was looking forward to the future.

It was fine for a few weeks. Nell was settling in, making a home for them in the bungalow and getting to know the other families. Blackie drove into town with the other guys for games or left for a few days on road trips, life was pretty good.

He was pitching well. His curveball was dropping in right where he wanted it, he was developing a good change of pace (a pitch that looks like it is going to be a fastball but is slow), and his fastball was blasting past batters and blistering the hands of his catchers.

In his first appearance in the regular season he was brought into a game to pitch to one batter in the ninth inning; just about the time that the temperature in the ballpark dipped below freezing. The Hens lost that game, but it had nothing to do with the couple of pitches he threw. But then he was beaten in all of the first three games he started.

Worse yet, it was his own team's failure to score runs that beat him. He lost all three games by one run, and in every game the other team scored the winning runs in the final inning.

Mad and depressed, Blackie quickly returned to old habits. The team traveled by train to games in some of the larger Midwest cities. The league included Indianapolis, Milwaukee, St. Paul, Minneapolis, Columbus, Kansas City, and Louisville, all of which provided plenty of the sorts of trouble that he craved. Even at home in Toledo he began to stay out almost every night. Nell and Rich didn't see much of him.

"Nell wouldn't come to the ball games," he said. "She wouldn't do this, she wouldn't do that, so I got a broad in every town. I didn't even try."

It was unfair to blame Nell. It's true that she didn't like baseball, but that had as much to do with the life Ralph led as with the game itself. The road trips and the temptations of the road to which he all too obviously fell prey, the seasonal nature of the work, and the unsteady pay all made her nervous. She wanted to raise a family, and for that she needed more stability than baseball seemed to offer.

It didn't help that the team was terrible. Just as everyone in spring training had figured, the Browns were ignoring the Mud Hens. Why put money into a ball club you weren't going to own next year?

They were the worst team in their league. They were worst in almost every category: team batting, runs scored, errors, and pitching.

In mid-June Blackie was injured. A line drive by a Minneapolis hitter smacked hard into his pitching hand and he had to sit out for more than a week, wearing a cast. He stayed drunk the whole time.

When he was healthy, and merely hungover rather than drunk, he continued to pitch well, mostly in relief, but he continued to lose.

"His record is kind of misleading," said Frank Mancuso, who was Blackie's catcher at Toledo. "He lost a couple of games in the ninth inning when we made some errors behind him." Four of his losses were by one run in low-scoring games.

"Geez, after one of those games he wanted to fight the entire team," recalled Mancuso. "Man, he was hot. I didn't blame him but you gotta get along with your teammates. Fight the other team, not your team. It was kind of difficult playing with a guy like that."

He'd always been somewhat thin-skinned and quick to fight. At the beginning of the season, still optimistic, he'd been funny, often joking with his teammates in a sarcastic way. But they began to call him "Dizzy" and he hated it. After the first month he was miserable, so he made everyone else around him miserable. All he could think to do was to drown his sorrows with booze and broads.

"Goin to the ballpark was such a drag," Blackie recalled. "It took four or five hours a night out of my social life." The more time he spent partying, the worse he played and the worse things got at home and he became even more miserable. He got into a lot of fights, and other than during games was shunned by the rest of the team.

He got a reputation for wildness on the field as well as off, something he tried to use to his advantage against batters. "Of course you don't throw 'em any strikes [they can hit] when they're so afraid," Blackie said. "They used to announce, 'Get all the married men off the field, Ralph Schwamb's pitchin' today.' But I wasn't really that wild."

On July 2 Joe Ostrowski, another Mud Hens pitcher, was moved up to the major-league Browns. He had been scheduled to start that night's game against the Milwaukee Brewers. The Hens' manager gave the start to Ralph, who had appeared in twenty-three games and been the losing pitcher in seven of them.

Hoping to get the attention of the Browns, Blackie concentrated on the game and on keeping his temper. He was a little wild, walking eight batters, but it was because he was trying to mix up his pitches and to get batters out with the location of the ball rather than simple brute force. He kept his cool and pitched his way out of a couple of tight situations. He even knocked in what turned out to be the winning run with a double in the fourth inning. It was an impressive performance and his first win of the season.

The good times didn't last. He was the losing pitcher in his next two games, one of them a close one that was decided in the eighth inning.

Most baseball people knew that he was a better pitcher than his record indicated. Walter Alston, who later had tremendous success as the manager of the Brooklyn and Los Angeles Dodgers, managed the St. Paul team in 1948. He was quoted in the *Sporting News* as saying, "Toledo's Schwamb was the toughest pitcher we faced."

Al Rosen, later a four-time All-Star with the Cleveland Indians, played for Kansas City against the Mud Hens that year. He said: "I couldn't get a loud foul off that big son of a bitch. I probably batted against him twenty times and he either struck me out or broke my bat and I popped the pitch up."

In the July 7 edition of the *Sporting News,* Browns' general manager Bill DeWitt said, "Schwamb is a star of the future for us."

The fact that he was pitching well was not much consolation to Blackie. But just about the time he was beginning to wonder what in the hell he was doing in baseball, the Browns called him up to the major leagues. "They just couldn't keep me down there in the minors, even though I was only one and nine. The manager George DeTore, an old-time infielder [he played in a total of thirty-three games for the Cleveland Indians in 1930 and '31] says, 'This donkey doesn't belong here, get him up there and maybe you can show him something.'"

The Browns weren't too popular in Toledo. They had called up three Mud Hens and replaced them with players that most Toledo fans and sportswriters figured would be even worse. In his column the day after the players were assigned to the major-league team, Bob French wrote, "The Browns' owners aren't particularly worried about the reaction of the Toledo public to recent events, for they won't be in here next year. They probably are not perturbed about any adverse attitude of organized baseball as a whole, for they are not likely to figure in baseball much longer."

Eddie T. Jones, a writer for the *Blade,* opened his account of the previous day's game by writing, "The St. Louis Browns, from whose tentacles the Toledo baseball club will be released in September, are enjoying their last days as masters of Swayne Field."

The unpopular masters of Swayne Field told Blackie to report to the big-league team in Washington, DC, on Saturday, July 24. He was scheduled to start the second game of Sunday's doubleheader against the Senators and he barely had twenty-four hours to get there.

The Capitol Limited was scheduled to roll into Toledo for a fifteen-minute stop between Chicago and Washington at about 12:30 A.M. Blackie had a sleeper reserved on it. He went home to tell Nell they were moving to St. Louis and to pack his bag for the trip to the major leagues.

"Nell just packed up and went home," he said. "When I went up to the Browns she wouldn't come to St. Louis."

CHAPTER 12

THE CAPITOL LIMITED PULLED INTO Washington, DC's, Union Station at about two in the afternoon on Saturday, July 24. Blackie was no rube and he appreciated grand architecture. He couldn't help but be wowed by his greeting to the big leagues.

When Washington's train station was completed in late 1907 it was the largest passenger depot in the world. It covered more ground than any other building in the country. Regarded as a particularly fine example of Beaux Arts architecture, it was designed as a gateway to the capital. The high, vaulted ceilings were covered in seventy pounds of 22-karat gold leaf. The complex was like a small city. Some five thousand workers staffed businesses and services that included a bowling alley, mortuary, baker, butcher, barber, YMCA, hotel, ice house, liquor store, Turkish baths, restaurants, nursery, police station, and a variety of shops.

Union Station was busier than usual for a Saturday afternoon. President Truman had called a special session of Congress that was going to open on Monday morning. Senators, congressmen, their aides, lobbyists, reporters, and all the thousands of people that seem to be necessary to the operation of the legislative branch of the government were pouring back into town.

Everyone figured that the president was going to try and push through his civil rights program. In the bars, meeting halls, and restaurants of

Capitol Hill and in the club cars of the trains arriving at the station, deals were being struck, strategies were being planned, and sides were being chosen.

It was an exciting time to show up in town for his major-league debut. Blackie took the streetcar three miles out to Griffith Stadium and showed up in the middle of that day's game. The Browns, his new team, were having one of their few good days. By the sixth inning they were leading the Senators seven to one. In the first inning they'd pulled off a very rare triple play.

Dizzy Dean was the radio announcer for the Browns. During the 1930s Dean had been one of the best pitchers in baseball, and certainly one of the most colorful. Outspoken, brash, known for clowning around, he'd come up to the St. Louis Cardinals from Lucas, Arkansas, a town so tiny that it scarcely shows up on any maps. For five seasons, from 1932 through 1936, he was one of the greatest pitchers in the history of the sport. Then a batter in the 1937 All-Star Game hit a ball right back at him that broke his toe.

The strain on a pitcher's arm is tremendous. The best fastball pitchers, guys like Bob Feller, Dizzy Dean, Satchel Paige, Randy Johnson, and Blackie Schwamb, can throw a ball so that when it crosses home plate it is traveling somewhere in the neighborhood of 100 miles per hour. To do that, the ball needs to leave the pitcher's hand at about 107 or 108 miles per hour. If a pitcher throws that ball just a little bit wrong or with his arm not quite in shape, he can rip his muscles, tear his shoulder's rotator cuff, even pop his joints out of place.

A curveball, though slower, requires a hard twist of the wrist. That puts terrible stress all up and down the arm. Everything a pitcher does puts stress on the back and the hips and the legs. The difference between a natural, fluid pitching motion and one that is just slightly off kilter is crucial. Throwing a ball from an eighty-degree angle rather than ninety degrees, twisting a wrist a tenth of a second too late or too soon, putting too much weight on a weak foot, or too little; all of that can make the difference between a long successful career and a short, painful one.

Dizzy Dean started pitching again before his toe had fully healed. It hurt. He changed just a few little things about the way he threw the ball so that it didn't hurt so much. That ruined his arm and cut short his career. Retired from baseball, he'd become the Browns' announcer just after the war.

Dean did have a brief comeback of sorts on September 28, 1947. The Browns, having lost nearly two-thirds of their games, were in last place. They were playing the Chicago White Sox. On the air he said that he could still beat most of the pitchers then pitching in the major leagues. Muddy Ruel, the Browns' manager, took him up on the boast for one game. Dean, having not played since 1941, was called in, pitched four innings in relief, gave up just one hit, no runs, and would have been credited with a save, if that particular statistic had been kept in those days.

Back in the broadcast booth he was wildly popular with almost everyone other than the St. Louis school system. His backwoods speech was at best grammatically incorrect and sometimes considered risqué for the times. Describing the remarkable feat of running and sliding by Enos Slaughter that won the 1946 World Series for the St. Louis Cardinals, Dean had said, "You shudda seen that Slaughter slud home." The Parents and Teachers Association regularly agitated to have him taken off the air as a bad influence on youth.

When Blackie arrived at Griffith Stadium, Dean got him up to the booth for a short interview. "He asked me, 'What are they calling you up for with a record of one [win] and nine [losses]?'" Schwamb recalled. "I told him, 'I just guess they don't want anybody to get killed down there.'"

The next morning, the day Blackie was going to pitch his first game in the major leagues, the Sunday papers reported that the United States had been testing bigger, better, and more atom bombs than most people had thought. Russia didn't have the bomb yet and the Atomic Age was more a source of optimism than anxiety in the country.

UFOs were another matter. Two Eastern Airlines pilots in a DC-3 over Alabama had reported seeing a big one on Saturday afternoon. It shot a forty-foot flame out of its back and flew away at five hundred to seven hundred miles per hour. The passenger plane was bounced around by the shock wave. "Wingless, Flaming Sky Monster Seen," shouted the headline on the front page of the L.A. *Times.*

It was a good time for aliens to visit America. The country's 142 million people had nearly forty billion dollars more spending cash in their pockets than they had before the war. They were using their money to buy all sorts of new gadgets and luxury products.

In Detroit the Tucker car, with its engine in the rear, safety belts, exceptional gas mileage, and a number of other futuristic features, was rolling into showrooms, although buyers didn't much care, they were too busy snapping up the better-known brands in record numbers. The new Packard Super Eight Sedan had more than enough room for seven passengers and cost $3,300, or more if you wanted white sidewall tires or delivery.

Despite the high price of $2,100 plus installation, General Electric could barely make enough of its GE Daylight Televisions; a "giant screen entertainment center" with a three-square-foot TV picture plus phonograph, and FM, AM, and shortwave radio tuner.

Philco had just brought out its new and highly coveted combination radio and phonograph console with FM reception.

Companies, in record numbers, were taking to the air. American Airlines was promoting its "Airconomy Plan—You can't afford an earthbound business."

A lot of people were talking about sex that July. *Sexual Behavior in the Human Male,* better known as *The Kinsey Report,* was on the bestseller list, having sold more than two hundred thousand copies in spite of its price—$6.50, size—804 pages, and weight—a little more than three pounds.

In Philadelphia the Progressive Party nominated Henry Wallace, who had been vice president during Roosevelt's third term, as their presidential candidate. The Communist Party, among others, supported him. That didn't do him much good with most voters. In far-off Malaya the communists were battling the British for their country's independence.

One country south, Indonesian rebels were fighting the Dutch for control of their nation. And the U.S. Olympic Team had just finished training for the July 29 start of the Olympics in London.

Blackie usually slept late because he'd been out late. He rarely had breakfast; it was tough holding down much of anything other than coffee or beer until later in the day. He looked over the paper on the way to the ballpark from the hotel. It was his habit to go straight to the sports pages then catch up with the news, comics, and entertainment sections later if he had the time. That Sunday morning the Browns were in seventh place, next to last. So far in the season they'd lost fifty-two games and only won thirty-one. The Senators weren't much better; they were in sixth, having lost forty-nine and won thirty-eight.

Blackie arrived at the ballpark in the early afternoon. He was excited. He was a little hungover, but nothing so bad that a beer or two couldn't hold in check. Griffith Stadium was the first major-league playing field he'd ever stepped onto, though in truth it wasn't much more impressive than Wrigley or Gilmore Fields back home in L.A. But as a baseball fan, he knew some of its history.

The stadium was built in 1891 and the Senators had played baseball in it since 1903. Two World Series had been played there and Walter Johnson, another big, lightning-fast right-hander, had hurled the ball the sixty feet six inches from the mound of dirt in the middle of the infield to the back of home plate with terrifying velocity. In the second game of that day's doubleheader, Blackie would be standing on that same pitcher's mound, facing down major-league batters with his own fastball.

It was a quirky stadium. The center field wall took an abrupt detour inward to make its way around five houses and a large tree that jutted into the playing field. The base path from home to first base sloped gently downhill. Washington's batters were notoriously slow and the groundskeepers were trying to give them an advantage. Like many teams, the Senators were sponsored in part by a beer company; a fifty-foot-tall bottle of National Bohemian Beer towered above the scoreboard.

Griffith Stadium could hold 32,000 fans but 10,618 were all that were on hand that day to watch two of the worst teams in baseball play each other.

Blackie put on his Browns uniform, he wore number twenty, and sat in the dugout through the first game, studying the Washington batters and reveling in the fact that he had made it to the big leagues. The Browns lost the first game, five to one.

Then, as the long, sultry Washington, DC, summer evening settled into place and swarms of mosquitoes formed clouds around the sweaty, wool-capped heads of the players, Blackie went out onto the field to warm up. He felt loose and good, his pitching motion was fluid and comfortable. His long, lean, strong body felt balanced and poised throughout the entire range of his movements. The ball thumped into the catcher's mitt with a deep, satisfying resonance.

Since the Browns were the visiting team, they batted first. An account of the game in the *Sporting News* provides a fine example of baseball's peculiar, at times opaque, lingo:

> St. Louisians made rapid getaway in after-piece, touching Harrist for brace of runs in first heat on Lund's ace, Priddy's double and another two-bagger by Kokos, who smacked nine hits in three-game series. Browns increased margin with another pair in third on Priddy's one-bagger, Lehner's walk and Kokos' triple. Nats pecked away at Schwamb, making first start following acquisition from Toledo, for single tally in third on Fleitas' pinch single, Yost's double and Partee's error on relay to plate. Early's long single in seventh scored Vernon and Wooten, chasing Schwamb in favor of Stephens. Stevens' boot on Priddy's toss allowed Vernon, who had singled and advanced on a sacrifice, to score from second in ninth with tying run, setting stage for Lund's blow on heels of single by Pellagrini and Kozar's bobble of Dillinger's foul-line looper.

What may be difficult to decipher from all that mumbo jumbo is that Blackie once again pitched an excellent game but wasn't the winning pitcher because of a bad play by his team in the ninth inning. He struck out three batters, didn't give up any walks, and his control was excellent until he got a little tired.

The *St. Louis Post-Dispatch* read: "It was a tough break for the tall rookie right-hander who pitched with amazing coolness until he weakened slightly in the seventh." The Browns managed to win the game, six to four, in the eleventh inning but Bryan Stephens, pitching in relief, got credit for the win.

Back in Toledo where Blackie hadn't made many friends, the *Blade*'s sports editor Bob French saw his major league debut as an opportunity to take another dig at the Browns organization. In his column on July 27, under the subhead "Defeats Help Schwamb Advance," he wrote:

> Pitcher Ralph Schwamb lost nine games and won one while a Mud Hen, and showed a juvenile disregard for training rules. As a result he gets promoted to the Browns.
>
> And to bewilder the fans still more, Schwamb pitched a good game for the Browns Sunday. He didn't go all the way, but the Browns won the game.
>
> This it would seem, bears out the idea of the Browns' front office, that the way to strengthen a ball club is to bolster it with players who didn't make good in a slower league.
>
> So a couple of questions remain unanswered. What qualifications are needed to earn a player promotion in the Browns' farm system, and just what is promotion in that organization anyhow?

After Sunday night's game the Browns hurried to Union Station. They had an 865-mile overnight train ride ahead of them. They were scheduled to play the New York Yankees back home just a few hours after the train pulled into St. Louis's Union Station.

At least the team traveled first class. They had a special dining car that turned into a lounge after dinner, and their own Pullman car with sleeping berths. The regular players got the more comfortable lower berths and the newcomers got stuck in the uppers. Still, the trips were terrible, long, and noisy; it was a rare player who got an actual good night's sleep on the train.

The players spent a lot of time playing cards and drinking. The team's manager, Zack Taylor, was a pretty easygoing guy, but he didn't want his team playing poker. It caused too many fights. So they played fan-tan, hearts, and gin at no more than a nickel a point. Sometimes there'd be poker games in the hotels, but quietly and only on occasion when the players had just been paid. There was one well-established regular game on the train between a few of the team's veteran players. Most rookies didn't dare try and get in on it.

"But Schwamb joins the ball club and we were on the train and within about ten seconds he'd muscled his way into the card game," recalls Chuck Stevens, who was the first baseman for the team. "I was sitting across the aisle reading and I looked up and there he was, right in the middle of it. The guys were kinda looking at him [funny]. That was his hustle. Some of the guys really resented that."

When the team got to St. Louis, Blackie moved into the Fairgrounds Hotel. Ballplayers with families rented houses, but the single players and the ones whose families didn't come to St. Louis stayed at the hotel. Built in 1927, for a time it had been one of the fanciest places in the city. By the time Blackie checked in, other than some of his teammates, a few of the St. Louis Cardinals, and visiting teams, most of the residents were elderly. There was a dining room and a quiet bar, but Blackie didn't spend a lot of time there.

"He'd be out all night," recalled Ned Garver, another rookie pitcher that year for the Browns. "He wouldn't come in until we'd be up in the morning. I didn't know too many guys who abused themselves like he did."

The hotel was across the street from Fairgrounds Park. The park had been built for the 1904 World's Fair, famous for, among other things, the song "Meet Me in St. Louis, Louis." During the fair's eight months nearly twenty million people had passed through the grounds. They were treated to such marvels as the public debut of air-conditioning; ice-skating throughout the hot, muggy summer; wireless telegrams to cities as many as fifteen hundred miles away; and exhibits that ranged from the Philippine jungles to Eskimo villages, from Japanese gardens to the holy sites of Jerusalem.

The neighborhood had enough taverns and dives that Blackie didn't need to wander too far afield to satisfy his constant thirst. He'd stumble in about breakfast time and head up to his room to shower and change if there was an early practice or game, or catch at least a couple of hours of sleep if there wasn't.

Garver remembers that at first all the players thought he never changed his clothes. He always seemed to be in the same suit. "Then he told us that he had five suits that were all the same," he said.

Despite the long train ride, the Browns beat the Yankees, four to one, in their Monday night game. The next night the Yankees beat the Browns. Win or lose, games against the Yankees were always fun for the team; it was pretty much the only time that they got big crowds out to the ballpark. The Yankees weren't having one of their better years, they were only in fourth place, but as much as the Browns were known as losers, the Yankees were known as winners. They also were rich with some of the game's biggest stars and the stars brought out the fans. Blackie enjoyed watching the games from the dugout and enjoyed having a big city to go out in afterward.

The Yankees left town after two games and the hapless Washington Senators came to play five. The Browns lost the first game in a close one. Then it was Blackie's turn to pitch. He was scheduled to start against Walt Masterson, who had pitched in the All-Star Games the past two years.

Maybe a few cheers echoed off the walls around the relatively uninhabited Sportsman's Park. The stadium could hold about 32,000 people, but on Saturday, July 31, only 4,556 were on hand to watch Blackie win his first game in the major leagues.

Blackie got off to a shaky start, giving up two runs in the first inning, and then settled down. Over the next five innings he gave up only one hit, struck out two batters, and walked two. Meanwhile his team gave him the support he needed, scoring two runs in the third inning, another in the fifth, and then going berserk and scoring seven runs in the sixth.

He got tired again in the seventh inning. Booze, chain-smoking, and heavy partying have never been known for their salubrious effect on athletic stamina. The Senators scored four runs on four hits and two walks. Blackie was taken out of the game for a relief pitcher. But the Browns held on to win the game ten to eight.

"I had my first major-league win," he said. "I was just a week shy of my twenty-second birthday. I had the world by the tail."

CHAPTER 13

BLACKIE WENT OUT TO CELEBRATE, though a night of celebration wasn't much different than any other night. There was plenty of booze, maybe some gambling, St. Louis had a good variety of jazz clubs and for a major-league-winning pitcher it was easier than ever to find willing women.

Nell and Rich were back in L.A., living with Janet, and he called to give them all the good news. By then Nell knew better than to be blindly optimistic, but everyone who knew him had long hoped that if he found some success, Blackie might settle down.

He didn't.

With four days until he was scheduled to pitch again Blackie took full advantage of his status. He showed up at the games as required, warmed up with the team, threw some balls to keep in shape, but mostly he drank. At night after the games it was whiskey washed down with beer; during the day and during games it was just beer. But he stayed drunk the whole time.

On the day of his next start he showed up at the stadium reeling somewhere in that harsh, dizzy daze between smashed and hungover.

"I got to the ballpark just in time to get dressed. I was sitting in front of my locker holdin' my head in my hands. Somethin' hit me in the head and it was a new ball. The manager, Zack Taylor, picked it up, threw it to me, and said, 'You're in there.' I thought, 'Well, that's nice.' So I went down to warm up. I threw about five pitches and they picked them up down by the backstop somewhere. I told them, 'I'm ready.'"

He wasn't ready for the Boston Red Sox who were in a tight, four-way battle for first place in the American League. Once again it was a small crowd, only a little more than five thousand, and this time Blackie was thankful for the absence of loud noise.

Dominic DiMaggio, the great Joe DiMaggio's little brother and a very good player in his own right, batted first. Blackie, hardly able to focus, walked him. He managed to get the next batter out, but then Ted Williams, the most dangerous hitter in baseball, came up to bat.

"I got right in the middle of my windup and stopped. The thought that went through my mind was, 'What if this sucker hits one jock high, right back [at me].' Sweat was just pourin' off of me. [I knew] he'd hit the son of a bitch someplace if I threw him a strike." He did throw him a strike and Williams hit a single that moved DiMaggio to third base.

Blackie threw the next ball almost into the stands behind home plate and a run scored on the wild pitch. After that the roof caved in. He walked the next batter and then gave up four singles in a row. In just one-third of an inning he had given up six runs, five hits, and walked two batters. The game was only twenty minutes old when he was taken out for a relief pitcher.

"Zack Taylor comes runnin' out to the mound, throws his hat on the ground, is jumping up and down calling me all kinds of names. 'Get the hell out of here, ya goddamn . . .' I told him, 'Zack take it easy.'"

The manager fined Blackie $250 for showing up to the game in no condition to play and for talking back. It was the first of many fines and at 5 percent of his annual salary, the bite hurt.

Oddly enough, once Blackie left the field and the Red Sox finished their rampage, the Browns scored seven runs in their half of the first inning and went on to win by a score of nine to eight. In baseball, often described as "a game of inches," even one game can make a big difference. That one loss quite possibly cost Boston the league championship for the year. They finished the season in second place.

This time Ralph didn't have the team to blame for his misfortune. He continued to binge, drinking up the four days until his next starting appearance. Even though he'd had two strong performances and just the one disaster, he wallowed in self-pity.

On Sunday, August 8 he trudged the three blocks, through hellish heat and dense humidity, from the hotel to the ballpark. He was scheduled to pitch against the league-leading Philadelphia Athletics.

The Athletics were often called the "Amazing As." Their entire infield of players cost them around $50,000 per year in salaries, which wasn't much. They'd put together a group of pitchers who were among the best in baseball that year for less than a good-sized signing bonus would have cost most teams for one promising player. The secret to their success was a remarkable old man.

Connie Mack, their manager, had been born in 1862, just about the time that General Ulysses S. Grant was laying siege to Vicksburg, Mississippi, during the Civil War. He was a relatively old twenty-four years when he started playing for the major-league Washington Nationals of the National League in 1886. Eight years later he was pretty young for the job when he started managing the Pittsburgh Pirates of the National League. By the time Blackie pitched against his team he had been the Philadelphia A's manager for forty-seven years.

He was also the team's owner, one of the very few who had no business interests other than his ball club. Under his management the As fielded nine teams that got into the World Series, winning five of them. As an owner though, he was a shrewd businessman. He once confided to a reporter that "It is more profitable for me to have a team that is in contention for most of the season but finishes about fourth. A team like that will draw well enough during the first part of the season to show a profit for the year, and you don't have to give the players raises when they don't win." (In 1948 his team fought for first place through much of the season, then finished fourth.)

Mack was an imposing, mostly quiet, presence on the field. While all the other managers wore team uniforms, he wore dark suits and ties. In a sport that was famous for its tobacco juice spitting, swearing, temperamental players and managers, he almost never raised his voice and was known for his impeccable manners.

Pitching, Mack figured, was about 80 percent of the game of baseball. He favored tall, strong, young pitchers he could sign cheap. Except for the disciplinary problems Ralph would have been just his kind of player. Dick Fowler, a six-foot-four twenty-seven-year-old right-hander was the best pitcher on the As. When he started the game against the Browns and Blackie, he had won ten games and lost only three. The game had all the makings of a classic duel between similar pitchers.

Once again attendance was disappointingly small, especially for a Sunday afternoon—just 6,990. By contrast, on the same day the other St. Louis team was playing the other Philadelphia team in Philadelphia. That game between the third-place Cardinals and the sixth-place Phillies drew a crowd of 27,457, nearly filling the ballpark.

The game got off to a good start for Blackie. He was relaxed and pitching well. In the first two innings the As got just one hit and the Browns scored a run. In the third inning, with two outs, Fowler came up to bat. Like most pitchers he was a terrible hitter, but Ralph threw him three straight balls and no strikes. Zack Taylor came out to the mound to calm down his young pitcher.

"He tells me, 'For crisssake Ralph, throw a strike. Who do you think you have up there, DiMaggio or somebody? Just throw a strike. This guy can't hit. Just lob the ball up there.' So I lobbed the ball and he hit the damndest, longest home run you ever saw." It was the only home run that Dick Fowler ever hit in his ten years of major-league baseball.

The next batter hit a single but the following batter made an out. After three innings the game was tied. Other than that one bad pitch, Blackie had been throwing pretty well. But Fowler's homer, which he blamed on Taylor, had made him mad.

The first batter in the fourth inning got a single. The next two made outs and Ralph was beginning to relax. Then the A's right fielder, Elmer Valo, was called safe at first base on a very close play. Blackie argued the umpire's call and came away unsatisfied and unnerved. He walked the next batter and the bases were loaded. Herman Franks, the A's second-string catcher who was a weak hitter, came up to bat. By then, fuming and very nervous, Blackie had lost control. He walked Franks on four pitches and Philadelphia went ahead two to one. Taylor took him out of the game and for the first time in the major leagues he was the losing pitcher.

Normally it would come as no great shock that a rookie pitcher would have a couple of bad days. It usually takes time to get comfortable in the major leagues no matter how much talent a player has. Blackie's first two starts had shown a lot of promise. The second two wouldn't have mattered much, especially since the Browns didn't have a hope of winning their league anyhow, except that Ralph's bad attitude made them important.

How a pitcher reacts in a jam is one of the most important aspects of the job. Keeping cool in a hot situation is one of the keys to success in baseball. Blackie didn't have the maturity to be a big-league pitcher. Taylor sent him to the bull pen, to sit around and wait to be called in as a relief pitcher when he was needed.

"By 1948 [the Browns] were just trying anything," said Ray Coleman, an outfielder on the team that year. "[They were] bringing young guys up, especially young pitchers, before they were ready."

Al Zarilla, who had played ball with Blackie around Los Angeles in the off-season and who was also a member of the 1948 Browns, said, "He was rushed up there and I think that helped screw him up. He just couldn't handle it. Pressure does funny things sometimes."

He didn't get into another game for two and a half weeks. He sat and stewed in resentment and booze.

> I'd always been a starting pitcher and no matter how much I
> drank, I always had great stamina. Being down in the damn bull
> pen I drank a case of beer a game. But I could still go out and
> throw strikes.
>
> Once in awhile the Browns would get in a close game. I'd be
> warming up from about the first inning on and it only took me

about ten pitches to get ready. You could get into a game where you had a chance to pick up the win, they didn't have saves in those days, but they'd send in one of the starters [to give him a chance at the win], and I'd sit down again.

So I'd get up to go in a game where we were playin' Washington to see who was the worst team in the history of baseball. Fourteen to two in the second inning and here's Zack Taylor calling me. So a few times I told him, "You want a pitcher in a fourteen-to-two ball game? Get your mother down here." They fined me and fined me. I never had any money but I had a couple of good friends.

"What a mouth," said Joe Schultz, who was one of the Browns' catchers. "I think he kind of drove Zack nuts. 'Just shut up and play ball,' he'd yell at Ralph."

Blackie could be funny and he was smart. On a team that was filled with misfits and players who didn't want to be there, he did get along well with at least a few of his teammates.

"He liked to fool around, kid around," recalled Joe Ostrowski, a pitcher for the Browns. "Some of the players seemed to enjoy his company. He was very outgoing with people. You have your buddy or buddies and after the game the two or three of you might associate and the others go their own way."

Ralph didn't have any regular pals on the team, but he did go out on occasion with Les Moss, one of his catchers. "Some guys on the team didn't like him," said Moss, "but I got along fine with him. We went out to dinner a few times. He was one entertaining guy, a very funny fellow. He told me of some of his exploits back there in L.A. He had an interesting life. I'm a country boy from Oklahoma so I just soaked all this in. I kind of envied him, to be honest. Never a dull moment with Ralph."

Bob Dillinger was the Browns' first-string third baseman, one of the team's few stars. He liked his liquor too, and he liked Blackie, but he took his baseball seriously and didn't mix the two. "Ralph and I hit it off," he said. "I liked the guy. Like most of us he was a little kooky, but he was more so than the rest of us. I didn't go out drinking with the boys and didn't stay drunk for three or four days on end."

A lot of the other guys either ignored Blackie, going home to their wives and families after the games, or didn't like him and steered clear of him off the field.

"He was different, you could sense that," said Don Lund, an outfielder on the team. "You never got to know him as closely as you did your other teammates."

By most accounts the 1948 St. Louis Browns were not a close-knit team. According to Ralph, "They were malcontents. What kind of team spirit could you have when you play a Fourth of July doubleheader and you get less than five hundred people?"

Sam Dente was an infielder with the Browns for just that one year of a ten-year career. "I wasn't there very long, thank god. We had some nice guys, but absolutely no chemistry. Everybody went his own way. No team unity. I was very happy to leave."

The Boston Red Sox traded Eddie Pellagrini, the Browns' shortstop, to St. Louis at the beginning of the 1948 season. "What a shock," he recalled. "A terrible ball club. The ballpark was all run down and the organization was pathetic. I hated the two years I was there.

"The Browns had all these young pitchers and they were all wild as March hares. Schwamb fit right in. He had a lot of ability but you could tell he was an oddball, a screwball. It was no fun hitting against that guy. He'd throw batting practice and knock guys down. His own guys! He had kind of an attitude."

Roy Partee, a catcher with the Browns, grew up in the same neighborhood as Ralph and went to the same high school, although a few years earlier. "He had a great arm but he just didn't fit in with the rest of the guys. I wouldn't associate with him after hours. He was one of those guys who would drink and then do crazy things. Ralph tried to act like a tough guy. He had a temperament problem but he didn't scare me. [He was] a real eccentric. The Browns thought they were getting the next Dizzy Dean, but Blackie was just dizzy."

Picking up on his behavior and the nickname his teammates had given him in Toledo, the newspapers began to refer to Ralph "Dizzy" Schwamb. He didn't like it. The longer he sat in the bull pen, the more frustrated he became, the more he drank; the less he liked a lot of what the other players and the manager were saying about him and calling him.

"He was an odd bird and would defend himself when his teammates would needle him," said Ostrowski. "He would not shy away from abuse, and the problem is that in baseball there is a lot of that sort of give and take. Ralph just didn't handle it very well. Physically, he was a very mature guy. But emotionally, he still had growing up to do. He knew how to get into trouble, but not how to get out of it."

"He was the nervous type," remembers Owen Friend, an infielder with the Browns in 1949 and 1950, who met Blackie in spring training. "He always had to be doing something, and that something wasn't always what he should've been doing. He liked excitement."

"He created his own problems," said Chuck Stevens, the Browns' first baseman and no friend of Ralph's. "He wasn't ready, he shouldn't have been there. You have to get along, especially as a rookie. Instead he seemed to go out of his way to stir up trouble, to break the rules. A lot of the older guys resented him. Frankly, he was a cancer on that team."

Ralph had grown up fast on the streets of Los Angeles and in naval prison and Ostrowski was right; in the course of it he'd left some important parts of his personal development behind. In some ways he didn't treat his teammates any differently than a child might react to the other kids on the schoolyard.

"The thing that bothered me the most about Ralph was that he just couldn't relax and be one of the guys," said Fred Sanford, one of the starting pitchers on the team. "He acted like a tough guy, but when players started to get on him, razz him, the usual stuff you hear as a player, he couldn't handle it.

"[We'd] call him things like 'Ears' or 'Dumbo.' He had big ears and ballplayers being ballplayers picked up on that. It's not very clever, but it's something you just have to laugh off. He didn't like being called

Blackie or Dizzy either. So then he'd run up to [general manager and owner Bill] DeWitt's office and rat on us. Now, you do that and you are going to have problems with your teammates."

"He just about drove everyone crazy," said Pellagrini. "Then he'd run up to DeWitt's office and complain to the boss man. You just don't do that! A tougher, better manager might have been able to get him squared away. With Zack there, he had no chance."

Zack Taylor was liked all right by his players, but not respected much as a manager. He'd been in baseball for twenty years, having broken into the major leagues as a catcher with the Brooklyn Dodgers. He was first hired to manage the Browns in the last month of 1946. He took over at the helm of a team that was going nowhere and didn't change its course; the Browns finished in seventh place. The next year he went back to being a coach for the team and then in 1948 he was promoted again to manager. It was a thankless task. Even if it hadn't have been, he probably wasn't up to a thankful task either.

"Zack Taylor was a joke as a manager," said Partee, pulling no punches. "He didn't know how to handle players. He'd let 'em get away with murder and then get mad about some piddly bullshit stuff."

"He had been a great coach," said Pellagrini, "but as manager he just didn't have it. He couldn't handle these young bucks. And he didn't know how to run a ball club. Once we were playing in Boston, my hometown, and he took me out of the game for a pinch hitter in the third inning. That's bullshit and I told him so. Kind of hard to respect a guy like that. It's no wonder he couldn't control the young guys."

Owen Friend didn't think much of Taylor's leadership either. He likes to tell a story to support his opinion: "Zack was an OK guy but not a good manager. [One time] the Browns were gonna play the World Champion New York Yankees. So Zack says, 'All right boys, hit the cutoff man, make good throws, throw strikes, don't swing at bad pitches. Let's get out there and look good losing!' He really said that. I was there."

The loser's mentality infected the whole team. After the last game of the 1948 season Eddie Pellagrini stopped for a little while on the field to talk with a player from the opposing team while the rest of the Browns went into their locker room. "Then I went into our clubhouse," he recalled, "and the guys are celebrating and spraying beer all over. I say, 'What the hell do we have to celebrate? We lost ninety-four games.' It turned out the celebration was because we had lost one less game than the 1947 Browns."

The Browns' tradition of losing demoralized the players. The only hope they had was to be traded to another team. "They would develop a ballplayer and then sell him," said Chuck Stevens. "The theme song when we were there was to bear down, elevate your salary to a certain level, and that's how you got away from the Browns. Everybody looked forward to leaving the ball club if they could because you knew you were never going to be a contender."

"Their big thing was to develop young players and then sell them," said Ostrowski. "That's how they made their money. For me it worked out great. They sold me to the Yankees for $50,000. It was a dream come true. That's how the Browns viewed their players, as cattle to be sold to the highest bidder."

"You'd play for the Browns figuring that if you did good they would dump you," said Dillinger.

Not long after his first two games, the Detroit Tigers made an offer to trade for Ralph. A clause in his contract, however, meant that the trade would have cost the Browns about $30,000, so they turned the deal down.

"Not that Detroit was all that great in those days, but they had a good solid ball club," said Blackie. "It's always been a great organization. When [the Browns] turned that down, I kind of just gave up. I lost all heart. I just pitched when they told me to pitch—'go on, get out there.' I don't think the glamour would have affected me as much if I'd been with a good team."

There was glamour to be had, even with the historically worst team in baseball. Ralph didn't have much money, but he rarely needed any when he went out at night. Men wanted to buy him drinks, women wanted to have sex with him, even though he was just a bull pen pitcher with a lousy team people wanted his autograph. He stayed almost constantly drunk. He didn't eat or sleep much and his health and stamina deteriorated.

On August 25 in Washington, DC, Blackie was the third of five pitchers that the Browns used against the Senators. He came into the game with the Browns behind five to nothing and when he was taken out a couple of innings later they were losing ten to nothing. After the game Zack Taylor told the St. Louis newspapers that his team desperately needed better pitching.

Two nights later in Philadelphia he was brought in to pitch in the eighth inning with the Athletics leading the Browns five to one. He threw gas on the fire and by the time the Browns managed to get three of the As out, the score was nine to one.

Two nights after that he pitched just one inning in Boston. When he came into the game the Browns were losing by a score of ten to two. He gave up one hit but no runs and didn't look too bad.

Then the team went to New York to play the Yankees. The city was the world capital of baseball. It had three teams, the Dodgers, the Giants, and the mighty Yankees, who had won more championships and fielded more big stars than any other team in the game.

Yankee Stadium, with seats for more than sixty-seven thousand people, was baseball's greatest monument. It was sometimes called "the House that Ruth Built," after Babe Ruth, whose prodigious feats in the early 1920s had made the New York team enough money to build its ballpark. Ruth had died on August 16 that year, at age fifty-three, of lung cancer. The stadium's flags were at half-mast and black bunting was draped throughout the stands.

Ralph, like most young ballplayers walking onto the field at Yankee Stadium for the first time, was awestruck. There were 41,335 people in the stands, the biggest crowd he'd ever seen. He didn't think that he'd get into the game unless it looked hopeless for the Browns, so he settled into his chair in the bull pen with a beer in hand.

In the eighth inning the Yankees were leading ten to four and Ralph got the call to pitch. He loved telling the story. It was, according to him, one of his few great moments.

"There was one out and men on second and third. The first hitter I faced was Charlie Keller."

Charlie "King Kong" Keller was on a hitting streak at the time. He'd already had a single and a home run in the game. He was a great fastball hitter and especially dangerous with men on base.

"So Taylor says to me, 'Don't give this guy anything good [to hit].' Which is a helluva thing to say to a kid pitcher whose control wasn't the greatest. Besides, I was really nervous. This was Yankee Stadium. I used to be a Yankees fan. I kept thinking, 'What am I doing here? This is my team.'

"I went for broke. I threw the first pitch straight down the alley as hard as I could. Keller swung and missed and Taylor ran out, his face white.

"'Fercrissake,' he says, 'what are you doing? Don't give this fellow anything good to hit.'

"'Sure,' I said, and I fired twice more, straight down the pipe and Keller swung and missed [both times] and then the next guy popped out, and I was out of the inning.

"Not every two-thirds of an inning was so good."

Not every two-thirds of an inning actually happened either. Moments of triumph were few and far between for Ralph Schwamb in his major-league career, so he seems to have made a few of them up.

In reality he did come in to pitch in the eighth inning of the game in Yankee Stadium. There were two outs and two men on base. Nervous, he walked the first batter he faced to load the bases. The next batter hit a short fly ball to the outfield for the third out.

Back in St. Louis a week later the Detroit Tigers were beating the Browns five to nothing when Blackie was called in to pitch. He pitched a good game for the first two innings and had got two outs in the third when it all blew up in his face. An error, a walk, and a single loaded the bases with runners.

Roy Partee was the catcher.

The next hitter was a dead fastball hitter. I knew it, Blackie knew it, everybody in the crowd knew it. But there's old Zack in the dugout, yelling, "Don't throw him a fastball! Don't throw him a fastball!"

It's a hot day, the umpire has missed a couple of calls, I'm having all I can do to handle Ralph's pitches, and I don't need any more advice.

So it gets to be three and two on the batter and Zack is yelling, and I signal for a curveball and Ralph throws a curveball. His curve was what we called a "nickel curve" (a "slider" in modern baseball lingo.) It was a hell of a pitch, but thrown at about the same speed as a fastball. The batter ripped it for a double and all three runners scored.

We got the next guy out and trot back to the dugout and Zack is all over me. "What the hell is the idea of calling for that fastball?"

So I tell him, "Number one it was a curveball. Ask your goddamned pitcher what he threw! And number two; don't call pitches for me. Keep your dumbshit mouth shut when I'm catching."

He and I are going to war and Ralph comes over and naturally he also gets into it with Zack. Joe Schultz says, "Boys, boys, don't fight."

The Tigers, [watching all this,] are just falling down laughing. Finally the umpire comes over and says, "Are you guys gonna play or are you gonna fight?"

I just walked to the other end of the dugout, took a long drink of water, looked up to the heavens and said, "Get me out of this loony-bin."

The Browns' pitching had been so terrible that Zack Taylor decided to enlist the help of the team's announcer, Dizzy Dean, to light a fire under the young pitching staff. He asked Joe Schultz to help get the pitchers and catchers out to the ballpark earlier than usual one morning. Schultz recalled:

> Dean was late showing up. Everybody's hungover and it's drizzling and we're all standing around at the pitcher's mound feeling sorry for ourselves, when Diz finally shows up.
>
> He launches into this spiel about how great he was, how great the Cardinals were and how the Browns were always horseshit. So this is going over real good, you know. After about twenty minutes of this he stops to take a breath, and I yell out, "Any questions?" And, of course, Ralph raises his hand.
>
> Ralph pipes up in this prissy voice, "Gee whiz, Mr. Dean. I read all these record books and they have to be wrong. They show you lost about one hundred games and, from what you're telling us, that can't possibly be true."
>
> Well Dean and Blackie get into a yelling match right there. Everybody is breaking up and finally even Dean starts to laugh. You had to laugh because it was just a ridiculous situation to begin with. So we broke it up and sent everybody home. It was the last time Dizzy ever volunteered to coach our pitchers.

For the most part Blackie and Dizzy got along pretty well. "He'd tell me about the mechanics of pitching," Ralph said. "[Sometimes] I'd be pitching in St. Louis when the catcher or Taylor would come out to talk to me and Diz would flip on the field announcement system and say, 'Leave that boy alone, let him fling that thing.' Then he'd turn it off."

On September 12 Ralph got a chance to leave the bull pen and start the second game of a Sunday doubleheader. Better yet, he was going to pitch against Bob Feller, one of the greatest pitchers in baseball, and the Cleveland Indians who had been battling for first place since the start of the season. (The Indians went on to win the American League championship and then the World Series.)

It might have been a show of confidence in Blackie by Taylor, or it could have been a test to see whether or not the team wanted to make much of an effort to sign him for the next season, or it is also possible that the manager wanted to give his other pitchers more time to rest between starts and it didn't much matter to him who was likely to lose to the Indians. Blackie didn't care what the reason was, he was happy for a starting assignment, especially against a good team.

Cleveland's Municipal Stadium was huge. It could hold more than 80,000 people and the Indians had been setting attendance records all year long. Even a game with the lowly St. Louis Browns drew a crowd of 55,616. In the eight games that the Browns played in Cleveland that year, 50,000 more people paid to see them in action than had come out to see the Browns play in all fifty-four of their home games at Sportsman's Park.

With its high round stands and slightly overhanging roof, the roar of a big crowd in Cleveland's stadium could be deafening.

The sound level during the first two innings must have been nearly unbearable for Blackie. Entering the last few weeks of the season, the Indians were in third place but still very much in the running for the league championship.

Just as the Indians' first batter walked up to the plate and Ralph finished his last warm-up pitch, a tidal wave of sound flooded the stadium. In their dugout the Cleveland players were grinning, cheering, and gesturing at the scoreboard. Blackie had to wait before he could deliver his first pitch, so he turned to take a look at what all the fuss was about.

In Boston, the fourth-place Philadelphia As had scored six runs in the last inning to beat the first-place Red Sox. That meant that Cleveland, which had won the first game of the afternoon, had moved up a notch in the standings and had a chance to move up another half point if they beat the Browns in the second game.

All the uproar rattled him, but the first batter hit an easy ground ball for an out. He walked the second batter, gave up a single to the third, and was in trouble again. The noise from the crowd was unlike anything he had ever heard before. The game was about to slip completely out of control and he was standing on the pitcher's mound right in the middle of it.

Then the Browns' left fielder, Zarilla, made a great catch to save a couple of runs from scoring. But the next batter hit a double and two runs scored. Another great catch, this time by the right fielder, Dick Kokas, got Blackie out of the inning.

In the second inning the Indians scored another run. In the third the Browns scored two in their half, but it was still three to two when Ralph was taken out of the game after walking the first batter in the inning. He went to the showers and Ned Garver, one of the Browns' best starters, took over.

After twelve innings the game was declared a tie because of darkness. There was a rule that any game that had been scheduled as a "day" game could not be continued under the lights if it went too long.

For the rest of his life Blackie got a lot of mileage out of telling people about the time that he battled the great Bob Feller to a twelve-inning tie. The lie got him bought plenty of drinks over the years.

The team won its game against Cleveland the next day, and then took the train back to St. Louis to play the As again. Blackie was angrier than ever. He didn't think that he'd pitched all that badly against the Indians. The game was still winnable, he'd just been a little nervous; who wouldn't have been in the same circumstances? If he'd have had a better manager, a better pitching coach, a better catcher, they could have calmed him down and he could have shown his stuff. Once again at his expense one of the regular starters had been brought in when he had a chance for a win.

On Tuesday he was back in the bull pen, contentedly sucking back beers and comfortably in the bag when Taylor called him in to pitch against the As. It was another hopeless situation; the Browns were losing ten to two in the seventh inning. At least it was quiet; there were only about three thousand people in the stands. He'd been in minor-league games with bigger, noisier crowds than that. He pitched for two innings, giving up two hits, two walks, two runs, and struck out one batter. He got taken out of the game when it was his turn to bat in the eighth inning and headed down to the locker room for a shower and one of the cold beers that was always available from the ice chest by the trainer's table.

Blackie walked out of the clubhouse and disappeared for a few days. The season was winding down and the Browns were pretty well set into sixth place. There was more satisfaction to be taken from booze and women than from the ball field.

He was fined again when he showed back up, but he'd expected that. It was just part of the routine by then. Zack Taylor hardly even bothered to get mad at him anymore.

A few days later he was back in the bull pen, a few beers chasing away his hangover, St. Louis losing at home to Boston yet again. There were only two weeks left in the season. The Red Sox were in first place but the Yankees and the Indians were breathing down the Boston team's neck. Even though the Browns weren't in the race, every game was crucial in deciding the American League championship. Ted Williams, the Red Sox's left fielder, was one of the biggest stars in baseball and was having a typically great year.

Still, only thirty-seven hundred fans showed up to watch the "national pastime" on a summer Saturday afternoon. Gorgeous George drew nearly three times as many people when he wrestled on the cards promoted by Sam Muchnick at nearby Kiel Auditorium.

In the sixth inning the score was eleven to four. The Red Sox had two outs but a couple of men on base, so Taylor, of course, signaled for Ralph to come into the game. He got the last batter out, and then didn't allow a run to score over the next three innings. He walked one batter, gave up three hits, and struck out one. It was a good performance for a relief pitcher with a bad team, but in the end it was meaningless. The Browns scored two runs in the seventh inning but still lost the game.

Another week went by in which the Browns lost six games and won only two. Blackie spent the time in the bull pen and his usual bars. On the morning of September 27 the team was on the Detroit Limited, waiting for it to pull out of St. Louis's Union Station on the season's last road trip. Blackie was nowhere to be found.

"We were about to leave without him," remembered Partee, "when he came staggering into the station. It looked like he had slept in a gutter and smelled like it too. I helped to get him on board and take him to a washroom where he slumped down on a chair.

"One of the players walked in and said something like, 'Looks like Ears really tied one on.'

"Blackie jumped up and grabbed something out of his coat pocket. I saw that he had a whiskey bottle and I figured he's about to smash the other guy in the face. So I grabbed his arm and we're all wrestling around in there. It's a wonder the conductor didn't throw the whole team off the train.

"Finally we got him into a berth and kind of tied him in with our belts, and he slept it off."

When the team got to Detroit, Taylor and Bill DeWitt told Blackie that he was suspended for the rest of the season and to go home. He waited a couple of hours in the station bar, got on the Twilight Limited to Chicago, then transferred to the Super Chief to L.A.

CHAPTER 14

B LACKIE COULD HAVE GONE BACK TO MEXICO. The team in Ciudad Obregón would have been happy to have him. But Nell wanted him home and he felt that baseball had let him down. The big leagues had been fun, but not all that he had hoped for. Besides, his gangster pals were busier than ever. They also could use his services and they paid better than anyone else.

Mickey Cohen and his associates were in the newspapers so often, popping up in both the news and society pages, that a columnist for the New York *Daily News* had begun using the phrase "L.A.'s Vicecapades" to describe the sheer lunatic criminality that centered around them. Following the murder of Bugsy Siegel in June 1947, Cohen's rivals, particularly Jack Dragna, figured there was a power vacuum to be filled.

On August 18, 1948, while Blackie was warming the Browns' bench in St. Louis, his friends in Los Angeles were fired upon in the opening salvo of what the press called "the Battle of Sunset Strip." Cohen and some of his "henchmen" were in his haberdashery. Mickey went to wash his hands, something he habitually did fifty to sixty times a day. As he closed the bathroom door, a couple of gunmen stepped in the front door and opened fire. Mickey barricaded himself in the washroom and later emerged unscathed. His right-hand man, Hooky Rothman, was killed and two of his other guys were wounded. Mickey told the press that he knew who had ordered the hit and would deal with it personally.

A few weeks later Mickey pulled into his driveway at home when some of Dragna's men in the bushes started shooting at him. He dove to the floor of his car and with a hand on the gas and one on the wheel steered himself nearly a mile to a busy street. He waited a few minutes then drove back home and walked in the door to be greeted by his dinner guests, including movie star George Raft. He was bleeding, but only from flying glass.

"Raft says to me, 'Jesus, what happened?' recalled Cohen.

"I said, 'Don't worry what happened. Let's sit down and have dinner.'

"He says, 'How are we gonna eat after this?'

"I said, 'What do you mean how? Get around the table and eat dinner.'

"So everybody sat down. But nobody was eating except me, see, even though we had a beautiful dinner set out."

Mickey was getting better press and more of it than ever.

Not long after the attempted ambush, Blackie came back to town. Other than a few bucks here and there for pitching in semipro ball games, no one was going to pay him to play ball in the off-season. One of the first things he did back in L.A. was to call Freddie and Joe Sica, looking for some action.

He could have had plenty of legitimate work. There was a lot going on in Los Angeles. The city was expanding at an unprecedented pace. Chester, his father, had more work than he knew what to do with and he wanted Ralph to come to work with him. He was building department stores, shopping centers, office buildings, schools, and enormous sprawling housing developments.

The sleepy, agricultural San Fernando Valley had woken up with a start. In Encino, where orange groves had covered the land just a year and a half before, nearly two thousand new homes went on the block in just one housing development alone in late 1948. Veterans could buy a house without a down payment for $48 per month including principal, interest, tax, and insurance. In Seaside Heights, on lots overlooking the ocean, two-bedroom homes were going for $39.25 per month, also with no money down for veterans.

There was plenty of cash spread around and a lot of inexpensive products to buy with it. Porterhouse steaks sold in the market for fifty-five cents a pound. At Lindy's, the popular late-night steak and chop house on Wilshire Boulevard, a good steak dinner with all the fixings might set a diner back three bucks or so. Buicks were cheaper than butter, at least on a pound-for-pound basis, according to the advertising.

Cars were beginning to clog the streets. The trolley lines, once considered among the finest public transportation systems in the world, were a sore spot; drivers complained bitterly about old-fashioned, lumbering trolleys getting in their way.

With everyone wanting to ease into the fast lane, corruption was a big issue in Los Angeles. There was an election for mayor coming up on April 5, 1949, and the campaign was already getting nasty.

Mayor Fletcher Bowron had first been elected in 1938. He swept into office backed by "reformers" who were in turn backed by Bugsy Siegel's crowd.

In some ways Bowron had actually cleaned up the city. The police department, while continuing to take its cut of criminal profits in exchange for turning a blind eye to protected rackets, had pretty much been forced out of the crime business itself. The cost of bribing the various city permits offices had come down considerably, smoothing the way for postwar development. City planning, though not highly regarded for its foresight, had for the first time been instituted.

To hear Bowron and his supporters talk about it, and to just take a cursory look around town at the goings-on, a casual observer would have thought Los Angeles was living in a golden age. But there was a flip side.

The police department was known for its brutality, its antiunion activities, and for protecting the gangsters who paid it off. It also wasn't very effective. In the first six months of 1948 there had been more than twenty-five thousand major crimes reported in the city. By comparison, New York, with four times the population, had reported less than half as many;

Philadelphia, with a population of about two hundred thousand more people than L.A., reported only about a fifth as many serious crimes.

City permits were cheaper and easier to get than ever and the rampant development that fostered was uncontrollable. While transportation and other public infrastructure fell into disrepair and most public services either deteriorated or failed to keep up with the fast-growing need for them, private enterprise made a mockery of any real attempts at urban planning.

Lloyd Aldrich, Los Angeles's city engineer since 1933, considered the father of the city's freeway system, was the latest reform candidate for mayor. His campaign hammered at Bowron for having turned the city over to mobsters and irresponsible developers.

Mayor Bowron, disingenuously campaigning to "Keep Corruption Out of Los Angeles," publicly returned Mickey Cohen's contribution, while accepting money from Cohen's associates behind the scenes.

According to Cohen, "Mayor Bowron was very important to me. I never got to a point where I was social friends with [him] . . . We kept it at a distance, but I could always reach him by phone.

"When I was in the mayor's corner, see, a certain amount was put into his campaign each time through my lawyers. I didn't care if any politician I was backing took a stand against me, which was what he was supposed to do. There was no other way that you could do those things, if you understand politics."

Cohen didn't just fork over campaign cash to the mayor; sometimes he was called upon for favors. According to his autobiography, in early 1949 he got a call from someone at the police commission wanting to set up a meeting. He met with the chief executive of the commission, Harry Lorenson, and Burt Mold, who was becoming a political big shot in the city. They met at Goodfellow's Grotto, a fish house at Third and Main in downtown that was known for its private booths in which all sorts of deals were regularly cut.

The mayor's problem was a radio repairman named Alfred Pearson, who had a shop on West Adams, near where Ralph had been born. Pearson had more than a hundred nuisance lawsuits pending against the city.

He'd also recently used legal means to cheat a widow out of her house because she couldn't pay his padded bill for repairing her radio. Pearson had bought her $4,000 home at a sheriff's auction for $26.50.

"So they're telling me that Los Angeles Mayor Fletcher Bowron wants this guy knocked around a bit, and I should call Bowron for verification," wrote Cohen.

He told Lorenson that it would be easier to simply kill Pearson, but the commission executive said that they just wanted the guy hospitalized and promised that they'd keep cops away from the area of the shop on the appointed day.

A couple of mornings later Cohen and seven of his thugs, later referred to in the newspapers as "Snow White and the Seven Dwarves," paid Pearson a very unpleasant visit. Satisfied that the radio repairman was sufficiently beat up, Cohen went back to his office, which was then in a back room at Slapsie Maxie's, leaving the Dwarves to clean up.

Two rookie cops, who hadn't got the word to steer clear of the proceedings, showed up and arrested Cohen's men. They got them down to the local stationhouse, where the district captain took charge, releasing the unofficial public servants without booking them, duly issuing apologies, and returning their weapons, along with some stolen radio equipment.

Eventually the incident led to indictments and corruption charges. Some policemen retired, others were suspended, but the new blemishes on the commission's reputation were hardly noticeable among all the old ones. Cohen and the Seven Dwarves went to trial and were acquitted, and his stock with the public went up when he got the widow's house back for her and presented her with the deed and a sizable cash gift.

Blackie's work for Snow White was less high profile. It wouldn't have done anyone any good to have a major-league ballplayer openly working for gangsters. He almost certainly would have been thrown out of the sport. But his association with the high-flying mobster gave him even more standing in some circles than his playing for the St. Louis Browns. As a gangster he got respect, girls, free drinks, and fancy dinners, just like he did as a major-league baseball player, but crime paid a lot better.

Through the fall of 1948 and the first two months or so of 1949 Blackie lived it up at a greater pace than ever before. He was almost never home other than on occasion to change clothes or drop off some cash. Nell didn't know for sure where he was getting his money, but she had her suspicions and wasn't happy about it.

In November he got his invitation to spring training from the Browns. It was going to start on March 1, 1949, in Burbank, a small town just a little less than twenty miles north of his and Nell's apartment.

Ralph had been to Burbank a few times before. It was a horse community, with a lot of stables and riding academies along the Los Angeles River at its southern edge. Mickey Cohen owned the Dincara Stock Farm and Stables there, where he bred horses out front and ran a swank illegal casino in one of the back barns.

The city of Burbank was excited about the Browns coming to play. Tickets for exhibition games against other major league teams went on sale more than a month in advance. The *Burbank Daily Review* reported on its front page, as if it were significantly newsworthy, that the Browns' second baseman, Jerry Priddy, had bought a house in town. The chamber of commerce threw a gala dinner reception for the team, arranged with the help of MGM movie studios, and featuring singing, dancing, and joke-telling stars of stage and screen.

People were excited all over the greater Los Angeles area about spring training. In a city that didn't have a major-league team, four teams were coming to work out. The Browns were coming to Burbank, the Chicago White Sox were going to train in nearby Pasadena, the Chicago Cubs at Wrigley Field just south of downtown, and the Pittsburgh Pirates were showing up in San Bernardino. It was a feverish time for Southern California baseball fans.

By the time he was supposed to report for training, Ralph was a wreck. He'd spent most of the past six months drunk, sleeping little and eating less. He was almost anorexic thin and other than a few sloshed attempts at pitching in semipro and exhibition games, the only exercise he'd gotten over the winter was with his fists in bars and alleys.

The Browns sent him his contract the week before he was supposed to show up. They were going to pay him $5,000 again, the major-league minimum. He called Bill DeWitt, who with his brother now owned the team, and demanded a token raise of $1,000 for the season. DeWitt told him that if he made the major-league team at the end of spring training, he'd give him the grand.

The Browns' owner had plenty of experience with how much trouble Ralph could be. So he asked Jack Graham, a first baseman who lived in Long Beach, to pick him up on his drive to Burbank every day, and to make sure he got to the training camp. DeWitt wasn't too happy with Graham, who had held out for a $7,500 salary instead of the minimum, before signing his contract. (Graham, playing for San Diego, had led the Pacific Coast League in home runs the previous year and had been paid $7,500 by the minor-league team.) Graham figured that being assigned as Blackie's minder was a sort of punishment.

"First day I drive up and there's no sign of this Schwamb character," recalled Graham. "So I go to his apartment and his wife says she hasn't seen him in a couple days. She's crying and trying to take care of a kid and all that. So I figure right then this is going to be a bad business."

He arrived in Burbank without Ralph and DeWitt wouldn't leave him alone. "So the next day I figure I'd better find him, dead or alive. Finally I found him propped up outside a bar.

"That's the way it went all spring. Some days he'd show, some days he didn't. Just about every day he looked like he hadn't slept and he smelled like a brewery. Not a pretty sight."

Blackie was obviously in trouble all spring, sick, messed up, incapable of pitching, but the team just ignored it. "The Browns just didn't take care of him," said Les Moss. "Now, of course, teams would bend over backward to keep a guy like that healthy and happy."

It was Owen Friend's first year in the Browns spring training camp. "I heard all kinds of stories about him," he said. "He had a very bad reputation and he looked it. He had that pallor look.

"If he hadn't done all that stuff he could have been a hell of a pitcher. He wasn't scared of anybody. When he got the ball in his hands he was in charge up there, he was the boss. He wasn't just an average pitcher with a bad reputation, he was a damn good pitcher with a bad reputation."

"The Browns screwed him up," said Joe Schultz. "That happened a lot back then. Nowadays, a guy like that would be worth the mint. He would get the right kind of coaching and they'd ship him off to rehab, get him a personal head doctor or whatever it takes."

Maybe he would have done better with another team. Bill Rigney, who batted against Ralph in spring training of 1948 and whose career spanned eight years as a player and eighteen as a major-league manager, remembered hearing that at one point the New York Giants were hot to make a trade for him. The Giants manager in the late 1940s was the hard-drinking, combative Leo Durocher.

"The funny thing is, a guy like that would have really thrived under Leo," said Rigney. "Leo loved the bums. The bigger the bum, the bigger challenge it was for Leo. He would have loved having him around. Leo was kind of twisted, I think he really wanted to be a gangster and was disappointed he didn't make it."

In 2003 the minimum salary for a major-league baseball player was $300,000. That is a pretty sizable investment in even the guys who mostly just warm the bench. Five thousand dollars a year was a lot more money in 1949 than it is now, but it was still little enough that players like Ralph were expendable, no matter how much ability they had.

Other than a very few stars, baseball players were hardly pampered. It didn't even make the front pages on March 14 when ex-major-leaguer Bill Cissell was found dead of starvation in his tiny apartment. The Browns beating the Cubs in an exhibition game at Wrigley Field got a bigger headline. Cissell had been a good, journeyman player for nine seasons. In 1928 the Chicago White Sox had paid $123,000, which was then a lot of money, plus traded a couple of players to get him.

The Browns didn't even have to start paying Blackie his salary until the regular season started. His teammates worried about him, but mostly they tried to avoid him.

"Usually, on the way to Burbank, I'd have to stop the car a couple times for him to puke," remembered Graham. "A lovely way to spend the morning.

"I was just a glorified baby-sitter. It pissed me off because I was trying to establish myself with the Browns and I sure as hell didn't need for anyone to think I was some sort of pal to this guy.

"He was scary. One morning I picked him up and he's actually where he's supposed to be when he's supposed to be there and I figure this is going to be OK. So we're motoring along and we stop at a traffic light and there's a gas station just opening for business. Ralph says, 'You know, we could knock that place off in about thirty seconds, get back on the road, get to Burbank and nobody would ever catch us.' For Christ's sake, I'm thinking, is this guy kidding? I'm not so sure that he was. He was casing the joint. For this I signed with the Browns?"

Ned Garver remembers going into the locker room in Burbank and standing next to Ralph at a urinal. He looked down and was horrified to see that he was pissing blood. "That scared me to death," he said. "I was just a farm boy from Ohio. I hadn't ever seen anything like that."

Frustrated, sick, drunk most of the time, Blackie got into a lot of fights. The ones with his teammates were broken up pretty quick by other ballplayers. The ones at night in Central Avenue and Gardena bars and nightclubs were more serious. Strong and fast, he won most of his battles, but not without a price. He was beaten up, both inside and out.

Fighting was not unusual among men in the late 1940s. The world was mostly at peace but American men seem to have spent a lot of time warring among themselves. On March 21 the Browns beat the Cleveland Indians in an exhibition game in Burbank. The same day Mickey Cohen and his Seven Dwarves were arrested, again, for the beating of Pearson; and Frank Sinatra, at the height of his popularity as a singer, was arrested for slugging a retired businessman who was tending bar at a party in Palm Springs. Sinatra had asked for a cocktail and wasn't happy for some reason with what he got. "It was just one of those things that can happen at any party," he was quoted as saying by the L.A. *Times*.

In the last week of March Blackie began to come around. He stayed sober for a few days, long enough to look good in practice and to pitch reasonably well in a couple of games. The Browns were scheduled to leave Burbank on the train to Phoenix on March 28 and work their way slowly, playing exhibition games all the way back to St. Louis by April 16, three days before the opening game of the season in Cleveland. Despite everything, Ralph was invited along for the ride.

The city of Burbank was sorry to see them go. During their one month of workouts, the Browns had attracted more than thirty-two thousand people to the town to watch them. Those people spent a lot of money in local businesses. The team had also lost nearly twelve hundred balls during practice sessions and games, a windfall for the local kids. The day before they left the city council unanimously resolved to adopt the Browns as Burbank's official big league team.

On March 30 the Browns beat the Cubs five to four in Alpine, Texas. Alpine is a little town about two hundred twenty miles of good grazing land to the southeast of El Paso. A wealthy rancher and brewery owner, Herbert Kokernot, who was called "Coconuts" by the ballplayers, was a baseball fanatic. He'd built himself a very nice little ballpark in Alpine. He owned his own semipro team that played there during the season. Every spring he'd invite major-league teams to drop by for an exhibition game on their way back east.

The games were popular with the players. They got paid a little extra to play. Coconuts liked watching pitchers and he'd pay them an extra ten bucks for every batter they struck out. "We'd play the Cubs," recalls Garver, "and the guys would arrange to strike out a couple of times and share the money." After the games all the players would pile into buses and head out to Coconuts' ranch where a whole steer would be barbecued in a pit and cold beer would flow like a dry wash after a hard spring storm.

WRONG SIDE OF THE WALL

Blackie enjoyed pitching in Alpine and he performed well. Filled to bursting with barbecue and beer the team left the ranch late at night to get to the train to San Antonio. Everyone had just settled in to sleep when Blackie woke up screaming. "He had a nightmare or something," said Garver. "He was hollering and carrying on. It scared everybody."

Even when things were going well, incidents like that kept his teammates wary of him. "We were on the same team," said Garver, "but that's about as far as it went."

In San Antonio the team split up, minor leaguers went one way, the guys who had made the major-league squad stayed together to play a few more exhibitions on their way to St. Louis.

"So Bill DeWitt calls me in," said Blackie, "and says, 'You made the club.'

"'Great,' I said, 'now where's my thousand dollars?'

"DeWitt says, 'Well, after you get a couple of starts under your belt . . .'

"So I tell him, 'You mean after I get a couple of belts under my start,' and I walk out."

A few days later DeWitt told him that the team would send him to Baltimore, its minor-league team in the International League. Blackie wouldn't accept it and told them he wasn't going to accept anything with the Browns organization. DeWitt threw up his hands and told him to make a deal for himself somewhere else.

CHAPTER 15

S EVERAL TEAMS WERE IN SAN ANTONIO to play exhibitions and settle
their regular season rosters. Gene Mauch, whom Ralph had grown
up with, and Roy Smalley, another friend, were with the Chicago Cubs.
They were in town and over a few beers in the hotel bar he told them
about his problems with DeWitt. They encouraged him to look around
and see if there were any other teams that would have him.

After Mauch and Smalley, who were roommates, retired for the
night, Blackie stayed up drinking with Tex Shirley, an ex-Browns
pitcher who was playing in Little Rock, Arkansas, for the Travelers, a
team affiliated with the Detroit Tigers.

"So, the next morning [Shirley's] knocking on my door and he has
Little Rock's manager, Jack Saltzgaver, with him," recalled Ralph.
"Jack says he needs pitchers, but says, 'you drink, don't you?'"

Saltzgaver, who'd spent five years playing second base for the New
York Yankees, didn't drink, smoke, curse, or play around and didn't approve of players who did. "So I say, 'do you want a winning pitcher, or
do you want a Baptist minister? Tell me one way or the other and get
out of my face.'"

Swallowing his misgivings, Saltzgaver signed Blackie to pitch for his
team. Bill DeWitt, who knew the Little Rock manager's reputation, was
incredulous, but agreed to assign his contract to the team. The Browns,

convinced that with some seasoning he could be a good pitcher, kept an option to take him back.

Blackie's signing was big news in Little Rock. The main headline of the sports section of the Sunday April 3 *Arkansas Democrat* was, "Pebbles Obtain Brownie Hurler Ralph Schwamb." The story's lead said that the acquisition of Schwamb "brightened somewhat a cold and rainy day here yesterday as the Little Rock Travelers lost another exhibition game to the weatherman, the third in a week's time."

That day's *Arkansas Gazette* sports section was headlined, "Rocks Rained Out; Buy Big Right-hander." The story said that Jack Saltzgaver, having signed Ralph, was smiling in the gloom of the hotel lobby in Shreveport, Louisiana, where the team had just had an exhibition game rained out.

Apparently Blackie's reputation had not gotten back to Little Rock's sportswriters. The *Gazette* story finished up with, "Happily, Saltzgaver has no discipline problems. It's a fine, clean-living squad—one of the best at Little Rock in years."

Blackie joined the team in Texarkana the next day, and loosened up pitching batting practice over the next four days. Arriving with the team in Little Rock he was called in to pitch in the fifth inning on Friday, April 9 in an exhibition game against the Indianapolis Indians. His team was losing by a score of nine to nothing and it seemed too much like the bad old days with the Browns. He pitched well though, giving up only two runs in the remaining five innings. The *Gazette*'s reporter was impressed:

> Cheering the slim turnout of fans who stayed around, however, was the loose, lively throwing of Ralph Schwamb. That young St. Louis Browns farmhand, here on option, earned the respect of the Indians quickly and got through five rounds with five hits and two runs charged against him.
>
> The six-foot, four-inch right-hander was pleasantly wild, as they say, in his first chore as a Traveler. He walked three in one inning but that spraying spree cost him only one tally, coming after a fly ball. Before he was through he was breaking off and

controlling his curve nicely. But his pert fast ball still appeared to
be the Los Angeles product's best pitch.

Spring rains had been drowning Arkansas, East Texas, and
Louisiana and that was Blackie's only chance to pitch before the regular
season started. Once the season did start, much to everyone's surprise
the Travelers won their first three games. They were in first place, but
even their manager figured it was a fluke. Saltzgaver told a reporter for
the *Democrat,* "We're not as good as some people think. We're awful."

Finally, on April 19 the team got on the bus for an eleven-game
road trip that would take them to Memphis, New Orleans, and Mobile.
Blackie walked out to the pitcher's mound to start the game that night.

More than eighty-three hundred Memphis fans had turned out in
the cold and damp and Blackie made them regret it. He won the game
in a convincing fashion.

The *Arkansas Democrat* ran his picture on the front page of the
sports section. Orville Henry, the sports editor of the *Gazette,* wrote,
"Schwamb was supposed to have control trouble, but in his first Traveler start he worked surely and confidently with a marvelous fast ball
and an adequate curve . . . [He] is awkward looking but has a graceful
delivery. He threw three wild pitches to lead-off hitter Roy Bueschen,
then settled down to retire the outfielder and take charge from there on.
He passed but one batter and had a six-hitter going into the ninth. He
fanned four and had them missing constantly."

On April 22 the Travelers boarded the bus and rode to New Orleans. Their manager may have called them "awful" but they'd won
their first six games and the mood on the team was high.

They won their first game against the New Orleans Pelicans, bringing their streak to seven wins. The next day, Sunday, before a crowd of
almost ten thousand Ralph won his second game, holding the opposing
team to six hits and one run.

He was feeling good, strong and happy and he was in New Orleans,
a city bursting at the seams with good bars and nightlife. He had money
in his pocket. Friday had been payday. He went out to celebrate.

Blackie hadn't been on the wagon, but he had been staying just sober enough to pitch well. After the games he'd go his own way. So long as he was winning and kept his drinking out of sight, Saltzgaver was willing to put up with him. The manager's risk seemed to be paying off.

"But they made a terrible mistake somewhere along the line and put New Orleans in the league," Ralph said. "We were there four days and I met a broad who owned a bar down on Bourbon Street. She says, 'You don't have to play ball, I'll take care of you.'" The team left for Mobile on Tuesday morning and Blackie almost didn't make it onto the bus.

The Travelers arrived in Mobile with a league-leading record of nine wins and one loss. Even the manager was, cautiously, changing his tune, "Good pitching, more power than expected, and a lot of youthful spirit," Saltzgaver said. "But we're still very much in the experimental stage."

The games in Mobile were all rained out. With three days of unexpected rest, and for Blackie three days of warming himself with booze from the inside out, the team headed home to Little Rock. Hungover and run down, he was scheduled to start the first game of the Sunday doubleheader against the Atlanta Crackers, who were managed by his old semipro catcher Cliff Dapper from Los Angeles.

Travelers Field, the ballpark in Little Rock, had recently been spruced up: painted, new grass planted, and new lights installed. It may have been smaller, but it was a far cry from the older and decrepit Sportsman's Park in St. Louis. And despite a capacity of only slightly more than six thousand, it regularly attracted more fans than came to see the Browns.

The game was scheduled to start at two in the afternoon, but it had rained all the previous night and that morning and it was dark enough that the lights were turned on at about 11 A.M. The game had sold out, however, and the team's owners didn't want to issue rain checks to more than six thousand fans who would then be able to just show up for a game anytime they wanted later in the season. The groundskeepers worked like crazy to get the field in shape.

At one o'clock a thundershower flooded the field, but the fans had already started filling the stands. By game time water was still inches deep in parts of the infield, something that would normally postpone any game. But the Traveler's owners, looking out over all the paying customers and thinking of the money they'd put into the stadium at the beginning of the year, decided that the show must go on.

The grounds crew hastily dug drainage ditches along the side of the field. They then poured gasoline on the bigger remaining puddles and set it on fire to the cheers of the crowd. Warmed by the flames as well as concession-stand beer and in some cases jugs of moonshine, they stayed put in their highly flammable seats huddled close around the blazing ball field. Once the fire died down, sandbags were brought in and emptied over the remaining wet spots.

The game started about an hour late and it was a mess. Fielders fell on their faces chasing balls. Balls hit puddles and came to a dead stop. Runners slogged through mud getting to base. The umpires had to change balls after almost every play. Ralph got into a very bad mood— a mood that didn't improve as the Crackers scored three runs in the first inning.

Cliff Dapper was the first batter in the second inning. He singled past the third baseman who couldn't get through the mud to what should have been an easy ground ball. Frustrated, Blackie blew up. Saltzgaver, suspecting that his pitcher had been drinking and none too happy with his language, took him out of the game. The Travelers went on to lose the game by a score of fifteen to four. The second game of the day ended in a tie after the fourth inning when it got too dark and wretched to continue.

The team lost their next seven games in a row. Their spirits dragged down. On Saturday, May 7 they got on the train to Chattanooga to begin a fourteen-game road trip. Blackie wasn't with them. After being taken out of the game with Atlanta he'd gone into the clubhouse to shower, torn the place up, went straight to the bus station, boarded a bus to New Orleans, and disappeared into the embrace of the bar owner he'd met there.

Saltzgaver suspended him from the team and told the Browns they could have him back. The Browns must have figured they could still get something out of him. If he could just live at least partially up to his potential, they could at least sell his contract to another team for a lot of cash.

Selling players and renting out their stadium to the Cardinals was the only way the team had managed to stay solvent over the years. The Browns had a good system of minor-league teams. They developed a lot of very good young players, brought them up to the major leagues for a year or two of seasoning, then sold them to other teams as soon as it looked as if they might have to pay them much more than the minimum. The team treated its ballplayers like a cash crop. They contacted Ralph and said that they'd take him back.

"But I got stubborn and I said, 'Not without the extra grand.' Maybe I was one of those self-destructive people you read about in psychology books, a person who isn't happy unless he's unhappy, a guy who does his best to do his worst. Don't ask me why. I don't know why. But that buried me [with the Browns]."

He still wanted to play baseball. The games he'd played in Alpine, Texas, for the amusement of the rich rancher had been a lot of fun. Better yet, even though it was only semipro ball, Coconuts was paying more money than minor-league teams. Tom Jordan, Ralph's catcher from Mexico, had retired from organized baseball and was managing the Alpine Cowboys for a thousand dollars a month, being put up in the nicest hotel in the area, eating thick steaks, and washing it all down with free beer. Blackie called him from New Orleans to ask if the team could use a pitcher.

The team did need a pitcher and Jordan told him that he'd think it over and call him back. "He would have been a big winner if we had got him," recalled Jordan, "but if we had him down there with the free drinks and all, it certainly would have also been a very big headache." Jordan turned him down.

The New Orleans love affair didn't last long either. A couple of weeks later he was back in L.A.

Still wanting to play ball, Ralph contacted the L.A. Angels of the Pacific Coast League. From the time he was a kid growing up in the neighborhood of Wrigley Field, he'd always wanted to play for the Angels.

While in those days no one would, or could send him to rehab, and no team pushed him in the direction of the headshrinking that he so obviously needed, he was a great enough prospect that over and over again teams were willing to take a chance on him. The Angels offered to sign him and the Browns agreed to assign his contract to them.

It should have been the answer to his dreams. The Angels would have paid him at least as much as the Browns, probably more in another year. He could practically walk to the ballpark from home. His hometown friends and fans could come to games to watch him pitch. The Angels were a great team and with just the slightest success he almost certainly would have got another shot at the major leagues, most likely with a better team than the Browns.

But he blew it, as usual. When opportunity showed up at the front door, he always found some way to run out the back. The prospect of life at home with a wife and child terrified him. He could barely take care of himself, how could he be expected to take on the responsibility of a family? As for his friends coming out to watch him play ball, that sounded great, sort of. But what if he messed up?

Blackie suffered an almost textbook-perfect case of masochistic (self-defeating) personality disorder. As described in the *Diagnostic and Statistical Manual of Mental Disorders,* it is "a pervasive pattern of self-defeating behavior, beginning by early adulthood and present in a variety of contexts."

Most of the listed behavioral indications of the disorder cloaked him like a well-made suit: "chooses people and situations that lead to disappointment, failure, or mistreatment even when better options are clearly available; rejects or renders ineffective the attempts of others to help him; following positive personal events, responds with depression, guilt, or a behavior that produces pain; incites angry or rejecting responses from others and then feels hurt, defeated, or humiliated; fails to accomplish tasks crucial to his personal objectives despite demonstrated ability to do so; is uninterested in or rejects people who consistently treat him well."

These days he would be treated with a combination of psychotherapy, possibly antidepressant drugs, and rehab for alcoholism. Analysis might lead him to realizations about what in his background caused him to act the way he did. The simplistic Psychology 101 way of looking at Ralph's behavior might go something like this: his father was an often mean drunk, demanding and brutal when in his cups but loving and attentive when sober. To a kid that's confusing, he just wants his father to be in a good mood and treat him well. Sometimes that comes out in the form of, "I need to mess up because my father needs to be better than me so he can feel better about himself."

But there was little or no chance that in the late 1940s he was going to get any of the type of care he really needed. His behavior, though exaggerated, fit comfortably into the social fabric of the time. A "real man" was supposed to drink, be good with his fists, and if he was an athlete or movie star and wasn't a womanizer, well there might be something a little suspicious about him. Babe Ruth himself, the most famous and beloved ballplayer of all time, was well known for booze, broads, and brawls; they were just part of his mystique.

So instead of signing his contract with the Angels, Blackie packed his bag and went to Canada.

Baseball had been played in Canada since the 1800s but the leagues and players to the south mostly ignored it. It was, however, high-quality baseball, due in large part to the fact that it had been integrated since the mid-1930s and featured a number of excellent black and Latin American players.

In 1935 Alfred Wilson became the first black player in the Provincial League in Quebec. He was a convicted murderer, played under an assumed name, and impressed people with what turned out to be a phony college degree. In his first year he also impressed fans by leading the league in batting. That got him work back in the United States, in the Negro Leagues. He eventually wound up back in prison.

Even though the baseball in Canada was good, and often paid as well as in the major leagues, ballplayers jumped at every chance they got to play in the United States. A number of them got that chance during the war. Roland Gladu, the grand old Frenchman of Quebec baseball, played briefly, before being injured, for the Boston Braves in 1944. The next year the Montreal Royals, the top minor-league team of the Brooklyn Dodgers, picked him up. He had a great year and his prospects for 1946 seemed very bright.

But then Branch Rickey, the owner of the Dodgers, made his first move toward integrating the major leagues. He signed Jackie Robinson and sent him to Montreal for a year of seasoning. The Dodgers didn't need Gladu, their regular third baseman was returning from the war, and the Royals needed to move out an infielder to make way for Robinson. Listed at thirty-three, actually thirty-five, Gladu was the oldest member of the team. Age is no advantage in professional sports, so the Dodgers assigned him to one of their lower minor-league teams.

The Mexican League was just starting up and its scouts were trolling for big leaguers to make the jump farther south. Gladu was among the first to go. He was one of the group of players who were banned by the commissioner for five years from playing in U.S. organized baseball.

A couple of months before the end of the 1947 season, the Mexican League's salary checks started bouncing. The ex-big leaguers, no longer welcome in the U.S. major or minor leagues, started hunting for work elsewhere. A lot of them found it in Canada, in the Provincial League. Roland Gladu went home to Quebec and became the player/manager of the Sherbrooke Athlétiques.

With the influx of talent, the Provincial League was suddenly very hot. The *Sporting News* picked up on it and ran an article on the league. Ralph read that article on the very day that the L.A. Angels made him their offer.

He called Tex Shirley, who had hooked him up with Little Rock and was by then playing for Granby in the Canadian Provincial League.

Shirley's team wasn't looking for any more players, but he told Blackie that Sherbrooke was, and that he ought to call Gladu.

The world of baseball is remarkably small. Everybody knows everyone else, or at least has heard of him. Ralph had a terrible reputation, but the Provincial League was full of guys like that—drunk, misfit, flaky, and temperamental. The team's great third baseman, Sylvio García, was notoriously hotheaded. A couple of years after Blackie played with him he was accused of shooting and killing his wife's lover. In 1983 he was elected to the Cuban Baseball Hall of Fame.

But Gladu needed players, no matter what their reputation. Because of an impending court decision, the boom times for the Provincial League were about to come to an end.

Danny Gardella, one of the players who had been banned from baseball for having jumped to the Mexican League, had filed a lawsuit against organized baseball to challenge the reserve clause. The reserve clause was contained in the fine print of a standard baseball player's contract. It bound a player to the team that signed him for the duration of his career. A player could either stay with his team until the team decided to trade or sell him to another team, or he could quit baseball. There was no alternative.

Organized baseball was horrified at the prospect of losing the reserve clause. So the commissioner's office settled the suit by reinstating the players who had gone to Mexico. (The reserve clause wasn't successfully challenged until 1976.)

As soon as the ban was lifted, the Sherbrooke team lost four of its best players. Ralph's phone call had the advantage of very good timing. Gladu offered him a thousand dollars a month plus all his expenses. They wanted him quickly and wired him the money for a plane ticket. He called the Angels, said thanks but no thanks, and left the next day.

Sherbrooke is about a half-hour drive north of the Vermont border and about an hour and a half east of Montreal. It's a pleasant little town surrounded by low rolling hills in the thick of the world's largest asbestos mining region. Driving out of the city to the north, in the direction of the towns of Asbestos and Thetford Mines, the countryside is dotted with large, multihued piles of mine tailings that have been accumulating since the discovery of the mineral in the area in 1876.

The mines were on strike when Ralph arrived. Miners had been off the job for much of the year, fighting over safety issues and medical benefits for asbestosis victims. Local mining interests, or businessmen who depended on the mines, owned the six teams in the Provincial League. The owners saw spending a little extra cash to hire outside talent as an investment in distracting workers from their job issues. It was the age-old "bread and circuses" ploy to pacify the masses.

Local sporting rivalries were intense. The teams played within about an hour's drive of each other and would travel to their games either in small buses or just a few chartered large cars, often tailed by a honking cavalcade of rowdy fans. The ballparks were small, with capacities of no more than thirty-five hundred to four thousand, but usually filled to bursting and plenty noisy.

Ralph arrived on the evening of July 8, much to the relief of manager Gladu. The Athlétiques were down to just two regular starting pitchers. He started his first game on the twelfth against the St. Johns Braves and turned in a creditable job over seven innings.

Blackie enjoyed the games and got along well with his teammates, but once again the distractions of the road got the better of him. Rarely in any state other than drunk or hungover, he didn't pitch very well. He appeared in twelve games, winning four and losing four. Over forty-three and two-thirds innings he gave up twenty-eight runs on thirty-six hits and thirty-two walks, while striking out twenty-two batters. They were not good statistics.

Meanwhile Nell wanted him home. She didn't like baseball, would rather that he was doing something else, but she could have lived with him playing for the Angels. She was getting very fed up with having an absentee husband.

Around the beginning of August Nell got sick and asked him to come home, at least for a little while. On August 2 he pitched his best game in

Canada, a five-hit, one-run winning effort against the St. Hyacinthe Saints. He played third base in the game on August 4. The next day he took his leave, telling Gladu that he'd be back in no more than a week.

The week stretched into the next couple of weeks. He kept in touch, calling his manager every few days to say that he would be back soon. Gladu scheduled him to pitch on the night of August 20. He didn't show up. He also stopped calling.

"She wasn't all that sick, she just hated baseball," Ralph said. "I had three or four hundred dollars burning a hole in my pocket. I began to drink in a bar on Vermont Avenue in Los Angeles and never flew back. In the first week of September my money began to run out."

CHAPTER 16

BLACKIE STOLE A 9 MM LUGER FROM A GUY at a poker game in early September. He tried to sell it to his old pal Ted Gardner and some friends of his he met in a bar on the evening of September 7. He figured it was worth at least twenty bucks. Nobody wanted it; there were a lot of German guns in circulation after the war. He stuck around to have some drinks.

The bar closed at midnight. A guy named Jerry knew someone who was having a party nearby, so Blackie, Gardner, and three other guys piled into a car and went.

It wasn't much of a party, just a record player, a few bottles of booze, and no single women. Ralph was bored. He was talking with Leonard Smith, Gardner's brother-in-law, and suggested that they rob someplace, anyplace. Smith, who was beginning to feel a little sick from too much to drink, didn't think it was such a hot idea.

Something had just snapped inside of Blackie after he got back from Canada. He'd given up all hope of going back to baseball. His pitching had been lousy, Nell was nagging him to give it up, and the pay wasn't any good anyway. It was all getting to be just too much. He felt fine when he was drunk, sick when he wasn't, and he was always out of money.

He couldn't see the point of trying to live any sort of straight life. It never worked out the way he wanted it to anyhow. He loved playing baseball, but everything in his life just plain seemed to work out better when he was a gangster. Besides, in his crowd there was almost as much glory in crime as in baseball, probably more than in playing for peanuts with a losing team, something that a lot of people told him was for suckers.

The last week of August he'd got together with Gardner and some other friends of his from the neighborhood. "We took off a couple of pretty good scores, a couple of poker games," he said. "We ripped them off. But that kind of money goes faster than you make it. You don't ever want to get arrested with a bankroll. If they're goin' to catch you, let them catch you broke." By September 7 Blackie was out of money again.

After about an hour at the party Smith, a guy named Richard Farley, and Ralph left in Farley's car. Smith was in the backseat, nauseated, trying to not throw up. The car pulled to a stop in front of the Signal Motel next to a gas station on the corner of Figueroa and the Imperial Highway. It was no more than a dozen tiny run-down wood-shack rooms strung along a driveway with a small two-room office just three or four feet back from the curb. It didn't look prosperous enough to bother robbing, but Blackie rousted Smith out of the back and brought him along into the office.

Edwin Cohen was the desk clerk that night. Blackie pulled out his Luger, pointed it at him and told him to empty out the cash drawer and hand over his watch while he was at it. Smith pocketed the nine dollars from the cash drawer.

There was a small bedroom behind the office and Blackie marched Cohen into it, telling him to lie face down on the bed. He told Smith to watch the clerk and not let him get up. Smith put his foot at the nape of Cohen's neck to keep him in place while Blackie searched the room. He found thirty dollars and a woman's ring in the bedside drawer. One of the two robbers kicked Cohen in the head just before they got out of there and drove off.

Planning was not any of those guys' strong suit. The car ran out of gas a few miles away. Farley decided to stick by it. Blackie and the queasier-than-ever Smith took a streetcar back to the party. When Smith eventually got home, very late and very drunk, his angry wife was waiting up for him. He gave her the nine dollars and told her that he'd been setting pins in a bowling alley all night. She didn't believe him.

The next day Ralph sold the watch and ring to Earl Bogardus, a neighbor. The police traced Blackie through the ring and arrested him on September 15. They searched his apartment and found the gun. They picked up Smith and Farley the next morning.

The three of them were charged with three armed robberies: the Signal Motel, the El Capitan Hotel a few days before that, and a liquor store on Central Avenue. The take from the El Capitan had been just a few dollars. At the liquor store they were all so drunk that they never managed to get the cash register open and ran out empty-handed.

The district attorney wanted Ralph held on $5,000 bail but the municipal court judge set it at $2,500. That was more money than Nell or the family could scrape together. So Blackie stewed in jail for a week.

Nell thought that sitting in jail might be the best thing for him; at least it would sober him up. But he insisted that she get him out. So she pawned some belongings, and some of Blackie's old neighborhood baseball buddies chipped in, and they raised the $250 for a bail bondsman. "She begged me not to make bail, but I did."

He should have stayed put. Out of jail, out of work, Blackie began to spin totally out of control. "I was getting so paranoid by then, I'd do anything for a dollar," he said. "I wasn't looking for work."

At least not honest work. He got another gun and went on a crime spree. He held up motels, gas stations, liquor stores, and private card games. He took on all the jobs he could get from Mickey Cohen and the Sica brothers. He didn't have a car and he didn't go far from home. Most of his crimes were committed around his own neighborhood.

There was plenty going on in the neighborhood. As the police continued their crackdown on after-hours and mixed-race joints along Central Avenue, more clubs moved west to Vermont Avenue just a block away from Blackie's apartment, to Western Avenue and south to Gardena.

In Gardena the Bal Tabarin and the Colony Club, under new owner-ship, were open until 2 A.M. and jam-packed nightly with burlesque-loving crowds. The Normandie Card Club, across the street from the Colony, was open around the clock as were a number of others nearby. Restaurants and bowling alleys never closed. Hollywood Park Race-track, more popular than ever, featured year-round race meets. Harness races were being run in the fall. Money was all over the place and the pickings were excellent for guys who didn't care what they did to get it. Almost every day the papers had at least one, and often several stories of people being held up on their way out of late-night Gardena businesses.

When he wasn't bumbling into hotels and liquor stores with Farley and Smith, Blackie's usual partner in crime was Ted Gardner, whom everyone called Bud. They'd grown up in the same neighborhood and known each other since they were kids. Gardner was four years older, but from about the sixth grade on Ralph had hung out with an older group of guys.

Gardner had spent four years in the marines during the war. He lived with his wife, Joyce, and their two kids in a small GI Bill house in Compton, about a fifteen-minute drive from Ralph's place. Joyce was twenty-four, a redhead with knockout good looks that four years of motherhood hadn't dampened. She was a salesgirl in a dime store by day and she and Ted went out on the town a lot at night. Ted listed his occupation as "carpenter" but he almost never seemed to get any work. Mostly he got by on gambling and petty crimes. He'd been arrested for burglary in February but the charges were dropped when the people whose house he'd been caught red-handed in failed to prosecute.

Ted played a lot of cards. Private games were better than the poker parlors; he could get a clearer picture of who the marks were and there weren't as many rules. If trouble broke out he usually had some friends on hand, he didn't have to worry about whose side somebody else's hired muscle might decide to come down on. Blackie backed him up sometimes. Sometimes he'd back Blackie up on a collection.

When Ted and Joyce went to one of the card clubs, it was usually the Normandie on Western. It was new, big, had cheap drinks, and often buzzed with what passed for high rollers in Gardena. The city's real high rollers had their own private clubs up in Hollywood, along the Strip and out toward the beaches. But Ted was small time and the size of the play in Gardena suited him just fine.

They also spent time across the street and down about a half block at the Colony. There was no cover, no admission, and three burlesque shows a night. The showgirls were good looking, but none so much as Joyce. Ted liked showing her off on the dance floor, watching the other guys try not to get caught staring at her. At the Colony he wore Joyce like he wore his flashy clothes and the big onyx ring that he liked to wave around.

Ralph never cared much for the display. He also had his suspicions about Joyce. He thought she spent too much time looking back at the men who looked at her, and she also seemed to like looking at the showgirls a little too much herself.

October was hot, clear, and dry. There were light, warm breezes across the basin but no Santa Ana winds yet. Not long after dark there was a mild, refreshing chill in the air. It was the kind of weather that brought the crowds out to Los Angeles. It put Blackie in a good mood. His arraignment on the robberies was set for Thursday October 13, but it was looking like two of the three charges were going to be dropped and he was optimistic.

There wasn't much to catch Blackie's attention in the papers on Wednesday morning October 12, Columbus Day. In the sports section, which he always turned to first, it was between seasons. The Yankees had polished off the Dodgers in the fifth game of the World Series three days before and football hadn't started yet. Jean Spangler, some TV actress he'd never seen, who the hell had a TV anyhow, was missing and the press was screaming about a "lust-maddened sex killer."

Some people were beginning to get TVs at home, but they were expensive and there wasn't all that much to watch on them. Gold's on Central Avenue at Washington was advertising "Giant Size 16 Inch Screen Admiral TVs" for $400, as if that was some sort of bargain. You could buy a twelve-and-a-half-inch RCA Victor for $314 and Le Roy's would sell you a slightly smaller Hallicrafter for $260 including installation. Blackie had seen them in shop windows and a few bars. He'd watched some of the World Series games on the TV at Jimmy's, a bar around the corner from his apartment, but the picture was small, fuzzy, and a lot of the time you'd get a better idea of what was going on listening to the radio.

The radio and the papers were full of scandal. The jury in the burglary case of suspended vice sergeant Charles Stoker, a whistle-blowing cop whom he'd heard some of his gangster pals complaining about, couldn't make up its mind. According to the paper some of the jurors figured the charges were a police frame-up. You'd have had to be an idiot not to have known that. The vice scandal revolving around Hollywood madam Brenda Allen, Mickey Cohen, and the police department, which had been fueled by Stoker's ratting out the police chief, was getting stranger almost every day. The papers tried to make sense of it, but it was just too hard to follow.

A couple of Mickey Cohen's guys, whom Blackie had met in passing, were missing. Cohen figured it for foul play. He was also having to liquidate the inventory at his haberdashery. In type bigger than the front-page headlines, ads read "Mickey Cohen Shoots the Works!" There were some deals to be had, suits for under a hundred bucks, name-brand coats and shirts for less than half price.

White Heat, Jimmy Cagney's first gangster movie since the thirties, was still playing nearby at the 5th Avenue Theater on Manchester. The new Randolph Scott picture, *Fighting Man of the Plains,* was opening the next day. Blackie always liked Westerns. He also liked Cagney, although he thought he was sort of ridiculous.

The L.A. *Herald Express* had a strange story headlined "Jap Humor Baffles, Americans Fail to Understand Nips." It was about how Americans in the occupation forces just didn't get what the Japanese found funny. "The difference between American and Japanese humor often puts occupation personnel in embarrassing positions," read the article.

"Sometimes it can make a person right uncomfortable." According to the story, the Japanese laugh, heartily, at even the most gruesome experiences they had during the war.

Blackie found stories like that funny. He didn't know if he believed them, but he enjoyed reading about the odd quirks of other people. He wondered about the Japanese. After the war they started moving back to L.A. and a lot of them were showing up in Gardena. A lot of them had been farmers before the war but their farms were plowed under for housing developments by the time they came back.

Power lines crisscrossed the city in long, narrow empty stretches from the generating plants down by the harbor to downtown and the factories just east of the Los Angeles River. No one, at least no one in his right mind, wanted anything to do with the miles of wasteland underneath them. Japanese farm families started leasing, and then buying the long, thin strips of soil beneath the humming electrical wires. They planted nurseries, creating garden belts that eventually stretched from the harbor to the foothills of the San Gabriel Mountains.

The south part of Los Angeles was changing rapidly. Oil was plentiful and the wooden derricks and grasshopper pumps that had drained the moderate rolling landscape of Gardena, Compton, Inglewood, and south-central L.A. were no longer as valuable as the land they drilled into. Wells were capped and oil fields were subdivided, waiting only for cheap loans to come through so that construction could start.

The building trades were working at their peak. Hollywood Park Racetrack's grandstands and clubhouse had burned down—"a quarter mile of conflagration"—two weeks before the summer race meet was scheduled to start. Just four months later, post time for the Columbus Day harness races at the rapidly rebuilt track was one o'clock. Bigger than usual crowds were expected for the midweek meet. Twelve years earlier President Roosevelt had declared October 12 a national holiday. There were nine races scheduled for the day and with the dry hot weather it was going to be a fast track.

Like a lot of doctors, Donald Buge regularly took Wednesdays off. He'd close his small general practice in Long Beach, next door to his mother's house, and he and his wife, Violet, would often as not go to the races, or a card club. They weren't big gamblers but they enjoyed it. Dr. Buge was forty-four, a friendly, cheerful, round-faced fellow who was reasonably fit and healthy. He had a prosperous practice and liked to show off his money. Waitresses and bartenders liked and remembered him, as he was a big tipper. Violet, a small forty-year-old matronly looking blonde, was his second wife. They'd been married eleven years and had no children, although Violet had a nineteen-year-old daughter from her previous marriage. They lived with their wire-haired white dog Wensie in a small, neat house just a short walk from the doctor's office.

The doctor had graduated from Northwestern University Medical School in 1929 and gone into general practice. For a few years before settling in Long Beach he'd worked for the U.S. Public Health Service in Panama. In 1943 he joined the Navy Medical Corps, entering the service as a lieutenant commander. For a while during the war he'd served at Great Lakes Naval Training Station, where Ralph was incarcerated. He practiced psychiatry in the navy but went back to general practice when he returned to civilian life in April 1947.

After the fire at Hollywood Park, the summer thoroughbred meet had been relocated to Santa Anita. That was a lot farther for Donald and Violet to drive, so they hadn't been to the races much that year. They were looking forward to the harness meet on Columbus Day.

CHAPTER 17

COLUMBUS DAY 1949 WAS A MIXED BAG for the bettors and the book-ies at Hollywood Park. Three of the favorites came in at low odds and the bookies liked that. A lot of people at the track bet on the favorites, but when they bet with a bookie they tend to look for longer shots. The best long shot of the day was in the third race when G. B., which George Main in the *Herald* had picked for dead last, came in first at $41.90 to one.

Dr. Buge and Violet had a good day at the races. They came out forty bucks and change ahead. Driving down Western on their way home to Long Beach they passed the Normandie Card Club. Violet felt like playing some poker with their winnings. That was fine with Donald. He didn't feel like playing cards, but he liked the atmosphere and was content with that and a few cocktails.

The Normandie was the only one of Gardena's card parlors that came close to living up to its billing as a poker "palace." It had plush carpet that was cleaned with some degree of frequency, crystal and brass lighting fixtures, dealers in tuxedos, waitresses in dresses that showed off some of their assets but within the bounds of good taste, and good, reasonably priced food in its restaurant. The drinks weren't watered down and the noise level wasn't too high. It had good ventilation so it didn't smell of stale tobacco smoke. It attracted as refined a crowd as could be found in the neighborhood.

Donald and Violet got there a little after seven in the evening. It was beginning to fill up with players who had also spent their day at the races. Violet found a seat at a poker table, Donald a stool at the bar.

Around eight she was a few dollars up. Donald came by the table to say that he was going across the street, to the Colony Club, to cash a check. He kissed her on the cheek, said, "Good luck," and walked out.

At the same time, Ralph was sticking close to home. He had to be in court the next morning for his arraignment so he figured that he'd better have a quiet night. After dinner he told Nell that he was going to go around the corner for a few drinks at Jimmy's.

Blackie was a regular at the small, always dark lounge on 81st and Vermont, just a block and a half from the apartment; (Jimmy) Oliveri's Club was more often than not the starting point for his nights out. A wood bar with maybe a dozen stools, a couple of booths with tables, a TV, a jukebox, and a pool table, Jimmy's was identical to hundreds, maybe thousands of other places around the city.

All the regulars had already heard his baseball stories, and some of his crime stories too, but with a few drinks under their belts they were happy to hear them again. Ralph, garrulous and insecure, was happy to tell them again. Sometimes there'd be a new customer who would hang on every word and buy the drinks. Sometimes Blackie would buy the drinks. He liked spending money when he had it.

Ted and Joyce Gardner had left their kids with her parents, planning to drive into downtown for a movie. On the way they stopped at the Colony Club for a drink. They hadn't been there long when Dr. Buge came in and walked up to the bar.

It isn't clear how or why the doctor hooked up with the younger couple. Men often started talking to Joyce and maybe that was it. Ted was always looking for an easy score and the prosperous-looking Dr. Buge had been drinking. It's also possible that the meeting was arranged. Ted had been helping Blackie with his collections. The doctor did gamble and like most gamblers at the time almost certainly placed bets with bookies.

"[He was] such a pleasant man, laughing and buying drinks," Joyce said. "He seemed so happy."

After a couple of drinks Ted asked the doctor to come along with them to meet a friend. Either it seemed like a good idea, or he was coerced, but Dr. Buge said okay. He went across the street to tell Violet that he'd be back soon. "I just met a nice young married couple and I'm going to have a drink with them," Violet recalled Donald saying. She was up seven or eight dollars by then and didn't want to leave her game.

Ted and Joyce got their car and were waiting in front of the Normandie. Dr. Buge got into the front seat with them. It was only about a ten-minute drive to Jimmy's, where they went to meet Ralph.

The four of them ordered drinks and while Dr. Buge talked with Joyce, either Ted took Blackie aside to tell him that the doctor had money, or Blackie asked Ted if he thought he did. They decided that he was flush and a mark, either for a stickup or to cough up for a debt he owed a bookie. It isn't clear which. Either way they figured they were going to part Dr. Buge from his cash.

They had another drink there and watched a little TV, then Blackie and Ted suggested they go somewhere else. Or maybe Dr. Buge asked for a ride back to the Normandie Club. That's also not clear. Blackie got into the backseat of Ted's car and lay down; he'd drunk a lot, fast, and his head was swirling. Joyce sat in the middle up front, between Ted and Dr. Buge.

What is clear is that Ted stopped the car under a large oak tree at the corner of a vacant lot at 124th Street and Menlo Avenue. A year or two before, the gently rolling slopes of the area had been an oilfield. But the wells had been capped. The city had laid new asphalt streets and built up four-inch curbs. Down on the next block of Menlo a couple of houses had been built and the land all around was subdivided for more. Developers were optimistically calling the area "Athens on the Hill." There were no streetlights yet. The only light was from the car's headlights and a dim porch bulb down the block.

Blackie had popped his head up from the backseat and told Ted to pull over. He told Dr. Buge to get out of the car. The doctor refused, so Blackie got out, yanked open the front passenger door, and dragged him out.

Ralph, Ted, and Joyce all told pretty much the same story up to that point. Then according to press reports, and later the trial transcripts, they started watching out for themselves.

"[Ted's] wife got all the trouble started," Ralph said. "This doctor was foolin' around with her in the front seat. I was laying down in the back seat, drunk. And [Ted's] tellin' him, 'Hey man, knock that shit off.' So I tell him, 'stop the car.' I tell [the doctor], 'get out' and I pulled him out and shoved him up against a tree and I knocked him down.

"[Joyce] ran down the street screaming and I ran after her. When I came back, I got her in the car. The doctor was layin' face up and I remember clearly that when I hit him he fell down spread-eagled flat on his face. I remember that clearly. But when I came back [with Joyce] he was laying face up, all spread out with his pockets inside out and his coat pulled open. Ted rolled him and had done a number [on him], either kicking him or punching him, his face was a mess. I didn't think anything about it except to get out of there."

Joyce had a different story. "We were having fun. I thought we were going to another bar. Ted drove to [124th Street and Menlo Avenue]. We stopped and Blackie told Dr. Buge to 'get out of there.'

"The doctor didn't move. Blackie reached in and dragged him out. Then he started beating him with his fists.

"I screamed. Ted got out and I screamed at him not to do anything but he hit the doctor several times. I jumped out and ran down the road screaming. I don't know how far I ran before Ted caught me. I didn't see them take any money."

Ted's story was pretty much the same as Joyce's. He explained his part in the assault, saying, "Blackie and the doctor started fighting and I cracked the doctor a couple of times to help. The doctor went down and Blackie put the boots to him."

There is a slim, but gruesome possibility that Blackie recognized Dr. Buge from his time in the brig at Great Lakes Naval Station. The two men had been there at the same time, although it was a very large and active place and the naval prison was kept well separate from the other facilities.

Blackie had always hated being analyzed and picked apart. He didn't react well to psychiatrists and there is a slight chance that the doctor had been in a position to evaluate his mental condition in naval prison. His navy records don't say and he claimed that he had never seen Dr. Buge before that night.

It would have taken a remarkable coincidence, but if Blackie did recognize the doctor, drunk and angry the way he often was when he was drinking, did he take it all out on a man he saw as one of his tormentors? The doctor did take a savage beating, the sort of thrashing that would lead at least one investigator to suspect that it might have come from someone with an especially sore point to make.

Whoever it was though who ran after Joyce and whoever it was who stayed behind, the fact is that someone rolled the beaten and unconscious Dr. Buge over and went through his pockets, tossing out a key chain and sixty-five cents in change. They took his wallet and split up the contents, fifty-three dollars, in the car. Ted got twenty-five dollars and the wallet that they figured was worth at least three bucks.

According to Ted, Blackie then said, "Let's get out of here." Ted said that they'd better turn their lights off because the doctor might be able to get their license plate number. Blackie responded, saying, "I don't think he will. I gave him some good ones."

They drove off, taking Blackie back to Jimmy's. On the way, Joyce said that she pleaded with Ted to go to the police but that Blackie warned them both not to do anything like that. After they dropped him off Ralph had a couple of beers before he walked home and went to sleep. The Gardners went home to their kids. They thought the doctor was alive, just badly beat up.

Dr. Donald Buge might have been alive when they left the scene, but he wasn't for long. His nose and upper jaw were shattered. His face was almost unrecognizable from the beating. His eyes were completely swollen shut and several teeth had been knocked out. Unconscious, the blood from the cuts on his face poured into his mouth and down his throat. He drowned.

Violet played poker until ten, then took up her winnings of about eight dollars and went into the lobby to wait for Donald. At one point she went across the street to the Colony Club to look for him. She had him paged, but when he didn't answer she went back to the Normandie to continue waiting. She stayed put until 2 A.M. then used her spare set of keys to drive home.

While Violet waited, Carl Reinhard, an oil worker, was driving home. He lived in the house with the dim porch light on Menlo Avenue. He drove down 124th from Vermont and just as he was about to turn right onto his street, the car's headlights picked out a body lying under the big oak on the corner. He stopped his car and got out to see if the guy needed help. As soon as he got near enough to see clearly it was obvious that whoever it was, was beyond anything he could do for him. He went home and called the cops.

Detective sergeants E. O. Kruger and G. H. Burrough of the 77th Street Police Station caught the call and drove out to the scene. Detective lieutenant Paul Phelps was put in charge of the investigation. The press heard about it on their police scanners and showed up soon after.

The police surveyed the scene, patrolmen trying to hold back the reporters, at least until everything could be noted and photographed. At first they thought that the victim had been murdered somewhere else, then the body dumped where it had been found. They didn't think there was enough blood on the scene to account for the beating. They didn't know until the autopsy about the blood that had filled the lungs and throat. They found a thin strip of blue metal from a car, another flat piece of metal, the broken-off top of a wine bottle with the cap still sealed in place, a matchbook, and the doctor's change and keys. They bagged all that, it could be evidence. The detectives made impressions of footprints and carefully photographed tire tracks.

On Dr. Buge's body they found a fountain pen, a watch, receipts for paid medical bills, and a letter from the Norwalk state hospital to his mother, Myra, asking about her ability to pay for his brother Irving's medical care. It wasn't hard to identify the victim.

A detective was sent to break the news to Violet and bring her to the police station. He arrived at the house in Long Beach just after she got home. Violet called her daughter, Betty, who came over and went with her to the 77th Street station house. Betty's husband, John Grissom, met them there. Later, at the morgue, he made the formal identification of the body.

Dr. Frederick D. Newbarr conducted the autopsy as soon as he could after the body had been brought in. He made note of a heel print on the forehead and concluded from cuts and bruises on the face that someone wearing a heavy ring had battered Dr. Buge. The beating was so severe that the victim would have bled to death if he hadn't drowned first.

Ted and Joyce woke up on the morning of the 13th to the news that the doctor was dead. The body had been found in time for it to make the morning papers. "Long Beach Doctor Is Slain In Mystery, Victim Of Savage Assailant," was the front-page headline of the *Herald Express.* "Long Beach Physician Savagely Beaten, Murdered and Robbed," stretched across the top of page two of the *Daily News,* along with large photos of the body and of Violet with her daughter, Betty.

The story would have gotten even bigger play if it hadn't have been for Shirley Temple's marriage to then retired Army Sergeant John Agar hitting the skids, and a holdup attempt in Hollywood that had turned into a gunfight.

"We were scared to death," said Joyce. "I asked Ted again to go to the police, but he was afraid." Joyce had to go to work. Ted gave her the blood-flecked gray pants and sport shirt he'd been wearing the night before and told her to take them to a cleaner near the dime store, which was about eight miles from their house. He also gave her the wallet and told her to throw it away.

Ralph got up early with his usual hangover. He wasn't happy about his arraignment that day, but he figured that he'd better be on time. Whether he'd read the papers or not, people who saw him in court described him as "cool and collected." He was, in any event, pleased with the result; the three robbery charges had been reduced to one, the Signal Motel.

Violet had given her statement the night before. In the morning detectives took her back to the Normandie so she could point out all the details.

On the evening of October 13th detective lieutenants Jack McCready and Rudy DeLeon went back to the Normandie and the Colony Club to poke around. They found a few people who remembered seeing a guy who fit the description of Dr. Buge leave the Colony with a man and woman. The woman was a short, attractive redhead who some of the witnesses thought might be named "Joyce." The man, who everyone seemed to know as "Bud," was a flashy dresser who most interestingly to the detectives wore a huge onyx ring. Irving Rosenfeld, the manager of the Colony, knew Bud and Joyce. They had introduced him to a doctor they'd been with the night before. He didn't know where they lived, but he thought it might be in nearby Compton.

The detectives started hitting the bars in Compton. At the Epicure Café on the corner of Wilmington and Olive streets they found a bartender who recognized the description of Bud and Joyce. He told them that the couple had been in the bar Wednesday night at about 10:30 and that the woman had been crying. He didn't know where they lived, but he thought it was probably in the veteran's housing project nearby. It was too late to start knocking on doors in a residential neighborhood so McCready and DeLeon called it quits for the night.

Friday morning, the fourteenth, Ted and Joyce woke up to the news that they were being sought. "Police Hunt Pair In Doctor Slaying," was a headline in the *Times*. "Couple Hunted In Medic Death," was on the front page of part two of the *Examiner*. Both articles identified the couple as Bud and Joyce. Not knowing what else to do, Joyce went to work as usual. Ted stayed home.

It wasn't too long before detectives McCready and DeLeon showed up at the door. A postman who recognized their description had pointed out Ted and Joyce's house. Ted answered the door and they asked him what he knew about the murder of Dr. Buge. He denied knowing anything. They noticed that his knuckles were scraped. His hands looked like they'd been in a fight. The detectives told him to stick around and then drove off to find Joyce at the dime store.

Joyce hadn't got around to taking Ted's clothes to the cleaners. The detectives found them in a bag by her purse in the back room of the dime store. They found Dr. Buge's wallet in the dumpster out back. She probably told them where it was after they found the pants and shirt. They took her into custody. At the 77th Street station she told her story, at least enough of it that they went back to the house and arrested Ted.

Confronted with the evidence, Ted broke down and gave a tearful confession to Lieutenant Phelps. Joyce corroborated his story. They implicated Ralph and told the police where he lived.

Lieutenant Karl Lee found Blackie in downtown at the office of his bail bondsmen. Following the arraignment he had to show up there to sign some papers. Lee slapped cuffs on him and took him in.

Ralph said, "That was the last time I saw the streets until 1960."

CHAPTER 18

BLACKIE MAINTAINED HIS INNOCENCE FOR SEVERAL HOURS, figuring he knew better than to just start talking when the police started asking questions. It is possible that the police tried to beat a confession out of him. It was a brutal time, a horrible crime, and that was a common practice. No court had yet stepped forward to restrict it. In press photos taken just after he was booked, he does look a little worse for wear.

He'd had enough run-ins with the police though, and was physically tough enough, that he didn't tell them anything until they showed him Ted and Joyce's statements. He knew when he was cornered and confessed. But he said it was Ted's fault, not his.

The police transferred him to the L.A. County Jail and booked him on suspicion of murder. They kept Ted locked up at the 77th Street station.

In their cells, they kept trying to pin the blame on each other. "We were both pretty drunk and we got the idea of robbing him," Ralph told reporters.

"The doctor, who I thought was an insurance man, didn't resist and Ted slugged him with his fists first and the doctor fell to the ground." He denied ever hitting Dr. Buge.

Ted claimed that he only punched the guy a couple of times and that Blackie did most of the dirty work. "I never meant to kill the guy," he said. "I never even meant to rob him.

"I was drunk and out of work and when Blackie suggested we clip him for his purse, it sounded like a pretty good idea."

Meanwhile, the police had released Joyce and given her a ride home. She was met by reporters on her front steps. She made a point of telling them that she didn't know whether or not Ralph had threatened Ted into not going to the police when they found out Dr. Buge was dead. No one had asked her about it. "Ted's not a bad husband," she told them, "but he drinks."

Over the weekend, while Blackie and Ted sat in jail, there were several more robberies of Gardena card club patrons. A seventy-five-year-old businessman was among the victims. He was badly beaten by crooks who had followed him home from a poker club. In Texas and New Mexico a manhunt was under way for another baseball player who was wanted for murder. Leonard "Lucky" Hawkins had never made the big leagues, but he had outrun the police in a wild car chase after killing a man he worked with in a café.

At Manchester Playground where Blackie had played baseball as a kid and then semipro ball as a hot pitching prospect for the major leagues, his ex-teammates and neighborhood buddies passed the hat. They all liked Nell, felt badly for her, and knew that she would need money.

On Monday morning the seventeenth, Ralph and Ted were brought to court for the coroner's inquest. They were given bedroom slippers to wear for the appearance; their shoes were being analyzed for evidence in a police lab. Violet Buge, waiting to testify, sat just behind Joyce, who was also waiting her turn on the stand.

Just before she was called to the witness box Violet leaned over to Joyce and whispered to her, "I want you to know that if Dr. Buge could be here he would tell you that he has nothing but forgiveness in his heart, and would ask for mercy for his slayers. He was the type of man who was always forgiving everyone."

Then, sobbing, Violet told the story of her last day and evening with Donald.

Joyce, also crying, then took up the story from where the doctor left Violet at the Normandie Club. Blackie and Ted sat impassively at their table. Following their lawyers' advice, they refused to testify.

The coroner's jury quickly decided that a murder had been committed and that Ralph and Ted should be charged with it. The next day the district attorney's office formally charged each of them with one count of first-degree murder and one count of robbery. They were held without bail. Arraignment on the charges was set for November 10.

On Thursday, October 20, Dr. M. J. Rowe, a Long Beach psychiatrist, was asked by the court to examine Ralph. The request was actually in regard to the robbery charge from September, but also went into the file on the murder case. Dr. Rowe met with him in the county jail on the morning of October 24 and turned in his report later that day. The examination was hurried and the report, based almost entirely on what Blackie said about himself, was full of errors. It does, however, contain some interesting details[7]:

> FAMILY HISTORY: Father and two maternal uncles drink alcoholics to excess. Other family history negative.
>
> PERSONAL HISTORY: Infancy and childhood were uneventful.
>
> SCHOOLING: He attended school from five to sixteen years, was an average scholar, took part in all school athletics and excelled in baseball, quit after completing the tenth grade, giving as a reason to enlist in the Navy, but other statements showed a lapse of one year before enlisting.
>
> OCCUPATIONS: For one year had several odd jobs of unskilled labor, quit without cause in each case after a few week's employment. Enlisted in Navy, was Seaman, Second Class. Had six courts martial, one for destruction of government property, others for A.W.O.L., of various length. Was given a bad conduct discharge. Has since played professional football for the St. Louis Browns and various minor league teams, receiving from six hundred to one thousand dollars per month of which he saved practically nothing.

---

[7] All quotations from the psychiatrist's report are verbatim, without correction.

ILLNESS AND TRAUMA: Had mumps and measles without sequels in childhood. Had a gonococcus [gonorrhea] infection in 1949 with complete recovery. No trauma.

ALCOHOL AND DRUGS: Began drinking at sixteen. Likes beer but drinks whiskey with beer for chaser for the effect. Drinks either alone or in company. States five ordinary drinks of whiskey will usually intoxicate him. Claims he is always cheerful and the life of the party when drinking but when drinking too much becomes quarrelsome and sleepy. Has no savings because of drinking. Drugs denied.

SEXUAL HISTORY: Has been sexually promiscuous since the age of thirteen or fourteen.

MARITAL HISTORY: Married, has one son, age three years. Marital life has been satisfactory except for the defendant's drinking habits as he neglected his family, spent all of his money, and at one time a divorce was considered. He has continued his promiscuity since marriage.

CRIMES AND ARRESTS: First arrest was when he, with companions, broke into a winter resort. The charges were dropped after he made restitution. Second arrest was when he was charged with suspicion of burglary which was dropped because of the defendant's drunkenness. Third arrest the charge was armed robbery. He was granted bail after the preliminary hearing until his fourth arrest, when the charge was murder. He states that he was drunk at the time. There was a quarrel and the victim was slugged but he says there was no intention of robbery.

MENTAL CONDITION: During the examination the defendant's attitude was friendly and cooperative. His expression was usually sardonic but he was responsive except when he believed that answers might adversely influence his trial, at which time he would usually say, "I am sorry". He is well oriented and has a good grasp on his surroundings. Tests for intelligence were quickly and well performed. He shows full appreciation of the nature and possible consequence of the charges now pending, and repeatedly volunteers that his conduct was influenced by drunkenness, claiming that he knew nothing of the events of the robbery until afterward when he and his companions were interrupted in a second robbery, but refuses to give details leading to the charge of murder further than that he had been drinking.

PHYSICAL AND NEUROLOGICAL EXAMINATION: Negative except for unequal knee jerks.

OPINION: The defendant was sane at the time of the alleged offense and sane at the time of the examination.

Blackie's sanity was not going to be an issue in his prosecution. At the time, however, California law allowed evidence of "diminished capacity" to be introduced at trial, separately from any consideration of a defendant's sanity. That meant that his level of intoxication could be relevant. If he was drunk at the time of the murder, a good defense lawyer might make a case to a jury that his intentions were not as bad as they would have been if he were sober.

In most states first-degree murder is charged when there is evidence that the crime was premeditated or when it takes place during the commission of another crime, such as robbery. The district attorney wasn't going to be able to show that Blackie and Ted had planned to kill Dr. Buge, but the fact that they had also robbed their victim was inescapable.

On Thursday, November 10, Blackie and Ted were brought back to the superior court for their arraignment. They were charged with first-degree murder and robbery and the DA made it clear that he planned to shoot for the death penalty at trial. Blackie entered a plea of not guilty. Ted didn't enter a plea. Both of them were held without bail and went back to jail.

Outside the county jail it was hot in Los Angeles, the usual brush fires were burning in the hills, and in late November the worst smog in its history squatted over the city. Air pollution was not a new phenomenon in the area. When the Portuguese-born Spanish explorer Juan Cabrillo anchored off of Long Beach and San Pedro in 1542, he noticed that smoke from the fires onshore rose a few hundred feet and then just flattened out to cover the land. He named the area the "bay of smokes."

The word "smog," combining smoke and fog, was coined in 1940. Throughout the war years, with the great increase in industry, the air quality deteriorated. After the war, with the huge influx of population and the consequent rise in the number of cars, the air became even thicker, uglier, and deadlier. The headline for November 23, 1949, on the front page of the *Mirror,* was "Worst Weep in History."

It was just beginning to be understood that the haze in the air wasn't so much a sign of progress, as a potential health hazard. In Sacramento, Dr. Clarence A. Mills, director of experimental medicine at the University of Cincinnati, told state legislators that air pollution had a much worse effect on men than on women. According to the doctor, men breathe more and smoke more than women, so their respiratory death rate is much higher.

Meanwhile, the smog in L.A. roiled and churned in billowing clouds all the way down to ground level. It looked like thick, brown fog and smelled of gasoline and soot. Ralph, who had been chain-smoking since he was twelve, coughed and hacked almost without stop in his cell.

The trial started on Monday, December 12 in Department 43 of the Superior Court of California, for the County of Los Angeles. Judge Charles W. Fricke was presiding.

The sixty-seven-year-old Judge Fricke had been on the superior court since 1927 and was considered one of the greatest authorities on California criminal law. He had written several highly acclaimed textbooks on the subject. He was a thin, frail-looking bald man with a wrinkly face and oversized, prominent ears much like Blackie's. In the courtroom he had a solemn demeanor and put up with no nonsense. Under his robes, however, he was known for wearing gaudy, colorful, flower-patterned neckties. Outside of court he was easygoing, friendly, and well liked.

Seven years earlier Judge Fricke had presided over the "Sleepy Lagoon Murder Trial," in which, because of wartime racism, seventeen defendants were convicted of a murder that most likely never actually happened. All of the convictions were overturned within two years on the grounds that the judge's rulings during the trial had effectively denied representation to the accused.

A year and a half before Ralph and Ted went on trial, Judge Fricke had sentenced Caryl Chessman, the notorious "Red Light Bandit," to death. Chessman later became world famous, as after defending himself in the trial he demonstrated a remarkable mastery of legal proceedings, managing to postpone his date with San Quentin's gas chamber for twelve years, during which time he wrote four popular books.

By the time Blackie and Ted came up for trial, the judge was known as "San Quentin Fricke," a reference to the large number of defendants who had passed before him on their way to the huge state prison on San Francisco Bay.

Before jury selection got under way, Ted had a surprise for the court; he changed his plea to guilty. It seemed obvious that he had cut a deal with the DA. The changed plea was accepted and sentencing was put off until after Ralph's trial.

It took two days to pick the jury, which isn't that unusual in a murder case. The prosecutor was deputy district attorney Manley Bowler. He was aggressive and efficient, with a strong record of convictions. Blackie's lawyer was David Silverton, a nondescript man given to wearing nicely cut gray three-piece suits, who had a fair, if not quite spectacular record of winning acquittals for his clients.

In his opening argument, Bowler laid out what looked like a solid case. He had two eyewitnesses who would testify against Blackie: Joyce, and now that he'd pleaded guilty, Ted.

Silverton played up the fact that Blackie had been drunk and told the jury that he would show that the fatal blows had been struck by Ted. He said that the evidence he planned to present would make a "big difference" in the outlook for his client.

The prosecution opened its case with witnesses to put Ted, Joyce, and Blackie together with the victim, Dr. Buge. Irv Rosenfeld, the manager of the Colony Club, then Violet Buge, then Jimmy Oliveri, the owner of Jimmy's, set the stage for Joyce, who took the stand on Thursday, December 15.

"Blackie Schwamb dragged Dr. Buge from our car," she testified. "I tried to hold my husband, but he got out too. I was hysterical and I don't know what was done to Dr. Buge, but I knew something was wrong.

"I ran up the road screaming, but my husband caught me and took me back to the car. Schwamb got in and we drove away."

"She was just chirpin' like a bird," recalled Blackie.

The prosecution finished up its presentation with Dr. Newbarr, who had conducted the autopsy. He showed three large photos of Dr. Buge's face. Violet and Joyce; Blackie's wife, Nell; and his mother, Janet, who were all sitting near each other in the courtroom, stifled gasps and turned away.

On Friday, Silverton, beginning his defense, played a tape recording the police had made at the time of Blackie's arrest. "I never hit that guy," Blackie said on tape. "I never kicked him. I never touched him except to roll his body over and take his wallet, then Ted and I divided the money.

"I was drunk, I didn't know what it was all about. Ted said to me, 'This guy is an insurance man and he's got lots of money on him, let's get it.' So I said, 'OK', and we did.

"Gardner hit him five or six times. But I never got out of the car until it was all over."

After the tape played, Blackie was called to the stand. He confirmed that it was his voice on the tape and that he'd been so drunk the night of the murder that he couldn't remember clearly what had happened. He pointed the finger at Ted as the ringleader, and said that the one thing that was clear in his mind was that he knew he hadn't hit the doctor. "When I saw the doctor lying on the ground and groaning," he said, "all that went through my mind was to take his wallet and get more drinks."

The defense then called Mike Harvey and Henry Clay West, who had been drinking at Jimmy's on the night of the murder. They both had seen Blackie and they testified that he had been visibly very drunk. West added that when he saw him after he had gone away with Ted and Joyce and then come back, he didn't see any blood on his clothes or cuts or scrapes on his hands.

The matter of what was on his hands was important. The detectives who had arrived at the murder scene and Dr. Newbarr thought that Dr. Buge's face looked like it had been cut up in the course of being slugged by someone wearing a large ring. Ted had his big onyx ring; Blackie just wore a small wedding band. There were also the facts that Ted's hands had looked bruised, like he'd been in a fight, when he was arrested, and the clothes that he'd worn the night of the murder were speckled with blood.

None of that really mattered to the final verdict. The murder and robbery were tied together and both defendants were equally guilty in the eyes of the law. The mitigating circumstances could, however, quite literally make the difference between life and death.

The defense rested its case. Bowler said that he planned to bring Ted Gardner to the stand as a rebuttal witness to Blackie. The court adjourned for the weekend.

It was the weekend before Christmas and all through the city there was the usual seasonal crime and violence. On Monday the *Herald* proclaimed the coming week with the headline "Crime Wave Hits L.A. on Weekend." In bold type the story's lead sentence was "Christmas came a week early for thieves, burglars, and hoodlums who gave Angelenos a bad time in creating a fresh wave of crime over the weekend." The *Express* headline was "Crime Wave Rages."

It was a bad weekend for a game of cards in Gardena, or to run a small shop or café, or to go out for holiday shopping. It was even a bad time to spend at home with loved ones. Family violence, which didn't usually reach its peak until Christmas Day, was already taking its toll. Two different husbands, one of them just a few blocks from Ralph and Nell's apartment, shot and killed their wives and then themselves under their living room Christmas trees. The police were working overtime on crime and domestic disputes, many of them violent.

Crime seems to be a constant in America. When times are bad it increases as people become desperate. When times are good it increases as people become opportunistic. Christmas 1949 was an especially bad season for crime because it was an especially good time for money. The economy was pounding along at full tilt. The Dow Jones Average had hit its highest point since the 1920s on December 2. Nostalgia for the Roaring Twenties was all the rage as the good times were back. There had been a brief economic slump in the first half of the year, but it was barely noticeable to most people.

For the first time on some routes air travel had become cheaper than rail. L.A. to New York was just $88 one way, or $167 round-trip. Still, railways were the strongest sector in the booming stock market. IBM, which made some of the most advanced machines for business, had just brought out the "Electronic Counter." The ads said that it could "compute arithmetical problems at tremendous speeds." It was based on a large unit that had nine electric tubes, a bunch of small light bulbs and thirty-two small connectors. Companies and accountants were lining up to buy them and the company's stock was selling for more than $200 per share by the end of the year.

The housing shortage had begun to ease off a little in Los Angeles, although there was still an enormous amount of building going on. A two-bedroom house on a large lot in Compton, much nicer than the one in which Joyce now lived without Ted, was selling for $7,250. A two-bedroom, unfurnished garden apartment in Blackie's old neighborhood rented for $75 to $90 per month.

Stores couldn't keep new record players or records in stock. Columbia had introduced the 33 rpm Long Play Record Album the year before and RCA introduced the 45 rpm record in early 1949. The "Battle of the Speeds" was raging. In September, Decca had thrown in its lot with Columbia and LP sales had begun to pull ahead. For Christmas though, RCA was offering ten dollars' worth of 45s free with the purchase of a $39.95 record player. Most manufacturers were covering all the bases, churning out machines that could play all three speeds, including the older 78s.

Other than record players, TVs and almost anything made from nylon were the big seasonal sellers. For the first time in years store shelves were also well stocked with imported goods and people were snapping them up.

Crowds were getting away from it all at the movies. That weekend's box-office champion was Nicholas Ray's tough film noir, *They Live by Night,* about a pair of young lovers on the lam from the law. *Bagdad* with Maureen O'Hara came in second. It was advertised with posters of scantily clad women and beefy men and the slogan, The picture of 1001 pleasures! . . .1001 adventures! . . .1001 delights!

They were smoking in the theaters too. A new Gallup poll had just been released showing that 44 percent of all U.S. adults smoked cigarettes, even though more than half of the smokers believed it was bad for their health.

The weather was turning cold. The thermometer headed down into the twenties in parts of town. The fruit farmers in the San Fernando Valley heated up the smudge pots hoping to keep their trees from freezing. It was the coldest beginning of winter in memory.

Monday morning it was cold and uncomfortable in the courtroom. The only person with a padded seat was the judge, everyone else had to sit on straight-backed wooden chairs. There was a lot of squirming and adjusting of position going on as Ted took the stand.

Ralph, dressed in a double-breasted gray herringbone suit with a white T-shirt underneath, slumped low in his chair, his long legs sticking out from under the defense table, staring at his childhood pal in the witness box. Ted just looked straight at Bowler, and occasionally glanced at the jury.

The DA led him through the events of the night of the murder and Ted told his story in a flat monotone. They met up with Blackie at Jimmy's, he said, and then, "Blackie asked me if the doctor had any money. I told him I didn't know but that we'd find out."

They got into Ted's car to drive somewhere else until "Blackie said, 'stop here, this is good enough.' So I pulled over and stopped.

"My wife asked me why I was stopping but I didn't answer. Dr. Buge said, 'What's this?' and Blackie opened the door and dragged him out. I stayed in the car a few moments and then got out because Blackie and the doctor appeared to be fighting."

He testified that he only hit the doctor twice, both times in the face, and then Joyce got out of the car and started running down the street screaming and he went after her. At that point Ted's voice caught and broke. He lowered his head and started sobbing. Blackie looked at him in scorn. His old pal, his crime partner, was ratting him out and was too weak to even pull it off without crying like a baby.

Bowler walked up to his witness, put a hand on his shoulder, and said, "Now just a minute, take it easy."

Ted continued to cry and Judge Fricke called a recess for him to regain his composure.

After about ten minutes the trial resumed and Ted finished his testimony. Silverton just had a couple of questions and then both the defense and prosecution rested their cases.

Final arguments in the case were heard on Tuesday morning. Bowler asked the jury of seven men and five women to recommend the death penalty for Ralph, saying, "This was a vicious and cruel killing which warrants the extreme penalty." Silverton told the jury that the prosecution had not proved beyond a reasonable doubt that Blackie had struck the fatal blows, or that he had actually done anything other than take the victim's wallet.

Two hours later the jury was back. Blackie was tense. He was standing and as the clerk began to read out the verdict he leaned back against his chair, gripping its arms behind him. When he heard the word "guilty" he slumped down, burying his head in his hands on the table. He stayed that way the whole time while, at Silverton's request, the jury was polled and one by one they all said "guilty." Behind him, in the front row of the spectator's seats, Nell and Janet wept. He'd been found guilty of both first-degree murder and robbery. Not quite sure though of who was really telling the truth, the jury recommended life in prison rather than death.

Judge Fricke set sentencing for the coming Friday and Ralph was led back to jail. Nell and Janet stayed in their seats for another half hour, weeping softly and holding each other.

Blackie's previous robbery case was still pending and he was brought back to court on Thursday to begin trial on that charge. Perhaps figuring there wasn't much point in fighting another conviction, he changed his plea to guilty and asked for immediate sentencing. Superior court judge Clement Nye, who years later was to set the final execution date for Caryl Chessman, complied, giving him five years to life in San Quentin.

At about nine in the morning on Friday, December 23, Blackie and Ted were led back into Judge Fricke's courtroom. Ted went first. The judge dismissed the robbery charge. It was probably part of his deal with the DA. "They promised Ted second degree if he'd testify against me and put me in the gas chamber," recalled Blackie. "He was supposed to get five to life, [making him eligible for parole in about three years], but they sentenced him to life."

Ted was staggered by the sentence. He looked like he might faint, like someone had sucker punched him in the gut. Asked if he had anything to say, Ted said, "I only hope my wife will wait for me." Joyce wasn't in the courtroom. He would be eligible for parole in seven years.

Blackie, standing straight in his gray suit, looked poker-faced at the judge. He was sentenced to life for the murder and five years to life for the robbery, both sentences to run concurrently with the five to life he'd been given the day before. He didn't say anything before being led away in handcuffs. He would also be eligible for parole after seven years.

Nell and Janet were once more, as they had been every day during the trial, sitting in the front spectator's row. They sat quietly, resigned to their husband and son's fate. They left the courtroom with Silverton.

In the hallway Nell ran into an old friend who greeted her with "Merry Christmas," then thought better of it and added, "Gosh, is that the thing to say at a time like this?"

Nell smiled, wanly according to a L.A. *Times* reporter, and said, "Well, in spite of a thing like this, we have to go on living, you know."

CHAPTER 10

I T WAS WARM, HOT EVEN, IN BLACKIE'S CELL at the L.A. County Jail. On Wednesday evening January 4, 1950, it was getting awfully cold outside. The temperature in downtown that night hit a record low of thirty-seven degrees for the date.

At about 7 P.M. the guards came for Blackie and whoever else was being transferred to San Quentin. Weekly trains made the prison run along the California coast from San Diego in the south to Richmond, across the bay from San Francisco. The prisoners were told to strip out of their jailhouse jumpsuits and were given the clothes that they'd been arrested in to change into.

Blackie put on his gray herringbone double-breasted suit over his T-shirt. He slipped on his expensive pair of loafers, which needed a good polish after their mistreatment in the police lab. When he was dressed, the guards cuffed him, put leg irons over his neatly pegged trouser legs, and chained him to a manageable group of four or five other convicts.

The prisoners shuffled single file down the hall to the freight elevator. It took them to the basement and a sheriff's department bus took them for the three-block ride to L.A.'s Art Deco Spanish-style Union Station.

They were herded into the coffee shop where they had their own section of tables already laid out with burgers and fries. There was a waitress to bring them Coke or coffee. It had to be a terrible job. According to the author and actor Edward Bunker, who had made the same trip just a few months before, the men all knew that she was one of the last women they would see for a long time, maybe forever. Their eyes followed her hungrily around the room.

Most of the time the train was made up of a single coach and the engine. If there was an especially large number of prisoners to transport there might be two coaches. The windows were blanked out with sheet metal that had been welded into place. There was a cage with an armed guard at one end.

The prisoners were unchained from each other once they got on the train, but their leg irons were kept in place and some of the ones that were considered especially dangerous were left handcuffed. Almost everyone smoked. There wasn't much of anything else to do. The coach reeked of stale and fresh tobacco, body odor, and the incredible stench from the open toilet stall across from the guard.

The train grew more crowded as it stopped along the way in Santa Barbara and San Luis Obispo to pick up more men. By then it could have been anywhere. Ralph had left the world.

In the county lockup an inmate could still get a slight sense of being attached to the outside. There were new prisoners all the time, lawyers coming in and out, and a wide variety of cops and guards. If a guy had family nearby they could make reasonably regular visits. Someone always seemed to have a newspaper and some of the friendlier guards would take requests to change radio stations.

Getting on the train was stepping into another world. Surrounded by other men in the same fix, by their noise and smoke and heat and smell, Ralph was just twenty-three and facing a lifetime of loneliness and boredom. He felt very sorry for himself and angry at the circumstances and people who had put him in his situation.

It wasn't much above thirty degrees the next morning when the train pulled in at Richmond. The prisoners stayed put in the coach while it was uncoupled from the engine and towed onto the ferry to cross the bay to San Rafael.

At the dock on the other side they got out of the train car, blinking against the clear morning sun and at first pleasantly cooled by, then overly chilled by the morning cold. They were put on a bus with wire mesh windows and driven a mile or so to the outer gate of the prison.

The outer gate was a simple, high chain-link fence that stretched a long way in both directions. About a half mile away, the institutional green walls and high gun towers were visible. The first gate rolled back and the bus drove on to the second gate. It was a lot like the first, although it was topped with knife-sharp rolls of concertina wire. It also rolled back and the bus drove through.

The bus stopped and the second gate closed behind it. As the prisoners were let out they had their leg irons removed. They were then herded down a tunnel that led toward the prison.

At the end of the tunnel was a big steel door with a small hatch that someone on the other side could look out of. Two benches lined the walls. The prisoners were told to strip. If they wanted to keep their clothes, they could pay to have them sent home. Otherwise there was a bin where they could toss them for donation to the Salvation Army. Blackie's suit, shoes, and T-shirt went into the bin. He didn't know when, or if, he would ever need them again.

The naked, shivering prisoners sat on the benches, waiting their turn to walk through the steel door that opened to admit two or three at a time. Inside they were thoroughly searched. Some still managed to smuggle money or drugs buried deep inside their rectums, where even the prison guard's flashlights couldn't shine.

They were photographed with an old view camera. The pictures would go onto two cards: an identity card that the inmate always had to carry, and a privilege card that could be taken away for breaking regulations. Without a privilege card there was no getting into the weekend movie, the library, the gym, or other recreational facilities, and no buying from the canteen or the handicraft shop. Privilege cards were precious and rules were easy to break.

San Quentin prison was ninety-eight years old when Ralph walked through the steel door. It had started as a prison barge, anchored in San

Francisco Bay, when the Gold Rush in California had produced more prisoners than the new state had room for. The convicts were rowed to shore to build the permanent facility. For a while the prison was privately run, something that is once again becoming a popular trend. But in 1860 there was a revolt against the conditions in the prison. The warden was taken hostage and marched out of the front gate surrounded by knife-wielding men. A group of local farmers jumped the escaping inmates and subdued them. The running of the prison was taken over by the state.

To help pay its operating costs, the state contracted with private companies to establish factories in the prison. The inmate-workers were horribly exploited, conditions in the plants were dangerous and harsh, and corruption was rife. It all led to a series of riots that were brutally put down.

Throughout its first eighty-eight years San Quentin was a nightmarish place. Violence was common, both among the prisoners and committed by the guards on the prisoners, who were routinely beaten with straps, whips, blackjacks, rubber hoses, and clubs. Food was scarce and not very nourishing, malnutrition was not uncommon, and diseases regularly tore through the inmate population. Punishment was swift and harsh for even minor infractions. Men were thrown into the "dungeon," a dank, pitch-dark, airless hole with a daily ration of a piece of stale bread and a bucket of water. Some of them were kept there for months at a time. More than a few of them went mad. For particularly severe violations of the rules, residents of the dungeon were sometimes slapped into a sort of strait-jacket and suspended in air from the ceiling for hours on end.

All of that changed within twenty-four hours on July 14, 1940. Scandals at the prison finally led the governor of California to fire the entire board of San Quentin Prison and appoint a new five-person board to investigate conditions. The warden turned in his resignation as soon as the new board showed up. Not having anyone to immediately take over, the new board appointed Clinton T. Duffy acting warden for thirty days.

At the time, the forty-two-year-old Duffy was secretary of the prison's parole board. He'd spent his whole life at San Quentin, where his father was a guard for thirty years. He married his high school sweetheart, who had also grown up around the prison; her father had been captain of the yard.

Duffy had his own ideas about how the prison ought to be run. "I was warden," he wrote in his autobiography, "and would be for thirty days more. Thirty days, with much to do, and nothing to lose by doing it."

Within minutes of his appointment, Duffy walked into the office and fired the much-hated, brutal captain and six other particularly violent guards. He appointed a new captain and ordered him to close the dungeon, tear out its iron doors, and throw them on the scrap heap. (The doors eventually became the prison's first contribution to the wartime scrap-metal drive.) He issued an order banning the use of whips, straps, rubber hoses, and all forms of corporal punishment. Sometimes inmates had been forced to stand at attention for hours within nine-inch circles painted on the floor; he ordered the circles painted over. He abolished head shaving for new prisoners, saying that they were humiliated enough simply by being brought to the prison. He got rid of the large, black numbers painted on the back and front of inmates clothes, saying that they were dehumanizing. Then, to everyone's astonishment, he walked, alone, through the prison yard that was full of convicts, many of them violent men with serious bones to pick with the authorities, to the mess hall. He sat down and waited for them to come into lunch.

Duffy ate lunch with the inmates. It was barely edible beef stew with hardly any beef in it. He went into the kitchen and told the head chef that from then on the beef stew would have more meat in it, as well as dumplings. He had fond memories of his mother's stew with dumplings. He ordered major improvements in the food starting the next day. He hired a dietician to supervise the meals.

Within the next few days he had plumbers build new, freshwater showers so that inmates no longer had to bathe in dirty saltwater pumped out of the bay. He got rid of the ban against newspaper subscriptions and eliminated censorship of the outside news. He set up a pressing plant so that pants and shirts could be ironed and inmates wouldn't always have to wear wrinkled clothes. That might not sound like much, but little things count for a lot in prison.

More than three thousand of the prisoners signed a petition asking the prison board to give Duffy a permanent assignment. On September 1 Duffy was appointed to a full, four-year term as warden.

Under his enlightened leadership, San Quentin had become almost a model of a modern prison by the time Ralph got there. It had excellent recreational and educational facilities, or at least as good as could be expected. The amount of violence within its walls had dropped considerably from past levels, although with more than five thousand inmates in a facility built for no more than three thousand, there were still plenty of problems.

Two men shared a cell that was about a foot and a half narrower than a king-sized bed and only about four feet longer. Cell partners couldn't be more than seven years apart in age and were always the same race. In each cell there was a bunk bed, a toilet, a sink, and two small shelves. Each bunk had its own set of radio earphones that got two stations. Inmates were responsible for keeping their own cells clean and they got a new set of bed sheets once a week.

After being searched, Ralph was sent to take a shower. He was given a white, one-size-fits-all jumpsuit with its pockets sewn shut, a pair of socks, and cloth slippers. New arrivals were called "fish," and he was given a "fish kit" including a toothbrush, tooth powder, a three-piece safety razor with two thin blades, a sharpened pencil stub, two sheets of lined paper, and two stamped envelopes. He was also given an application for mail and visitors. It allowed him to see or write up to ten people not including his lawyers. Last, every inmate was given a copy of the booklet *The Department of Corrections, Rules and Regulations* and made to sign for it. There were more than one hundred rules in the book and it was recommended that prisoners memorize them all.

The walk from the admitting area into the main part of the prison was deceptively pleasant. Inmates shuffled along concrete paths through a small, well-tended garden. When Blackie took the walk it was winter

and there was nothing in bloom, but in the spring the garden is cheer-
fully colored with bright pansies.

On the other side of the garden the convicts were sent to their cell
blocks. The south block, also known as the Old Spanish Block, was the
oldest building in the prison. It was said to be the largest prison cell
block in the world. It was certainly the noisiest, dirtiest, and most decrepit in San Quentin.

For the first three months, however, Ralph, along with most of the
fish, was assigned to the guidance center. In the past at San Quentin,
and at most prisons, newcomers were just thrown into the fray and left
to fend for themselves. The guidance center was one of Warden Duffy's
reforms. It was intended to help an inmate actually make something
useful out of his time in prison. Prisoners were evaluated to assess what
jobs they were best suited for in prison and once they got out, what educational opportunities they might best take advantage of, whether or
not they needed psychological help, and of course, just how dangerous
or not they were to figure out what to do with them once they were released into the general prison population.

Ralph was given a battery of both physical and mental tests. A lot
of emphasis was placed on the Minnesota Multiphasic Personality Inventory, a test with some twelve hundred yes and no questions that was
used to classify the prisoners psychologically. The test concluded that
"he has a fairly stable personality with some tendency toward hyperac-
tivity." He scored well on intelligence tests, despite having quit school
after tenth grade. He was classified as "high average intelligence" and
ranked by the vocational counselor in the "upper percentiles of clerical,
manual, and mechanical ability."

Outside the guidance center, on the main prison yard, a lot of inmates were looking forward to Blackie's arrival. Another of the warden's reforms had been to start up a prisoner-written-and-produced
weekly newspaper, the *San Quentin News*. The prison hadn't had a
paper before, although it did have a print shop that was closed down in
the early 1930s when it was discovered that several enterprising inmates were using it to turn out high-quality counterfeit money.

The *News* had gleefully reported the arrival of a former major-league baseball player. There was a prison team, the San Quentin All-Stars, and the prospect of a big-league pitcher playing for it was exciting.

Sports, and particularly baseball, had been played in prisons since at least the 1890s. It had started in youth reformatories where it was noticed that organized sporting events were helpful in rehabilitation, teaching delinquents how to work together as a team. So, some adult penitentiaries decided to give it a try.

Around 1900 the need for recreation in prisons also became more pressing. Businessmen and workers were increasingly complaining about unfair competition from prison factories. As the amount of time that prisoners spent on the job decreased, something had to be done to keep them occupied. Idle, bored convicts were a lot harder to control than those with something to do.

Inmates had been playing baseball at San Quentin since the early 1900s. Until 1912 the prison team, even when playing against outsiders, wore old-fashioned prisoner's stripes rather than uniforms. James A. Johnston was appointed warden in 1913 and he quickly built up the prison's athletic program, with an emphasis on baseball. He issued the first privilege cards that entitled inmates to participate in or watch recreational activities unless they were being disciplined. He initiated Saturday "minor league" and Sunday "major league" games and managed to get the prison team accepted into the San Francisco Recreational Baseball League. At the close of every season the warden threw his "Grand Annual Baseball Banquet," at which he presented the players awards and laid on a much better feed than the usual prison fare.

At the banquet Warden Johnston liked to tell his players about "the exemplars of clean living such as Ty Cobb and Babe Ruth." Cobb was a great player but he was also a racist thug who was known to occasionally threaten people with a gun, and who once savagely beat a legless war veteran who had heckled him from the stands. Ruth was possibly the greatest player of all time, but he was an ill-disciplined, jovial, womanizing lout who did all that he could to excess. Both great players, if their talents hadn't taken them elsewhere, could very well have found themselves in the warden's audience listening to his well-intentioned speech.

In 1929 Ruth did go to prison. The New York Yankees played several exhibition games at Sing Sing State Prison, about thirty-five miles north along the Hudson River from Yankee Stadium.

Sing Sing was also famous for its electric chair in which 614 prisoners died between 1891 and 1963. Condemned prisoners account for a share of prison baseball lore.

At the state prison in Carson City, Nevada, Patrick Casey's last request wasn't for a special meal. He wanted to umpire a baseball game. The warden granted him his wish and he was hung the next day.

Warden Johnston of San Quentin recalled a sports competition day where the judges were several major-league baseball players who were in San Francisco during the off-season. One of the contests involved throwing a baseball for distance and the easy winner, by at least ten feet, was a powerful black convict named Alabama. The men from death row, in leg irons, had been brought out and allowed to sit on a bench and watch the events, but they weren't allowed to participate. One of the condemned inmates, who had played ball as a kid, asked Johnston if he could throw the ball against the winner. The warden decided to allow it. After five throws each, the doomed white man who was hung just a few days later, won the contest.

"As he walked to his place on the bench," wrote Johnston in his memoir, "the prisoners cheered him to the echo. About to die, he had the gratification and glory of being declared the victor.

"I walked to the end of the field where the balls landed. I saw that the winning throw was shorter than the ones made by Alabama when he was in competition with the others. That man, a Negro convict, handicapped by his color, branded as a felon, stigmatized as an outcast, was, with it all and in spite of it all, a good sport."

Prison baseball, perhaps because of the limited pool of talent, was integrated from the start, which was one of the reasons that prison teams so often beat visiting, segregated teams from the outside.

In the 1930s San Quentin got its first major-league inmate. Red Downs, an infielder for three years with the Detroit Tigers, Brooklyn Dodgers, and Chicago Cubs, was sent up the river for robbing a jewelry store. He was fifty years old when he showed up to help the San Quentin All-Stars, but he did a great job. During one four-year period the team lost only five games to the best outside teams the San Francisco Bay area had to offer.

At Sing Sing, Alabama Pitts, a convicted robber, was offered a contract by the Washington Senators to play for one of their minor-league teams when he was paroled in 1935. Judge Landis, the stern, moralistic commissioner of baseball, said that he wouldn't be allowed to play. There was an immediate uproar. Letters of support for Pitts came from all over the place, including one from the warden of Sing Sing and even one from one of Pitts's robbery victims. Landis reversed his decision and Pitts signed for $200 a month. He knocked around professional baseball for five years but never made it to the major leagues. In 1941, at the age of thirty-one, he was stabbed to death by the jealous boyfriend of a woman he was dancing with in a roadhouse.

Prison baseball even made its way into a popular song. In 1930, Arthur Fields and Fred Hall wrote "Eleven More Months and Ten More Days" and recorded it with Columbia Records. The final verse of the song, sung in the voice of a man in jail, is:

> Now, we play baseball once a week
> And you should see the score.
> Ev'ry player steals a base—
> they've stolen things before.
> There's lots of folks would like to come
> and see us when we play,
> But they've built a wall around the place
> to keep the crowd away.

While Blackie was being poked, prodded, and tested every which way in the guidance center, San Quentin's baseball season got under way. The opening game was against the Keneally Yanks, a local semi-pro team. The All-Stars lost by a score of sixteen to three. They also lost their second game. The prison's baseball fans were getting anxious to see their new pitcher in action.

In his column "Second Guessing" in the *San Quentin News,* inmate Lou Menney wrote, "The tentative date for the beginning of the San Francisco Recreation Summer Baseball League, of which the All-Stars are a member, is Sunday, April 23. There is a league stipulation that no man can be used until he has been out of organized baseball for two full years. It could affect our Mr. Schwamb unless we get some sort of a waiver or stipulation."

In late February and early March the doctors and counselors in the guidance center issued their assessments of Blackie and their recommendations for how he should be treated in the prison.

The guidance counselor, W. J. Pedler, wrote, "Subject had a somewhat interested attitude. He seems very resistant toward understanding himself and his problems. He appears to be a selfish, egotistical individual with a nice personality with a persuasive manner. He was not particularly well-liked by the group, mainly because he did not like them. He associated only with two of the more poorly adjusted members of the group." Pedler recommended that he be transferred into the main prison at a level of "medium custody."

V. A. Kirk, the prison psychologist, wrote, "He has high average intelligence and appears alert. Personality tests including the MMPI [Minnesota Multiphasic Personality Inventory] and the Goodenough indicate the presence of an overactive and psychopathic trait. During the interview he was quite calm and controlled. He answered all questions adequately. There does not appear to be any serious emotional disturbance requiring immediate psychiatric attention." He also recommended transfer to the main prison at medium custody.

The psychiatrist, L. B. Pilsbury, said that Blackie "has not been an ornament to society aside from exciting admiration for his prowess in the baseball field." He concluded, "No psychosis, paranoid trend or neurological defect. Is in need of counseling and taking sober thought of himself."

D. Farling was the correctional officer who issued the "Custodial Abstract" on Blackie. He wrote, "Still carries tendency towards a 'big shot' attitude. He appears to hold great animosity towards crime partner (Gardner) for assertedly turning states evidence. This seems to prey on Schwamb's mind as he mentioned during interview possible trouble between them if in close contact. Requests transfer to Folsom to avoid this contact. Of high average I.Q. he should not prove to be a custodial problem."

His overall institutional prognosis was, "No disciplinary problems anticipated," and all of the reports recommended medium custody. It was also recommended that he should be assigned work in the athletic department. In spite of that, R. L. Eklund of the classification bureau attached a supplement to the report that stated, "In view of the offense, information in the Guidance Counselor's abstract, and in the Custodial Abstract regarding "Big Shot" attitude, writer [Eklund] questions assignment to athletic department at initial classification."

In the end he was recommended for "close custody," meaning greater supervision of his activities and a general industrial work assignment with the usual time off for baseball practice. If no general industrial job could be found for him, the alternate assignment would be to the athletic department.

Blackie hated all the testing and psychological mumbo jumbo. He wanted them to leave him alone, let him out into the general population where he could just serve his time. He couldn't even get a drink in the guidance center and he knew from word on the streets that he could get a lot of whatever he needed in the regular prison, so long as he had the cigarettes or something else to pay for it.

CHAPTER 20

PRISONER NUMBER A-13670, RALPH RICHARD SCHWAMB changed from white to blue coveralls and walked out of the guidance center into the general population at the end of the first week of March 1950. On the eleventh he started his first game for the San Quentin All-Stars.

The ball field was on the lower yard and despite having to be squeezed into an area that was far from perfect for the purpose, it was no worse than some of the semipro fields Blackie had played on. The infield had wooden bleachers lining both baselines. The pitcher's mound was regulation height and all the distances were correctly laid out. The infield was dirt; the outfield had a few patches of grass.

Right field was open all the way to the prison wall, a good four or five hundred feet away and topped with a gun tower. Center field had a fence some three hundred feet from home plate, then the wall with a walkway patrolled by three sharpshooters. Left field came to an abrupt halt at the lower, outside wall of the jute mill, just two hundred or so feet from home plate. Balls hit over the wall were called "jute mill singles," and the runner was only allowed to advance one base.

The jute mill had been in operation since 1882 and provided more jobs for prisoners than any other industry or department in the institution. Jute is a fiber made from hemp plants. The mill produced burlap and canvas sacks from giant spools of raw jute imported from India.

Ball games were held on Saturday and Sunday. The Saturday games were called the minor leagues and took place among teams from within the prison, or against nonleague teams from the outside. They were popular, but not nearly so much as the games on Sunday, when semipro teams from outside the prison would come to play. The San Quentin All-Stars had long been part of the San Francisco Recreation Department American AA League. (There was also a National AA League.)

Like many semipro leagues at the time, especially in California where the weather was often cooperative and there were no major-league teams, the baseball they played was very competitive. The teams were renowned for producing major-league prospects and fielding big leaguers who wanted to stay in shape during the off-season. The outside teams liked coming to the prison to play. The games were well attended and the crowds of inmates were appreciative of anyone who showed up to provide distraction from the daily routine.

"Over 200 teams have written in requesting a date on the San Quentin 1950 baseball schedule," wrote Lou Menney in the *News*. "Inasmuch as we play approximately 40 games a season, about 160 requests cannot be fulfilled. Imagine that, around 160 teams or 1,440 players are going to be disappointed because they can't get INTO San Quentin."

Blackie's first game was against Modesto Junior College and he quickly struck out the first three batters to face him. There were nearly three thousand guards and inmates watching and their cheers rang off the walls. Even in prison he was pitching in front of crowds about the same size, or even larger, than he did in home games with the Browns. He tired quickly, life in the guidance center had been sedentary, and he wasn't in good shape, but before being taken out for a relief pitcher in the sixth inning he had struck out three more batters and got a hit.

Eleven days later he pitched against Marin Junior College. Once again he struck out the first three batters he faced. He left the game after five innings, having struck out thirteen.

On April 2 the All-Stars beat the Lodi Guild Wines, a semipro team that had been the champions of the Sacramento Rural League the year before. Blackie struck out eleven batters and got a couple of hits. The prison yard was buzzing with anticipation of the coming season.

Adjusting to prison life was easier than he had thought it would be. He knew he didn't have much choice, so he wasn't going to fight it. And, so long as he stayed out of trouble and was a hotshot ballplayer, he had certain privileges, including a plum job assignment.

Somewhere in the course of his various odd jobs he had learned to type. Because of that and his sports background he got work as a clerk for the athletic department. He even got his own small office in the gym on the fifth floor of the old brick industrial building.

Nell had stuck by him throughout the trial and did her best to show up on visiting days with Rich whenever she could. San Quentin was four hundred miles north of the apartment in L.A., so it wasn't easy. She and Janet also sent money when they could. Prisoners were allowed up to $65 per month, not in cash but in coupons that could be spent at the canteen for cigarettes, candy, instant coffee, peanut butter, or similar items, or at the handicraft shop for prison-made goods that could be used to decorate or fix up a cell.

Cash was rare in the prison; it had to be smuggled in, so cigarettes were the most common currency. There was an accepted exchange rate for everything from tattoos to laying bets with the two bookies that worked the yard. In the early 1950s it took four cartons of cigarettes, or ten dollars in cash, to buy a small bindle of heroin, enough for one good fix or maybe two smaller "tastes."

A quart of home brew cost just five packs. Blackie quickly caught on to that.

"Sure I made brew," he said. "I put up three or four gallons every couple of weeks, just yeast and sugar and the juice of three or four oranges and let it sit three or four days. It was like cheap wine, maybe ten percent. Drink a whole gallon and you could catch a little buzz."

Brewing booze was against the rules and if a prisoner got caught he'd get punished for it. But a lot of guards turned a blind eye as they figured it was something that helped inmates pass the time. If it kept some of them happy, it kept them out of trouble.

"It was a different kind of prison culture," recalled Ed Bunker, who was in San Quentin at the same time as Blackie. "The joint was really free. You could go many places; it was like a big city. I used to have parties. I'd go around and visit everybody; you could go to the hospital and most any place within the walls without a pass. We could do anything we wanted from 8 A.M. to 4:30 P.M. unless we had a job.

"There was an alley down some stairs from the upper yard to the lower yard and all the shops were off of it, the plumbing shop, the paint shop, the metal shop, the workshops; down near the other end was the barbershop. I used to go down there and hang out with friends of mine. It was a convivial place."

Reform-minded wardens like Clinton Duffy were beginning to have an impact on U.S. prisons by the early 1950s. Rehabilitation was considered a real possibility if only the right mix of psychology, education, and healthy recreation could be blended for the prisoners. Though prisons were overcrowded, with the booming economy and subsequent rise in tax revenues, more money was available for them than ever before.

"You could learn anything you wanted to learn," said Blackie. "Masonry, body and fender work, carpentry, name it; electricity, painting, you could even take college extension courses or get your high school diploma and take [regular] college courses.

"There was an excellent library, or you could order from the San Francisco Public Library. I was a voracious reader. I would go through periods of reading garbage and then I'd go through other periods. I got very involved reading Nietzsche. Which isn't the finest thing in the world for a prison mind. But what else are you going to do? You can only read so many Louis Lamour books. He can't write them fast enough.

"I have no doubt that if I'd had broken my right arm or my right shoulder the first month I was there [rather than playing baseball], I would have learned something useful. I picked up bookbinding in nothing flat. It was a good paid trade. If I had wanted to take the time, I could have learned Linotype or a lot of other skills."

While Blackie approved of the educational and recreational side of rehabilitation, he didn't have much stomach for the psychological ingredient. "When I got there they had one psychiatrist and he was the nuttiest son of a bitch that's ever lived in this world. He could write things in your jacket [file]. He would ask you, 'Does being in prison upset you because you're not able to sleep with your mother?' He wanted to see your reaction. He wrote in my jacket that I was a homicidal maniac. I'd still be there if someone else hadn't pulled that out of my file."

Regardless of what the prison shrink thought of him, Blackie ingratiated himself with the rest of the prison staff by making ball games more popular with the inmates than ever before. "After we got the team going and winning you could fire a machine gun in the upper yard on Sunday and not hit anybody. Every weekend I was keepin' about twenty-five hundred guys off of that big yard where there was nothin' to do other than walk and walk or play dominoes and try to cheat each other. Kept them down on the lower yard, watching the ball games, no fights, no nothing.

"Sure, gambling went on, heavy, you'd be surprised at the amount of cigarettes that were bet on a Sunday. And I had plenty of offers to dump or manipulate the scores. I didn't need to do that; it was never in my bag of tricks. I'd make bets. I'd signal to friends of mine that I'm going to strike the next guy out, or something like that. But as far as situations where I could manipulate the score, which I could do through walks or hit batters or easy pitches, I never did that because that's a good way to get killed."

Duffy's reforms had decreased the amount of violence in San Quentin, but they hadn't stopped it. If Blackie had deliberately lost a game it might have been good for some gamblers, but it would have been bad for others. The ones who had lost money couldn't permit something like that to go unpunished. The other prisoners would have seen it as a sign of weakness and looking weak has always been one of the most dangerous things an inmate can do. The most elemental laws of the street apply in prison, only more so.

"There were always killings," said Ralph, "but the guys that got killed, nine out of ten of them were supposed to get killed."

An inmate didn't have to do his own killing if he didn't want to. There were always killers available for hire. The rate, in cigarettes, varied according to who the victim was and for what reason. Some guys would kill snitches (informants) almost for free.

When Blackie got sent to San Quentin, the police held onto Ted in L.A. for an extra month. Because Ted had testified against him, the authorities figured that they'd better do their best to keep the two of them separated. In the guidance center they told Blackie that if anything should happen to Ted in prison, they'd know who to look for.

"I hadn't been there a week when I had ten guys offer to kill him for five packs of cigarettes the minute he walked through the gate," Blackie said. "They knew it was a snitch job. So I just said, 'No, I don't want anything to do with that.' When he did finally come up he wanted to talk to me and I told him, 'I don't ever want to look at you again.'"

The fact that he got along well with the guards, the staff, and the warden and wasn't doing anything to get back at Ted made some of his fellow prisoners suspicious. Some even thought he might be a snitch himself. But by and large he kept on everyone's good side by minding his own business and performing well on the playing field.

"He was pretty polite," recalled John Moore, a guard at San Quentin. "He would always say hello to you when he passed you on the yard. Talented guys like "Slick" Schwamb were the upper class of the prison. They didn't hang out with the lowlifes and the lowlifes didn't bother them much."

On April 16 the All-Stars got the welcome news that their star pitcher had received a waiver and would be allowed to pitch in the Recreation League games. That same day he came in as a relief pitcher in the sixth inning of a game against Reliable Drugs of San Francisco and struck out eight of the ten batters he faced.

On April 23, in the opening game of the semipro season, the All-Stars beat Galileo Salami. Blackie struck out fourteen and got two hits of his own. A week later against Moffat Manteca, a powerhouse in the league, he narrowly lost his first game but still struck out eight batters.

Blackie was feeling loose and good, pitching the way he wanted without any coaches pestering him to do it their way. He had great control, sizzling speed, and it wasn't just that he was a big fish in a small pond. Members of the opposing teams who had seen, and in some cases played against, a lot of major leaguers, were awestruck by his stuff. The fact that he wasn't always drunk, hungover, or distracted by other temptations was surely the reason for his newfound success. For the first time in his life he could really concentrate on what he was doing. And when he did that, he was good, really good.

In the *San Quentin News*'s "Second Guessing" column of May 5, Menney wrote, "Ralph "Blackie" Schwamb, our All Star pitcher whose arms are so long he needs only to bend down an inch to scratch a snake, has now struck out 73 batters in 44 innings."

A little less than a month later he had 113 strikeouts in 72 innings and also had the second highest batting average on the team. The Stars were on a roll. Inspired by their new pitcher the other team members played to the best of, if not even beyond, their abilities. On Sundays anywhere from three to four thousand inmates, guards, and staff gathered in the lower yard to watch the ball games. Those were the biggest crowds in the league.

The All-Stars kept winning and Blackie kept mowing down opposing batters. By the middle of June he was undoubtedly the best pitcher they'd ever seen in the league and he was also leading his team in batting. He didn't, however, have San Quentin's record for the most strikeouts in one game. That was held by "Sugar" Cain, an inmate pitcher in the 1930s. Cain once dedicated a game to a fellow prisoner and big baseball fan who was being paroled. He struck out twenty-two batters in that game, one for every year the convict had spent behind bars.

On June 26, in front of the largest crowd of the season, the All-Stars beat New Pisa Café to become the champions of the San Francisco Recreation Department American AA League. Blackie was the winning pitcher, striking out nine, getting two hits himself, and stealing home. Sam Levine, a well-known sports announcer from San Francisco, came to the game and gave a play-by-play account over the loudspeaking system.

No one could recall the prison team ever having this kind of success. Even the most hardened, cynical convicts felt the stirrings of pride. "New Pisa Restaurant, Holly Packers and Moffat Mantecas are seeded the number one, two and three teams in the State Semi-Professional Tournament now being played in Atwater, California," wrote Menney. "I wonder where they would classify San Quentin since the locals beat New Pisa twice, Holly Packers once, and blew one to Moffat's on errors? It's a little late in informing you but the Bill Erwin American Legion baseball team of Oakland piled up a record of 28 wins in 31 meetings last year in blazing to a National championship. The San Quentin All-Stars whipped them a couple of months before they won the U.S. title."

Blackie was the losing pitcher on July 2 against the San Francisco Fire Department, but he did strike out thirteen batters. On July 9 he started the game playing third base; he always enjoyed playing the infield and in spite of his size he was quick enough to be good at it. In the eighth inning he came in as a relief pitcher and struck out all six of the batters he faced.

The All-Stars were scheduled to play Carlo's Inn on July 23 for the overall championship of the San Francisco Recreation Department league. The day before the game the San Francisco *Examiner* called the Stars "one of Northern California's strongest clubs," and said that they were favored to win.

They did. Blackie struck out fourteen batters and got three hits. The prison yard went wild.

The "Second Guessing" column in the *News* crowed, "Our nine starting players have a team batting average of .367. That plus a pitcher who has won 11, lost three; has struck out 184 would-be-batters in 135 innings; has an earned run average of 2.50 and who strokes the ball at a .455 clip, leads us to shout: Bring on the Northern California semi-pro champions—the Salinas Rodeo Buffets!"

Blackie was achieving the success he'd always wanted. The problem was that it was far from the limelight. Though he had settled into it quicker and better than he had thought possible, life in prison was still a mind-numbing routine.

It was always noisy; there was no escaping that. After a restless night's sleep inmates were woken up early and fed a breakfast that more often than not was cold grits, a cold fried egg, or sometimes pancakes and weak coffee. Then, at eight thirty they'd either go to their jobs or out into the upper yard to spend the day walking around, playing cards or dominoes, reading, working out with weights, or just hanging out. Lunch was at 11:30 and was usually a simple sandwich with more weak coffee or water. On Wednesdays there was a "health salad" of carrot pulp with a few raisins. There was no privacy, no quiet, the prison was overcrowded, and it was impossible to be just left alone.

At four thirty in the afternoon everybody went back to his cell. A loud bell rang, a guard pulled a big metal bar, and the cell doors would slam shut. Inmates had to stand up and grip the bars with both hands while guards walked down the corridors counting heads. Once the count was finished it was time for dinner.

The mess hall was an enormous high-ceilinged room with a metal catwalk up near the top. Two guards with high-powered rifles patrolled from above. A cafeteria line snaked past huge steam tables. The prison served 15,300 meals every day. The inmates were fed a quota of thirty-eight hundred calories per day. Ten different meals had been planned by a state dietician in Sacramento. One menu was a bowl of chili, salad, green beans, five slices of white bread, the ubiquitous weak coffee, and a piece of spice cake. Another was spaghetti, string beans, three pieces of white bread with margarine, tapioca, and coffee.

Meals were served in the loudest place in the whole prison. Everything was made of metal—metal forks and spoons with metal plates, trays, and cups; metal dippers and serving spoons with big steel cauldrons; and gigantic metal dishwashers that let loose a constant barrage of steel drum–like rattling and ear-splitting bursts of steam.

After dinner it was back to the cells to hang out, read, play cards, or kill time in any other way the limited options would allow. At about ten taps was blown on a trumpet, and it was lights out for the night.

With an approval from the senior librarian, prisoners could subscribe to a reasonably good newsstand's variety of magazines. Sports magazines and publications where there was a faint hope of the occasional photo or illustration of a scantily clad woman were the most popular. On weekends there was a movie, half the prison population could go on Saturday, the other half on Sunday.

During the season the All-Stars were allowed an hour of practice every day. That helped break up the routine. Blackie did a lot of the coaching. He was patient and well liked by his teammates.

"There were a lot of changes I had to make in my attitude," he said. "So many of those guys have got real bad attitudes. Their mistakes were so glaring, but if you go and say something and one of those donkeys comes back with a [threat], well, what are you going to do? On the outside, you'd just say, 'turn in your uniform, be on the bus to Tuscaloosa in the morning, come back when you get your attitude straightened out, we'll call you.' What do you do [in prison]? You just call him something back and then for three days you keep turning your head to see who's gonna hit you with a pipe.

"I didn't have much trouble though. Everyone knew I was a square shooter and I wasn't a snitch. I wasn't goin' to go one way or the other. I wasn't gonna tell the bulls anything and I wasn't gonna tell the convicts anything. It's the only way to deal with it."

The team did have some very good players. "We had one kid, Frank Nubin," recalled Blackie. "He was a shit-disturber, a radical, but a good ballplayer; good arm, great speed. I wrote to one of the chief scouts for the Braves and told him that Nubin only had about a month left [before parole] and I'd like him to take a look at him. He was very impressed, so he gave Nubin a thousand dollars to sign. Coming out of prison, that was pretty good. And he gave him something like $320 a month, and sent him to Ventura in the Cal State League. He got going pretty good and then some pitcher threw at him. He got in a big beef and then somebody else threw at him. It went right around the league just like that, throwin' at him. So he finally hit some guy with a bat and that was the end of him and baseball."

Coaching a prison baseball team presented Blackie with some peculiar problems, but applying his intelligence to what he had learned from his life of crime helped him to understand the inmates he was playing with.

> What would amaze you is that the same guy who would walk up behind you in a line at the barbershop or the chow line and stick a sharpened screwdriver through you, or hit you in the head with a pipe and not think about it, if you hit a ground ball at him there is no way he is going to field it. He's going to get out of the way of it, backhand it or step aside. [Guys like that] have got very little guts.
>
> The violent criminals were more intense, but they lost a lot of their talent through that intensity. They couldn't control themselves. [When they weren't doing well] you could see the goddamn sawdust [from them banging their bats]. They lost a lot of their effectiveness. The more violent criminals were first-ball hitters. Like they wanted to smash it and get out of there. Maybe it's the thought that the second pitch might be at their head. Maybe they'd be afraid the pitcher would retaliate if they took a real hard swing at the first pitch and knock them down with the second one.
>
> The guys that played the best were the guys that might have played a couple of years in high school or something like that. But they were mostly chronic [bad] check writers or white-collar criminals. They played because they wanted to play; it broke up their routine. There were a couple of pretty good ones. There were more good hitters than fielders.
>
> All those years [in prison] I had one catcher who might have been able to catch in the minor leagues. That was a problem because [the pitcher and catcher] complement each other. You can give me the greatest pitching staff in the whole world and [a lousy] catcher and I'll show you some losers.

By the middle of summer the Korean War was in full swing and the naval bases and forts in northern California were filling with sailors and soldiers in training or in transit to and from Asia. A lot of good ballplayers came through the area and they played for military teams or the local semipro teams.

"We started getting some real good ball clubs to play against," recalled Blackie.

Tommy Morgan [who the next year was called up from the minors to pitch for the Yankees] was pitching for Fort Ord. The Alameda Coast Guard team had six or seven guys [who had been or were about to be major leaguers]. We beat them all. Well, I beat them all.

Our team got better and better and the word spread. The scouts used to come in there to look around, or they would bring the young turks from the Bay area [to play against us] so they wouldn't be looking at them play some small-time team. They brought in Tony Spatafore and another little guy, best double play combination I ever saw. They brought in a guy who had led the Southern Association in hitting. They brought in a Yankees bonus baby. They wanted me to check his flaws. He was a big guy, a pitcher, and I had the team start bunting him. They signed him anyhow and he went to Kansas City, which was their top minor-league club then. He had great stuff until somebody finally got smart and started bunting and he went pfft, never won another game in professional baseball.

The scouts wanted to see what these guys could do. They brought in Billy Martin, who I had played with in the Arizona-Texas League. He was a proven factor, but they wanted to check on a few things and they were teaming him at the time with Gil McDougald [who had led the Texas league in batting that year and was brought up to the Yankees the next year].

Outside players were always surprised and pleased at how good the competition was when they came to San Quentin. But all the security and gun towers and thousands of milling men in same-colored coveralls also gave visitors the creeps. "That day I had a strange feeling in my gut," recalls McDougald. "I really knew how lucky all of us were to be on the outside after the game."

The Stars kept beating all comers. In five games between July 23 and August 20 Blackie struck out seventy-three batters in forty innings and led the team in batting with an amazing average of .461.

At the end of summer the jute mill went on an emergency schedule for war production. The mill needed to fill an army contract for 390,000 jute sandbags by October 15 and all the inmates pitched in.

The major league's World Series between the Yankees and the Philadelphia Phillies began on October 4. In his column in the *News*, Warden Duffy announced that the championship games would be broadcast over the loudspeakers in the upper yard of the prison and that prisoners wanting to listen didn't have to go back to their jobs until the games were over. Following the successful baseball season, the warden was full of praise. "I don't think I have ever been connected with a group of men more united in a common interest for good sportsmanship and team competition than you of this institution."

The jute mill successfully filled its contract on time and one week later the All-Stars lost the last game of their season. Blackie didn't pitch, he played second base. The Stars finished the season with a record of twenty-nine wins and eight losses. Blackie won nineteen of those games and lost only three. He struck out 281 batters and walked 55 in 203 innings, and in a league filled with good hitters had an excellent earned-run average of just 2.04. He was particularly proud of the fact that he also led the team in hitting, with a batting average of .457.

Basketball season started just after baseball ended. Blackie had never played much basketball, but because of his height was encouraged to join the team. It was also called the All-Stars and also played games against teams from the outside. He liked the exercise but wasn't all that good at it. Baseball was his real love.

Over the fall and winter he got busy in his clerk's office working to improve the baseball program at the prison. "They had a good budget but they didn't know how to order anything," he said. "So they more or less let me take it over. They were spending the money on the wrong things, bunch of junk. I contacted Wilson Sporting Goods in San Francisco. The general manager at the time was Frank Kneilly. He came to the prison and I told him what we wanted and what kind of discounts we would expect considering our budget and the fact that we were a penal institution. He sent me all the current catalogs. I ordered better uniforms and decent gloves. Instead of ordering seventy-five six-dollar gloves, I ordered twenty-five eighteen-dollar ones. The same with the bats, and we switched from balls that when you hit them went lopsided, to official Coast League balls."

Bill and Charley DeWitt, the owners of the St. Louis Browns, were not on his approved list of correspondents, but Warden Duffy gave special permission to write to his ex-bosses on behalf of the All-Stars.

Dear Mr. DeWitt:

I would like to begin this by congratulating you and Bill on the great job you are doing with the Browns. I have followed you all year through *The Sporting News* and the local papers and I can't help but feel that by 1953 a lot of people who have been throwing dirt in your faces will be eating crow. It will be a long, uphill battle, but knowing you and Bill, I am confident you will succeed. Right now, with a little pitching, you have a potential first-division club in my opinion, and you may get just what you need from Bill Kennedy and Lou Sleater. With these two, plus Ned Garver and Cliff Fannin, who will come around, you will have four starters that will be the envy of the league.

We had quite a ball club here at San Quentin this year. We entered the San Francisco Class AA Recreation League and, for the first time in the institution's history, we won the championship. We had one drawback, though, and that was the bat situation. The budget the athletic department has to work with just couldn't quite make it. The Institution does not ask for donations as a rule, but I spoke to Warden Duffy the other night and he told me that, under the circumstances, he would sanction this letter. I am hoping that you will be able to see your way clear to send us a few used bats you might have lying around, now that the season is over.

Even a dozen will be greatly appreciated more than I can tell you, not only by the baseball team, but by the hundreds of men who look forward each week to seeing us play on weekends. Please let me know at your convenience, by writing to the Warden, Clinton T. Duffy, San Quentin, Calif. He will convey your message to me.

Give my regards to Mrs. DeWitt and also to your son, and Bill.

Believe me, I'm sorry I let you, Bill and the Browns down as I did.

Very sincerely yours,

Ralph Schwamb.

DeWitt replied quickly, writing, "I imagine that your team (which won the championship) probably has the best pitcher it has had for some time, if you are doing the hurling." He said that he would send bats immediately and complimented Blackie on his analysis of the potential pitching strength of the Browns in the coming season.

By the time the coming season started, the DeWitt brothers had sold the Browns to Bill Veeck. Of the pitchers Blackie mentioned in his letter, only Ned Garver had a good year, managing, incredibly, to win twenty games for a team with the worst record in baseball, one of the worst won–loss records ever.

"I figured they get so many bats, dozens after dozens after dozens, and some of them are made from a little inferior grade of wood," said Blackie, "I thought it was a cinch to get two or three dozen of these. So I get a letter from Bill DeWitt, 'We're glad to hear your evaluation of our team, and we're happy that you're able to play ball and we know that you're probably the best pitcher on the team and blah blah blah, and we're sending six bats.' And they were all used at that."

CHAPTER 21

B Y THE END OF 1950 BLACKIE WAS FEELING PRETTY GOOD, or at least as good as could be expected. It had been more than a year since he'd been in the outside world, but he'd been locked up longer than that before in the navy and under much worse conditions. Life in San Quentin was far from ideal, but it wasn't all that bad. He had the success and accolades he'd always wanted from baseball and he felt physically better than he had in a very long time. He could drink enough from time to time to get a slight buzz on, but there were many days of involuntary sobriety and that, even he had to admit, had its benefits.

Remembering the torturous monotony of life in the brig, he had expected to be bored stiff in the penitentiary, but there were a surprisingly large number of activities to keep him occupied. He saw more movies than he had when he was on the outside. He played more sports and worked out more frequently. He read more books, attended lectures, tried his hand at writing the occasional piece for the *News* and even some creative writing.

Prisoners were so thankful for any distraction they could get, that a variety of outside groups were happy to come to the prison for events. Theater troupes and sports teams made up of people with disabilities were popular with inmates, and the performers also found that the prison audiences were especially appreciative of their efforts.

One of the favored opponents for the basketball All-Stars was the Oakland Silents. "The Oakland Silents are a team made up of deaf mutes," explained the *News* in covering one game, "some of whom can catch the vibration of sounds, such as a whistle or buzzer. The Silents were amazingly alert and active on the court and used combinations for different set-ups that baffled the Stars for the first quarter."

In the 1930s a blind baseball team had come to the prison several times to play the All-Stars. They hit the ball off of a batting T, rather than having it pitched to them. They never won a game but they did surprisingly well.

The San Francisco Blind Actors' Guild showed up at least twice a year while Blackie was in San Quentin. They premiered some of their productions at the prison and also helped to put on acting workshops. Their pre-Christmas performance of a play by Jerome K. Jerome called *The Passing of the Third Floor Back* won them a standing, whooping, and hollering ovation and numerous curtain calls. "Some of the actors had tears in their sightless eyes as they remained on stage to take bows," wrote the reviewer in the *News*.

Blackie was also kept busy by his clerical work. He had improved the equipment situation for the baseball program, and had done so under budget. So the athletic director gave him more to do. He wasn't in charge of the prison's athletic programs, but by the beginning of 1951 he was doing more than anyone else to keep them running.

He was also studying, not on his own behalf, but despite having never graduated from high school he was helping his cellmate and a few other guys get their degrees. He didn't do it for free, his students would pay him in cigarettes or favors, but it was another way to pass the time. In a few cases it was a thankless task.

"[One guy was] a second-degree burglar doing one to fifteen," recalled Blackie. "He was going to do twenty months maybe, at the most. So he gets his GED and I'm real proud of him and he's out maybe two weeks before there he is, comin' in again with a new batch of fish."

Baseball practice started again in February. The season got off to a bad start on March 9 when the Keneally Yanks beat the Stars eight to two in eleven innings. Ralph was the losing pitcher.

The night before the next game the Blind Actors' Guild had come back to premiere their show *Springtime for Henry*. The front-page headline for the *News* that week was, "Blind Actors Wow Quentinites, Hilarity Reigns at Guild Play."

The writers on the sports page weren't laughing. Blackie had started the second game of the season and got clobbered, losing by a score of twelve to three. The Stars then lost their third straight game, fourteen to five. Ralph played second base to rest his arm for the game against a tougher team the next day.

His arm was sore. He hadn't thrown the ball over the few months of winter and he threw too hard when he first seriously picked the ball back up in March. Unlike in the major leagues where teams have a trainer who helps pitchers take care of their arms, in prison he was on his own. It was almost impossible to get ice to calm down inflamed muscles.

On March 18 the Stars and Blackie got their first wins. It wasn't the best game he'd ever pitched, but at least it broke the losing streak. They went on to win the next four in a row and he was getting back to form, striking out a total of thirty-two batters in two of those games. The fourth win was against the very tough Sixth Army team that fielded several ex- and future major leaguers. After winning that game and getting three hits to help himself out, the *News* dubbed him "Slick" Schwamb, a name that he liked better than Blackie and that was to stick with him through his years in San Quentin.

The official coach of the baseball program was John Apostol. In mid-April Apostol was appointed athletic director of the whole prison. That put Ralph into an even better position than before with regard to his work.

The Stars lost their next game, and then won the game after that when Blackie knocked in a run with a single in the seventh inning. It was the last "Jute Mill single" ever hit in the prison.

On Thursday April 18, eight hundred men were returning to work from their lunch break when smoke began pouring out of the jute mill. Within a minute flames burst through its roof and windows and into the air. Quick work by the prison's volunteer fire brigade and inmates who pitched in kept the fire from spreading to any other buildings. But the jute mill and all of its machinery, by far the largest source of jobs in the prison, were totally destroyed.

Between twelve hundred and sixteen hundred prisoners were thrown out of work. The idle crowds, aimlessly walking or just milling about in the upper yard every day, grew much larger and much more restless overnight. Tensions in the prison mounted, fights became more frequent. Recreation became more important than ever.

The Stars resumed their season on May 4. The outer jute mill wall was still standing and balls hit over it were now called "Junk Yard singles." The Stars won the first two games after play got back under way. Blackie struck out twenty-one batters in the second of those games.

On May 20, in a game that was the talk of the prison for several weeks leading up to it and at least a week after, the Stars beat the defending Northern California Semipro Champions, the Salinas Rodeo Buffets. The previous season the Salinas team had come within one run of winning the overall state championship. Blackie struck out ten batters and started the winning rally in the eighth inning with a single.

A week later the San Francisco Recreation AA League season started and the All-Stars and Blackie went wild. Against even tougher competition than the previous year, the team won its first fifteen games. They easily won the league championship for the second year in a row.

On September 3 the Stars played the Tiburon Pelicans, one of the strongest semipro clubs in California. The Pelicans, who were in a different league than the All-Stars, had won their last seven games, almost all of them against teams that were better than any of the teams, other than Salinas, that the inmates had played. Blackie pitched a no-hitter and struck out fifteen batters. The All-Stars were sitting on top of their little patch of the world.

By the end of the season on November 4 the Stars had won thirty-two games, lost seven, and tied one. During the year they overcame the loss of five of their players, including three of their best, who were paroled. Ralph's won-loss record was twenty-three and seven. He had appeared in thirty-one games and struck out more than three hundred fifty opposing batters. At one point he pitched thirty-two consecutive scoreless innings. His batting average was .371. It was an incredible performance, at any level of play.

He didn't play, however, during the last month of the season. His arm hurt, but more significantly, he was depressed. The World Series, between the New York Yankees and the New York Giants, started on October 4. Ralph knew at least eight of the players, and probably more, who played in the series. He'd been on teams with most of them, played against a few others, and, despite his aloofness when he had been in pro ball, counted a lot of them among his friends. Thoughts of what he might have been began to eat away at him.

"I was wishing they had got [the death penalty]," he said. "[Prison] might not be worse [than death] for a guy who never had anything, but imagine me pickin' up the paper every morning and reading about my friends; somebody doubled in the second and a guy you never heard of, who pitched with me at Toledo, wins twenty in the Coast League. I know exactly what town they're in, what restaurant they're going to."

Throughout his life, when Blackie got depressed he got into trouble. In San Quentin, a little bit of trouble just meant the loss of privileges until things got sorted out; more trouble meant "the hole."

You carried two plastic cards, a privilege card and an identification card. The privilege card allowed you to go to the canteen if you had any money coming in from anybody. It allowed you to go to the movies and ball games and the library, things like that. But if you lost your privilege card you didn't get anything. You got your meals, of course, but no extracurricular activity. The guards would stand next to the door going into the mess hall; if you needed a haircut or you were violating the dress code, they took your card. You knew which bull had your card, so you'd go get a haircut or straighten out what needed to be straightened and then go get it back. There was no going to the warden's office or anything, it was just man-to-man. Friday morning if you happen to get up and look in the mirror and think "I need a haircut and I want to see that movie tomorrow," you went and got a haircut. If you did what you were supposed to do, you just went back to the bull and he'd give you your card.

It was simple. You knew you could do this or that and exactly what the consequence was going to be. One thing might cost you five days in the hole; another is going to cost you ten. [Having] any kind of weapon is going to cost you thirty, the maximum. You know all this from the start.

After Warden Duffy got rid of the dungeon, solitary confinement in the hole wasn't as terrible as it used to be. "It wasn't a hole really," Blackie, who was sent there on several occasions, recalled, "it was bright and airy. It was a cell, there's no doubt about that. You sat on the floor all day; you got a mattress from six P.M. until six in the morning and just two meals a day. But as far as Devil's Island or something, it wasn't that."

Mostly the hole was boring. The Bible was the only thing to read, there was no radio, no visitors, no mail, and the food, while nutritious, was deliberately no better than merely utilitarian. Dinner was an extremely bland, chewy meat loaf. "Two or three days of the meat loaf meal are usually enough to improve the behavior of a man who likes to eat," wrote Warden Duffy in his memoir, "and the effect is likely to be lasting. If you ever have a guest in your home who pales if you merely mention the words 'meat loaf,' he could be a San Quentin grad."

The prison was going through a lot of changes in late 1951. Warden Duffy left to take up an appointment with the state Adult Authority Board. Five years later he became the president of a foundation to help ex-convicts when they got out of prison and also went on several national and international tours to speak against capital punishment. In 1954 the movie *Duffy of San Quentin* was released. Duffy was played by Paul Kelly, who had been an inmate at the prison for a little more than two years in the late 1920s after he beat to death the former boyfriend of his wife. The movie was shown, to great acclaim, in the mess hall.

The new warden was Harley Teets. He had a more bureaucratic, less personal approach to running the prison. He brought in more psychiatrists and gave the associate wardens more power over what used to be minor disciplinary matters that had previously been handled directly by the guards. Ralph, who had gotten along well with Warden Duffy and was liked by many of the guards, was rankled by the changes.

"All these namby-pamby gray-suited jerks started coming in," he said. "You didn't know where you stood."

By the beginning of 1952 the grim reality that he might spend the rest of his life in prison was beginning to sink in. Some days were worse than others. On the good days he threw himself into his work and into getting ready for baseball season. On bad days he could barely get himself to leave his cell and he would drink as much home brew as he could make.

Nell and his mother would come to visit when they could. Sometimes they'd bring Rich. But it was getting emotionally tougher for him to see them. It didn't take much effort to talk Nell into filing for divorce.

Baseball practice started on February 1 and the first game of the season was on the twenty-fourth. Three of the previous year's starting nine All-Stars had been paroled over the winter and the team had a hard time finding good enough replacements.

The Stars lost their first two games, although Blackie did strike out nineteen batters in the second of the two. Then they started winning again. Ralph took out his frustrations on his arm, throwing harder than ever, striking out twenty batters in one game, eighteen and nineteen in others. But then his pitching arm got sore and he spent most of April playing second base.

He pitched again on April 27, against the San Diego Naval Training Center Bluejackets, a team that included several players with major-league contracts in its starting lineup. He won the game, striking out thirteen and getting two hits of his own. But his arm still hurt and he went back to playing second base for most of May.

Blackie took the pitcher's mound again in a game on May 30 against a team from Fort Ord, the army base south of San Francisco. The army team had a record of twenty-five wins and one loss and their starting lineup included five major leaguers and four triple-A minor leaguers. They had another major-league player and a couple of other triple-A players in reserve.

In front of a crowd of 3,612 Blackie pitched a great game. In the sixth inning he got hit hard in the ankle by a bullet of a batted ball. But, said the report in the *News,* "the town's ace right-hander was tougher than a two-bit steak when the chips were down." Despite being in terrible pain, he stayed in the game, striking out twelve batters and getting three hits of his own off the opposing pitcher, Glenn Cox, who later played in the major leagues. The Stars won the game by a score of three to two.

Ralph started the game two days later, but with his ankle badly swollen and tightly bandaged, he didn't last long. Before leaving the game, however, he did get a hit, bringing his batting average up to .400.

A week later, his ankle feeling better, he pitched his second no-hitter. This one was a gem, a perfect game in which no opposing player reached first base and he struck out nineteen batters. "Didn't even break into a sweat," he told the *News.*

On July 11 Nell filed for divorce. Her attorney was David Silverton, who had been Ralph's lawyer during the murder trial. The complaint stated that there was no community property and requested that Nell be given full custody of Rich.

Baseball season ended in November and the Stars and Blackie had chalked up their usual impressive statistics. The team had twenty-nine wins, eight losses, and one tie for the season. Ralph won thirteen games and lost five. Pitching 163 innings he had struck out 261 batters, he had an earned run average of 1.55, and had the second-highest batting average on the team at .377.

On the same day that the *News* published the season's final statistics, exactly three years and a month after the murder of Dr. Buge, Nell was granted her divorce. Blackie hadn't contested it.

Nell, and on occasion his mother, had been his only visitors. No one else came on visiting day. "My Dad had gotten pissed off when it happened," he said. "He was a big man in construction with Broadway department stores. And my uncle was vice president in charge of personnel with JC Penney. They'd been braggin' for years, 'my son, my nephew the baseball player,' now it was 'my nephew the killer.' None of them took it too well." Blackie was truly alone.

He did see his old grade school friend and crime partner Ted Gardner, although they didn't speak. Hardly anyone spoke to Ted. Inmates who had testified against other inmates were not popular and the prison grapevine was very effective in letting everyone know who was who.

"I saw him on the yard, I saw him all the time," said Ralph. "He knew he was going to get killed, so he spent all of his time leaning against walls."

By 1953 Ted was still alive, but he wasn't looking healthy. "He was real skinny and he had a big patch on his neck. A guy who worked in the hospital told me he had Hodgkin's disease. I said, 'Whatever that is, if it hurts I'm glad.'"

Ralph was convinced that a friend had done him a "favor" by giving Ted the disease. "The guy that ran the lab in the hospital was a psycho convict who had killed his whole family. He was a homosexual and he had a crush on me. I never had anything to do with him, but I used to go up there because he'd give me straight alcohol, put it in grapefruit juice, and I'd have a little touch. He had seventeen years in then and he was only about thirty-four. He was never going anywhere. But the lab had gotten a culture of live Hodgkin's bacteria to study. So this guy would call my crime partner up there for a blood test and he'd geeze him full of the bacteria."

Hodgkin's is a type of cancer of the lymph nodes and even today no one is quite sure what causes it. Like almost all cancers, however, it is not contagious or infectious. Although it is theoretically possible, it seems highly unlikely that Ted could have developed the disease thanks to an injection of malignant cells. Still, Blackie was not unhappy to see his old friend wasting painfully away.

Baseball season got under way on March 1 in 1953. The big news was that the San Francisco Seals, a very strong Pacific Coast League team, was scheduled to play the All-Stars on March 20. The Seals roster included seven former major-league players and some of the greatest big-league prospects in California. Joe Dimaggio, Willie Mays, Lefty Grove; three of the greatest players in the history of the game had all once played for the Seals.

The *News* came out the day before the game with a large front-page headline of "Red Carpet Rolled Out For Seals' San Quentin Diamond Appearance." A two-column-wide cartoon just under the headline showed a befuddled-looking seal holding a bat and watching as a fastball zips past him. It was an obvious reference to the All-Stars' fireballing "Slick" Schwamb.

That day the prison was humming with the discreet sound of wagers being laid. Inmates were betting everything they had, not just on who would win, but on how many Seals Blackie would strike out, the point spread, scoring on an inning-by-inning basis, and any other variation that was open to disagreement. Fights broke out between skeptics who were betting on the visitors by a six-run margin and All-Star boosters and players who were more optimistic.

The San Francisco Bay Area was suffering one of its longest droughts on record, but the inmates started closely following the weather. The 1:30 P.M. bulletin said, "probable showers . . . Seal game in doubt." The 3:30 bulletin said, "probable rain . . . Seal situation fluid." At 6:30 the news was, "light rain . . . tomorrow Seal visit now liquid." On game day the inmates awoke to a weather bulletin issued at 12:01 A.M. that finished up, "abandon ship!" The biggest game of the year, the biggest game in the memory of any prisoner, had been rained out.

"It would be an act of flagrant deceit to attempt to conceal the collective disappointment of 5,000 men who watched, with mingled chagrin and resignation, the pelting rainfall," said an editorial in the next issue of the *News*.

"On the day of the 19th, an undesirable, unpredictable nimbus formation with a cruel sense of direction chose that untimely moment to loose the gate valve of its atmospheric tear ducts directly over San Quentin's short center field.

"It was not a 'little white cloud.' It was a complete gloomy overcast that matched the mood of the inmates. We hope the Seals won't abandon any plans for future visits to our shores as a result of the unseemly conduct of the weather."

Whether or not the Seals would try for a return engagement, no one wanted to count on being there for it. "They had to refund all the tickets because no one wanted to admit they would be around to use their tickets if the Seals agreed to make it next year," wrote a columnist in the *News*.

Baseball, more than most other activities, was important to the inmates. It provided them with one of their few outlets for a sense of, and the occasional expression of, freedom. The editorial that had voiced disappointment in the cancellation of the game against the Seals, also read:

> We use that weekend opportunity to blow off accumulated steam. Under the auspices of Baseball's unwritten "Bill of Rights" we assert our guarantee to disagree with anyone in the park, and most specifically, the Umpire.
>
> The world of the died-in-the-wool fan, the true professional and the simon-pure transcends prejudicial considerations as individuals discover a common affinity in the pleasure of the game.
>
> Remembering freedom . . . a majority of the men perched on the lower-yard bleachers, listening for the called strikes, experience a sensation of verisimilitude. A day at the ball game . . . inseparable from a moment of fun, whether it be in San Quentin or Ebbets Field [ballpark of the Brooklyn Dodgers].

Despite the heartache of the rained-out Seals game, baseball season continued. It wasn't the team's best year. Ralph was pitching well, averaging more than ten strikeouts per game, and giving up very few earned runs. The Stars, however, kept losing. They weren't hitting well and in the field they were making huge numbers of errors.

At the end of May the team lost Blackie. He injured his right elbow while pitching against the San Luis Obispo army post. He'd also hurt his ankle earlier in the year during a basketball game. He was out for the rest of the year and very frustrated.

The only highlight of the season came in June when three inmates, who were working on a construction project in right field, escaped over the wall during a game. They didn't get far before being caught.

By November Ted was fading fast. "There was a lieutenant who had a lot of faith in me," said Ralph. "He knew that I didn't belong there. He took me up to the hospital and said, 'I'm going to give you a chance to ask Ted to make a deathbed statement, to say that he lied [during the trial]. Maybe we can get you out of here.'

"But Ted wouldn't do it. He said, 'I've gotta think of my kids.'" Ted died at about nine in the morning on December 5 of complications related to his Hodgkin's disease. He was thirty-one.

Blackie's elbow and ankle had healed by then and he was playing basketball. He had been inactive throughout the summer and fall, so as soon as he felt better he started working out harder than ever. His efforts paid off and he became one of the best players on the basketball team. But then he injured his heel coming down hard from grabbing a rebound and was back out of commission.

He nursed his sorrows trying to get football approved for play. He'd always liked the sport a lot better than basketball, almost as much as baseball. It was an uphill battle. From the warden on down no one thought that a very rough, contact sport was a good idea in a prison.

Meanwhile, baseball season was postponed. The prison had received funding to clear away the remnants of the jute mill and build a new, larger recreation field on the lower yard. Baseball couldn't start until the construction was finished.

Finally Ralph won permission to write letters to try to get football equipment donated to San Quentin. The response from local colleges was good and at the urging of John Apostol, the supervisor of recreation, who had played the game in college, football got the go-ahead.

"I guess we had about thirty-five hundred guys turn out to try out for football," said Blackie. "It only took about two weeks, and about thirty broken legs, to cut that down to fifty. The program prospered." Football season was scheduled to start in late September.

Renamed "Coughlin Field" after Lieutenant Dan Coughlin who had really put San Quentin's athletic program on the map during the 1920s, the lower yard, freshly planted with grass, reopened to play at the beginning of August. The new field was better suited to baseball than the old one, and had a lot of new, more comfortable bleachers for spectators. But, long and relatively narrow, it was even better suited to football.

The All-Stars had sharp-looking, new black-and-white uniforms with numbers on them for their delayed season opener on August 8, 1954. They also had a new name, the San Quentin Pirates. Blackie, wearing number twelve, pitched and won the first game, striking out ten. For the rest of the shortened season he mostly played the infield.

For the first time since he'd arrived at the prison, baseball games were not well attended. Everyone was excited about football and saving up their cigarettes, money, and favors to bet once that season started. Interest in baseball was so low that the final two games of the season were cancelled so that football practice could start early.

San Quentin's football team was also called the Pirates. It was coached by a young, ambitious lieutenant. "The coach got us in over our heads as to who we were going to play," recalled Ralph. "They had a semipro league out there, and they played everybody, all the colleges and others. These guys were all college football players who graduated and didn't make pros. In fact he had the audacity to bring in the Fort Ord team that had some [pro players] on it."

Blackie, the prison's star athlete, started out playing quarterback, the most glamorous position on a football team. "I didn't want to play quarterback, I wanted to play end. But they didn't have anybody."

In front of an even bigger crowd than had ever shown up for a baseball game, the football Pirates lost their first game, twenty-six to thirteen, against San Francisco State University's team. With his long, strong arms, Blackie threw the ball way too hard and too far. He was a lousy quarterback. For the second game the coach switched him to end.

In football, the end runs out to catch passes from the quarterback. Until recently, it has been a position that is usually held down by squarely built, quick, agile, and fast guys who are often as not shorter than the other players on the team. For someone of his height and build Blackie was remarkably quick, agile, and fast, but he was not solidly built. In his second game he blew out his knee. It was broken, he found out many years later, but he didn't know that at the time. Still, he was on crutches for five months and it was the end of his football career.

By the time 1955 came around he was more miserable than he'd ever been. The months of inactivity were driving him crazy. The football team had been crushed by all of its opponents. For the first time the approach of baseball season was not causing any excitement on the yard and he wasn't sure he'd be able to play anyhow. A lot of the guys he hung out with had been paroled, and a lot of new, younger, more violent fish were being brought in to the prison.

"I'd done five [years]," Ralph said, "and I was so sick of San Quentin, I couldn't stand it. The gamblers were starting to put pressure on me to dump games. They were getting so many kids in San Quentin, every time some seventeen- or eighteen-year-old broke a window [nearby], they were sending them to San Quentin and lettin' them run in gangs.

"I wanted to go to Folsom. You do your own time in Folsom. But they didn't like to send anybody to Folsom until they were thirty or thirty-five years old because Folsom's motto was, 'All you who enter these gates, abandon all hope.' I tried to go, but they wouldn't send me."

He began to take chances, making and drinking more home brew, gambling more, always looking for corners to cut, ways to make his time easier even if getting caught meant trouble. He got transferred out of his clerk's job.

"I worked in the icehouse and next door was the butcher shop," he said. "We kept food for the officers and the mess and I was stealin' meat from the butcher shop and cuttin' it up. I had made a knife to cut my meat with; it was never inside the grounds. It was hidden way up in the louvers. You had to climb up on a compressor to get it. Somebody snitched me off."

It's easy to make a knife in prison. It just takes a relatively flat piece of metal, like a file, and the patience to hone it into a blade against any available concrete. "They got crazy in the 1950s and used steel knives in the mess hall," recalled Ed Bunker. "[They were] regular table knives but they could sharpen down real easy. They weren't very big but you could make 'em real sharp."

"He got dirty, picked up with a blade," recalled John Moore. "When a prisoner is caught with a knife he is brought up on charges to the disciplinary committee. Usually they're guilty and are given twenty-nine days in isolation. By law you can give them up to thirty days, but they always made it twenty-nine. After he gets out they refer the matter to a district attorney who usually assumes that there is some problem, whether the inmate is violent or just trying to protect himself."

Ed Bunker doesn't buy Blackie's meat-cutting story. "I figure that he had some beef with someone, probably over gambling debts, and got it for protection."

Whatever the reason, in June, thirty days after he'd gone into the hole for possession of a weapon, Blackie was transferred by bus about a hundred and ten miles northeast to California's highest-security, toughest prison.

CHAPTER 22

THE DRIVE FROM SAN QUENTIN TO FOLSOM State Prison is deceptively beautiful. North and east through the inlets of the San Francisco Bay and into the southern reaches of the Sacramento River Delta. Past low-lying rich farmland crisscrossed with streams and irrigation canals. Into the rolling foothills of the Sierra mountains that begin gently just east of Sacramento. Up along the American River, the small country roads shaded by large, old California oaks. Past the entrance to the Folsom Lake State Recreation Area. Through the charming historic town of Folsom itself. Down East Natoma Road which is heavily forested on both sides. Left on Prison Road across a wooded stream, through gently undulating pastureland where cattle and deer feed in the same fields. At the final bend in the road, on a clear day you can see the snow-covered peaks of the High Sierras to the east.

The first part of the prison you see is the top of the southwest gun tower. A high turret sticking above a stone wall is garrisoned by at least one guard with a high-powered rifle. As you drive forward into the parking area the walls seem to rise in front of you, ancient looking, formidable. The prison was built in 1880 but appears medieval. A tall fence topped with razor wire surrounds the parking lot. There is a guard booth with a heavily reinforced arm across the road before you even get to the first of the two sets of heavy iron gates set into the two lines of three-story massive granite walls.

Folsom was designed for the inmates that San Quentin couldn't hold, those with very long sentences, habitual criminals, and incorrigibles. Before the 1920s, when the walls were built, Folsom had a reputation for particularly bloody escape attempts and riots. In 1920 three inmates hijacked a prison train and used it to smash their way out. Only two of them were captured. In 1937 an inmate carved a realistic-looking pistol from wood and took the warden hostage. The warden and two inmates were killed. Up until the year before Blackie got there, the guards would fire a full belt of ammunition from a large, tripod-mounted machine gun on the first day of every month. That helped to keep the gun ready and was also meant to have a psychological effect on the prisoners.

The machine gun was pretty much the only psychology they got. Warden Duffy's style of reform hadn't breached Folsom's walls. There was no guidance center for new arrivals. Inmates were locked up, and then for the most part left alone if they followed the rules.

"It was the end of the world," said Blackie. "It was all old men. Everybody was doing a hundred years. Nobody bothered anybody. Sure they had their homicidal maniacs, but they had their own prison, a prison-inside-the-prison with the snitches. So you went ahead and did your own thing."

They'd been playing baseball in Folsom since 1897. The weather is better there than it is at San Quentin, so they played year-round. There were far fewer other forms of recreation at the higher-security prison, so baseball was taken very seriously.

The area around Sacramento, which included Folsom, was a hotbed of top-notch semipro baseball. There were three industrial leagues, all of which had reputations almost as good as the leagues in Southern California for producing excellent major-league prospects and for fielding a lot of big leaguers during the off-season. The Sacramento Solons of the Pacific Coast League were not one of the league's better teams, but they still produced their fair share of major-league players.

Folsom's team was called the Represa Eagles. (Folsom prison is actually located just outside of the town of Folsom, in the smaller town of Represa.) The prison team played in two of the local semipro leagues, the Tri-County League and the Rural League, and regularly played the Solons in exhibition games.

Ralph, his elbow, knee, and ankle all in good working order, got to Folsom in late June 1955. He played in his first game for the Eagles about a week later.

"Ralph Schwamb, whose feats on the San Quentin mound are almost legendary, suited up and played a few innings at short and first and collected a hit before leaving the game," said the report in the *Folsom Observer*. "He hasn't played in a long time, but visiting teams are due for an unpleasant surprise, it is believed, when he gets in shape. Schwamb, himself, isn't doing any threatening. All he'll say is: 'I've heard a lot about the Eagles from the teams we've played at Q. I hope I can help a little.' He will."

A month later, having played infield in his first few games, Blackie pitched his first game for the Eagles. It was the first game he'd pitched in nearly a year. He was the winning pitcher, struck out fourteen batters, walked one, and got two hits. Three days later he struck out thirteen from a team made up of Sacramento Solons rookie players. The week after that he struck out eighteen in a game against the tough Vallejo All-Stars, with no runs or walks scored against him and a home run of his own.

He was happy to be in Folsom. Once more he'd got a job as a clerk in the athletic department, his cellmates were older prisoners who kept to themselves, he was healthy and playing the best baseball of his life. He kept winning all through the end of summer and into fall, seldom striking out fewer than ten batters per game. Ball games were on Saturdays and Sundays, but he was able to work out on the field five days a week.

It was not what is called a "pitcher's park." There was no grass, it was just dirt and sand and ground balls took crazy hops that drove fielders nuts. It was surrounded on all sides by the high prison walls and they weren't as far from home plate as any pitcher would want them to be. The farthest away was center field and it was no more than about three hundred feet, close enough that any good high school hitter could at least bounce a ball off it, if not poke one over it. The left field wall was a mere 266 feet from home plate, although Blackie liked to point out that at the Polo Grounds, home of the major league New York Giants, the right field fence just inside the foul line was eight feet closer to home. "It was like playing in a phone booth," he said. Most games were high scoring, with a lot of hits.

In late November Blackie pitched two one-hit games in a row and then on December 4 the Eagles played the Carmichael Firemen. Woody Held, an infielder with the New York Yankees, was the player-coach of the Firemen and they were a very tough team. Blackie threw the third no-hitter of his prison career. Held almost got a hit in the ninth inning, but a diving catch by the prison team's center fielder saved the day.

One of the powerhouses of the Tri-County League, the Firemen played regularly at the prison. "They couldn't get out to play," recalled Held, "so one time they'd be the home team [batting second] and the next time they'd be the visitors [batting first]."

Schwamb was a real nice guy. He was tough, had a good curve, he threw real hard and had good control, [which was a] good thing [because] being in prison [if you get hit by a ball] you don't want to get out of line and charge the pitcher or anything. There were some vicious criminals up there. He did say one time that he wished he was playing where I was.

I enjoyed going up there. You always got a good meal afterwards, chicken-fried steaks and stuff like that. They had some good chefs. We always tried to get the game over so we could go and eat. The prisoners didn't eat with us, just our team, the warden, and some of the guards.

I do remember one exhibition game when a bunch of us professionals went there to play. I got a double and was standing on the base when I noticed some commotion around the first base line. Apparently one of the prisoners in the stands got stabbed, and next thing I know they're carrying the guy past me at second base.

Cece Carlucci, who had umpired games in the Mexican league when Blackie played for Obregón nine years before, came to Folsom to officiate games from time to time. "They had one hell of a ball club," he recalled. "One day, it was funny as hell. In the first inning [the prison team] got its first batter on base. The prisoners were all there in the bleachers. The runner was this little fast guy and the pitcher tried to pick him off of first base. So some big prisoner hollered, 'Hey chucker, what you trying to do with that man, took the FBI ten years to catch that man and you trying to get him on one pitch.' Everyone busted up laughing."

A week after his no-hitter against the Firemen, Blackie beat the Solon Rookies again. It was his ninth win in as many official league games. He'd been averaging more than thirteen strikeouts per game and given up only six earned runs during the whole season.

There was a break in the season for Christmas and New Year's and then after a few games in January and early February of 1956, the Eagles won the championship of the Tri-County League with a record of thirteen wins, one tied game, and no losses.

Bill Collins, the sports editor of the *Sacramento Bee,* was in the crowd for the last game of the season at the prison. He'd seen plenty of baseball played at all levels. After the game he told a writer for the *Observer,* "I had heard that you had a good team up here, but this, this is more than I bargained for. These fellows are all good ballplayers. And there is no denying it, Schwamb is outstanding. He has poise on the mound, his speed is terrific. I have never seen better control. And to go with it all he has that curve that makes a batter break his back trying to hit it."

George Barnes, the Eagles' left fielder and third baseman, had led the league in batting with a ridiculously high .510 average. Ralph finished the season having won eleven games and lost none, striking out 154 batters and walking seventeen, with an earned-run average of 0.656 and the second best batting average, .447, on the team. Barnes won the trophy for most valuable player in the league that year. Blackie, by an overwhelming majority, was voted the best pitcher in the league.

There was about a six-week break before the Rural League was scheduled to open at the end of April. The Eagles were considered a strong contender for the championship.

During the break the *Observer* picked up some new reporters for its staff. On March 29 they were announced in a column on the front page:

> A victim of the draft was Ralph Schwamb. He will be the *Observer's* new Sports Writer. Neither in Represa nor in any area compassed by the Tri-County League does Ralph "Slick" Schwamb need an introduction—he is THE Schwamb, the wizard pitcher!
>
> But perhaps some of the readers are not aware that Schwamb is as much a hot number in the writing field as he is on the pitcher's mound. Well, he is! He can shoot over a sports story with as much live steam as he puts onto a ball when he sizzles it over home plate!
>
> It happened that Schwamb already had a job-assignment—Clerk of the Athletic Department. However, at length he was persuaded to handle both chores. This arrangement should be of advantage to the readers—they will get sports news straight from the horse's mouth.

Blackie's first column, called "Shorts in Sports," was on page four of the March 29 *Observer*. He covered everything from wrestling and boxing to horseshoes and softball. He'd always enjoyed writing and his style was well appreciated by his readers.

Under the subhead "Wrestlers," he wrote:

> 'Jarrin' John Thomas, the athletic department's chief grunt and groan-ologist, tells us that his lusty crew are doing a fine job of attempting to rend one another limb from limb in the hope of winning a spot on the July card.

The wrestling picture will brighten considerably any day now as cauliflower alley is about to be presented with a new mat. This will be received happily by all concerned, as the old mat is so thin in places that Mother Earth has been taking a terrific beating lately with the bouncing of so many heads upon her none too spongy contours. With the arrival of the new mat there will be plenty of room for men, especially those with a touch of mayhem in their hearts, who would like to get into this program. Just drop up to the hill and see John. If you don't know him, just look on the mat—that's him—the monster trying to braid somebody's legs!

Wrestling and boxing were both very popular in the prison. So was softball.

The Represa Hawks were the prison softball team. They played on Saturdays during the summer and, like the baseball Eagles, were also a powerhouse in their league. In 1955 they'd beaten the California state championship team, Coca-Cola, in both games that they'd played against it. If the Hawks had been able to leave the prison to play in the tournament, they almost certainly would have been the state champs and represented the state in the national championship.

Ralph wasn't much good at softball, but he enjoyed playing. "I never could hit a softball," he said. "I had a terrible uppercut. But they had a real A-number-one softball team. They had a great pitcher. We played some fine outside teams. In 1956 they held the world championship in Sacramento and the winners, Raybestos of Connecticut, came to [the prison] to play a game. We tied them one to one."

In his job as the clerk of the athletic department, he was keeping up his contact with Frank Kneilly, the general manager of the sporting goods supplier in San Francisco. It was one of the few things that gave him much hope for the future. "Over the years I'd given him an awful lot of business," Blackie said. "And we more or less had an unwritten agreement that if I got out in a reasonable period of time, he would take me into his organization, because he knew I had purchasing down pat."

Ralph was upgrading the prison's athletic equipment and the playing field itself was also getting a makeover. Between the end of the Tri-County League season and the start of the Rural League, grass was planted and plans were drawn to build a backstop that would prevent foul balls from disappearing over the wall behind home plate, into the lower yard, and what was called the "Spud Yard."

The Eagles lost their first Rural League game, but the new playing field got rave reviews from both teams. Then they picked up steam and it seemed like they couldn't lose after that. When he was healthy, Ralph was, as usual, mowing down opposing batters. But in June he pulled a muscle in his groin. That healed, but then in mid-August he tore a muscle in his side. Folsom had a good team, but without him on the mound they usually lost their games.

Back at San Quentin, the Pirates were also hurting without Blackie's services. In his column in a July issue of the *Observer,* Ralph wrote, "San Quentin recently opened their season with a twenty man squad, averaging about 25 years of age, and were soundly trounced by the Oakland Old Timers."

The Rural League season ended on August 30. The team didn't win the league championship, in part because of Blackie's injuries, and also an injury to George Barnes, their big-hitting outfielder. Once again though, Blackie led his league in all the pitching categories and also had a huge impact as a batter with a slugging percentage of .855, leading the league in both home runs and doubles. A little less than a month later he won his one-hundredth game in prison baseball.

The Tri-County League started play again in the fall and on October 28, the Eagles, without Blackie, were beat by Russell Brothers. Otto Meyers, the chief scout for the big league Washington Senators, was in the crowd. "When the contest was over," Ralph wrote in his column, "he was all agog. As the ball players stood around with bodies all atremble, Mr. Meyers nonchalantly pulled a contract out of his coat pocket, unscrewed the cap of his gold Papermate, and said, 'Well, I didn't see any prospects, but I'll give you a thousand dollars for your new backstop.' Actually, he was highly impressed with the team, and the field."

Ralph still held onto his hopes of one day making it back to the big leagues. Bill Rigney, who was managing the New York Giants, recalled that he got letters from him in 1955 or 1956. "[He was] telling me what a great prospect he is, how he's striking everybody out there in prison. I know some of the other teams got them too.

"Horace Stoneham finally came to me and asked me about it, like, 'Do you think we can sign this guy?' And I said, 'Are you kidding? He murdered a guy. Don't we have enough troubles on this team without signing a murderer? The newspaper guys would have a field day.' Horace had a lot of goofy ideas. But that's Schwamb. He could throw. My oh my, he could throw."

As an ex-major leaguer who corresponded from time to time with guys in the big leagues, Blackie was sought out by other prisoners for predictions about baseball. His opinions were always in demand from gamblers, especially around the World Series. Baseball, with its long season and games without time limits, is probably the hardest of all sports to accurately predict, but it's a long-standing tradition for columnists to try.

Ralph was no exception and in "Shorts in Sports" on January 6, 1957, he did no better or worse at crystal-ball gazing than most other sportswriters. In the American League he figured that the Yankees would win the league championship, then the World Series. They did win the league, but they lost the Series. He guessed Cleveland would come in second, but they came in sixth. He picked the White Sox for third but they came in second. And he picked the Detroit Tigers at fourth, which is right where they were when the season ended. His National League picks were: the Milwaukee Braves in first, Cincinnati Reds in second, and the Brooklyn Dodgers in third. The Braves did come in first, and then beat the Yankees in the World Series. Cincinnati came in fourth and the Dodgers did indeed wind up in third.

Meanwhile the Tri-County League season was frustrating. Blackie missed a lot of games. At the end of January, a short item headlined "Sports Writer in Local Repair Shop," took the place of his column in the *Observer*. He was in the hospital with a knee injury.

The Eagles didn't win the league that season. Besides Ralph's all-too-regular absences, five games into the season they lost one of their best other players. Blackie wished him farewell in his column: "Before the next issue hits the Yard, the Eagles will have lost one of their most popular and hustlingest ball players. Virg "Cowboy" Edes is again departing for another shot at the free world. Virg is the kind of guy that a manager wished he had twenty of. Will play anywhere and turn in a good job. Our very best wishes Cowboy, buy yourself a car and stay out there this time."

Despite the so-so season for the Eagles and Blackie's injuries, when it ended in mid-February he was once again given the trophy for most valuable pitcher. He'd only appeared in seven games, but averaged thirteen strikeouts per game and had an earned-run average of 0.837; the next best in the league was 3.465.

Blackie stopped writing his column early in 1957. Other inmates wanted the job and in prison it is never a good idea to hang on too tight to something someone else covets. He was getting a little tired of it anyhow, all too often it reminded him of how he had fallen from the big time to the little time.

His attitude was moderating, calming down. Technically he would be eligible for parole after serving seven calendar years of his sentence. It was rare that even the most reformed lifers were released that soon, but the evaluation process did get under way. In December 1956 he had been assessed by Walter Aldrich, a prison psychiatrist. The doctor reported, "This man has been here about 18 months and has done quite well. There is history of difficulty at San Quentin prior to this time. His attitude is good and he has no hostility toward anyone. Believe he is making good progress and should be seen again in six months." The doctor also noted that his health was much better than it had been on admission to Folsom.

Once the 1957 baseball season started Blackie stayed healthy, but the Eagles, at least during the first half, had only an okay year. Late in the season "Shaky" Horton, who had once played in the minor leagues, took over as manager of the team, and the Eagles became almost unbeatable. On September 22 they beat Sacramento Cartage, the County League champions, who had seven professional players on their team.

At the end of the year Blackie had won eleven league games and lost six, he'd averaged more than thirteen strikeouts per game, and was second on the team in batting with an average of .414. It was another impressive year and baseball people all over California knew about it through the game's very effective grapevine.

He underwent another psychiatric assessment late in the year. According to the report, his attitude had changed. Perhaps he was in a bad mood the day he met with Dr. Kirksey, another prison psychiatrist. Or maybe somehow the chemistry just wasn't right between the two men. But the doctor diagnosed him as having a "sociopathic personality, antisocial." In his report he stated, "Subject is quite self-centered and a bit presumptuous in presenting his case. He assumes the attitude that he is being unjustly or at least too severely punished . . . Concerning his job assignments at Folsom he explains that he does work which he likes and 'keeps his nose clean' and that is sufficient. It apparently does not occur to him that anyone else might think differently. He commends himself highly for not having had any disciplinary infractions recently."

The report concluded, "This subject could be considered for parole under close supervision when he has completed sufficient time for his crime. His present attitude is not a fortunate one."

At about the same time Blackie was on the shrink's couch, an event occurred that would make him even less happy with his life in Folsom. On November 3, 1957, Folsom's athletic coach Norman Smith was arrested for smuggling drugs, amphetamines mostly, into the prison. Smith was a civilian, not a guard, and the union that represented the guards had long wanted all the prison programs to be run by its law enforcement members. The arrest gave the union the leverage it needed to put a guard sergeant in charge of the prison's athletic programs.

The new coach liked softball better than baseball. More inmates could play and the balls and bats lasted longer, so it was cheaper. The next year there would still be baseball at Folsom, but there was going to be a lot less of it and the game would be phased out. Ralph was not happy about that.

His hopes, however, were high. He had technically been eligible for parole after serving seven years of his sentence. Even if he had a perfect good-conduct record, which he didn't, it would have been unlikely that he would have got out in January 1957, but 1958 was a different matter. It was his first real chance for freedom.

He had his hearing in December 1957 and was denied parole. But the board recommended that he be reviewed for transfer to a minimum-security prison. "I really didn't want to go because I knew that the rules would be so tight," he said. "I was so regimented then, after eight years of hard time in cells, and I hate dormitories. [In minimum security the prisoners slept in dorms.] [In Folsom and San Quentin] you'd get a cell partner, and if he was messin' up you'd talk to him, 'keep the place clean.' If he doesn't you bounce him off the walls or something. It's your business. But you get in a dorm and what choice have you got? You don't even think of throwing a punch. All the bulls talk about is, 'We'll roll you up.' That means back up [to Folsom] and there go your parole dates."

Ralph told the board that he would rather stay at Folsom, but in early March they sent him to the minimum-security prison at Tehachipi.

Steve, who didn't put a last name on his byline, was writing two columns for the *Observer*. In "Battin' 'Em Out" in the March 13 paper he wrote, "The mountain region surrounding Tehachipi will look somewhat dwarfed when Big Ralph Schwamb arrives in that part of the country. Slick Ralph has been the big man on the mound here since his arrival from Esque [San Quentin], and we say that a man of his ability will be missed by all lovers of the game, along with the team."

In the same issue of the paper, in his "Hot Stove Stuff" column, Steve reminisced about some of Blackie's greatest moments. "Big Ralph Schwamb, Represa's Ol' Reliable, was turning on the heat with his fast one. Ralph calls one particular pitch the 'bovinator,' and when questioned about it he cracked, 'I call it the herdsman because it sails past the batter in such a streaky manner.'"

Tehachipi is a dry, dusty town in a valley in the cattle- and sheep-grazing mountains that separate Los Angeles and Southern California from the state's great, agricultural central valley. It was just 125 miles north of home.

"I saw it as a way to get out quicker, so I went," said Ralph, who really didn't have any say in the matter. "They had a baseball team and they were in a good league. Bakersfield [the nearest city of any size] had a real good industrial league; they had some excellent ball players. We won the league but I didn't have any fun playing there, none whatsoever."

If an inmate made use of what was available, prison was a good place to learn a variety of skills. Figuring that he had a good chance for a job with Frank Kneilly when he got out, Blackie spent a lot of time studying marketing.

Another friendship that he had cultivated since he was in San Quentin was beginning to look like it might also pay off. Bob Hunter was a widely read sports columnist for the *Los Angeles Examiner*. He'd followed Ralph as a prospect throughout the late 1940s and then wrote a sympathetic story about him when he went to prison.

> We have all been in scrapes in our lives, bar fights and that sort of stuff. It just seemed to me he wasn't guilty of first-degree murder. Involuntary manslaughter, maybe.
>
> Anyway, I wrote something in a column, and Ralph wrote back from San Quentin and we became, pardon the pun, pen pals.
>
> I remember how well he wrote. And I liked his approach to life. He was a maverick, an outlaw, a colorful guy. It was a lot of fun getting those letters from [prison].
>
> We carried on back and forth in letters. I mentioned him a couple times in columns when there was a slow news day. It was kind of catchy, the exploits of the best pitcher in the penal system.

Hunter's occasional stories helped keep Blackie from being entirely forgotten by professional baseball. In late October 1958, just a month before his next parole hearing, he devoted his entire column to his imprisoned pal. Three months later the column was reprinted in the February 1959 issue of the nationally read *Baseball Digest,* under the heading "The Year's Most Dramatic Story: I Served My Time; Now I Want to Pitch Again!"

More than half the column was taken up by the transcript of a recent letter from Ralph to Hunter:

> To begin with I was convicted of first-degree murder in December, 1949, in Los Angeles and sentenced to life in prison.
>
> I now have served eight years, nine months and three weeks, and will be eligible for parole in January, 1959.
>
> I have been a member of special counseling groups for the past 18 months and honestly feel that I have a fine insight into my problem.
>
> Baseball-wise I have played ball for eight seasons in the institutions—San Quentin, Folsom and now Tehachipi.
>
> I have been named the most valuable pitcher in six different leagues, and have beaten independent Armed Forces teams made up of many ball players from the professional ranks.
>
> I am now 32 years of age, as of last August, and know I have lost something off my fast ball, but feel that I am now a much better pitcher than I was in the majors in 1948.
>
> Two years ago at Folsom I pitched a no-hitter against a team managed by Woody Held, striking him out three times.
>
> My over-all pitching record for the last eight seasons is 131 wins, 35 defeats, 240 walks, 1,565 strikeouts and a 1.80 earned run average.
>
> During the eight seasons, I played almost a third of the games at shortstop, and have led three different leagues in hitting.
>
> I was refused reinstatement into pro ball in 1957 by Commissioner Ford Frick on the grounds that he would allow no man on parole to play Organized Ball.
>
> However, I kept writing to him, and after his decision on the Ed Bouchee case, he told me that if I had legitimate offers from

professional clubs he would take my re-entry under further con-sideration.[8]

I'm sure now he will rule in my favor.

I was declared a free agent in June, 1955, and since that time have been in contact with many ball clubs.

In 1957 and 1958, at the time of my appearance before the parole board, the Sacramento club would have taken me at once. I will have no trouble hooking up with a team when the time comes for me to get my parole.

I want to thank all my friends on the outside who never gave up their faith, or lost confidence in me.

Sincerely,

Ralph Schwamb

His parole was denied again in 1958 for 1959. But a psychiatric evaluation on December 18, 1958, made a strong case for his release before too long. The report, by Tehachipi's staff psychiatrist Ralph Varne, stated, "Examination revealed a rather gaunt, friendly man. He has a dynamic type of personality with evidence of much drive which up until the past year or so has been poorly controlled and directed. Currently he appears to have considerable insight into his basic diffi-culties. He appears to have received the maximum benefit of his pres-ent incarceration. Fair prospects when released for overcoming the obstacles presented by his basic personality and a dependency stem-ming from his extended incarceration."

In the spring of 1959 he once more went before the parole board. Along with the most recent psychiatric evaluation and above average work grades, he had a job offer to work as a warehouseman and driver, at $420 per month, for the Pacific Cement and Aggregate company in

---

[8] Bouchee, a first baseman for the Philadelphia Phillies, had spent the first three months of the 1958 season in jail in Washington state. He was allowed to rejoin his team as soon as he was released.

Sacramento, which fielded a good semipro baseball team. He had $80.88 in his prison trust account, which wasn't a lot, but along with his release money was considered enough to get him an apartment when he got out. This time the board set a date for his release. He wrote to Hunter, who published some of the letter in his column on May 23, 1959.

> We have new uniforms this year and they really are sharp. They have the Yankee pin stripes. All the accessories are black, too. Now all we need is for a few ball players to show up.
>
> We haven't been able to even go out and get in a little throwing lately. I feel it would be better just to sit still instead of throwing and coming up with a sore arm . . .
>
> Last Wednesday I went to the hospital to get the tattoos taken off my right hand. They will be healed in another week. I'm sure glad it's over with. I have no tattoos showing now as long as I wear long sleeves. A guy is sure foolish when he is young.
>
> The board has reviewed my case in regard to getting a time cut, but have informed me that first-degree murder convictions, and crimes with excess violence, are not eligible, so now I have 227 days to go. Ain't nothin'.

He also had high hopes for a comeback in baseball. A prerelease evaluation at the end of October 1959 reported, "Schwamb still has some desire to play professional baseball. Bob Hunter, of the *Los Angeles Examiner,* has been interested in his release program, although they have never met, and has contacted Ford Frick regarding possibilities of being reinstated. It is also verified that Tommy Heath, manager of the Portland Baseball Club, has recently expressed interest in offering Schwamb a spring tryout in coast league baseball. Schwamb is quite interested in trying to get back into professional baseball, but if his efforts in this direction prove fruitless, he is quite content to go along with his job offer as shown with the Pacific Cement and Aggregate Inc. Apparently he is beginning to make progress in some critical self-examination of his personality conflicts."

By the end of the year everything was falling into place for his release. Hunter had helped him get a job as a clerk with Ted Bentley Productions in West Hollywood. The job was only going to pay fifty dollars a week, so Hunter had also gotten Blackie an interview for a better paying position. A prerelease document makes note of the fact that he was to be given a tryout with the Portland team of the Pacific Coast League sometime around March 1, 1960, if he was reinstated in professional baseball by the commissioner. His proposed residence was with his mother in Hawthorne, not far from his old stomping grounds.

On January 5, 1960, at thirty-three years old, 3,741 days after he had last been on the streets, Ralph Schwamb was going to walk out of prison.

CHAPTER 23

H IS MOM AND HER BOYFRIEND PICKED HIM UP at eight Tuesday morning at the front gate of Tehachipi. The California Department of Corrections had issued him a sports coat, a pair of slacks, a shirt, a tie, and a pair of oxfords. "Obviously very cheap, but good enough if you want to go look for work," he said. They gave him $16.71 and he'd get another thirty bucks when he reported to his parole officer.

"We stopped in Mojave at a nice coffee shop for breakfast," Ralph recalled. "I was so tense, I felt like everybody was looking at me. But to sit there and look at a menu, to have hash browns and eggs, a piece of ham, two or three cups of coffee, and take your time . . . "

After breakfast they drove straight to downtown L.A. and met Bob Hunter in front of the *Examiner* building. It was about sixty degrees, sunny, and the air was sparkling clear because gale-force winds the night before had not just knocked down trees and power lines, but had blown all the smog out to sea.

Hunter went with Blackie to check in with his parole officer. The three of them then went to Blackie's interview with Vern Underwood, whom the parole officer, Lyonel Chew, described as a "millionaire sportsman and Los Angeles Turf Club vice president." Underwood also owned Young's Market Company, a chain of stores and the biggest liquor distributor in Southern California.

"He took me over to [Young's Market and] wholesale liquor and introduced me to the president," Ralph said. "It wasn't the greatest place to start me off, in a [booze] warehouse. I had my choice of working downtown at a liquor store on Central or down in Long Beach. I didn't want to work in downtown L.A. and start runnin' into ex convicts every five minutes."

Blackie took a job as a warehouseman in Long Beach that paid about a hundred and fifteen dollars a week. The job wasn't supposed to last long anyhow. Blackie had high hopes for his tryout with the Portland Beavers in March.

Chew was a little skeptical. In his initial evaluation he wrote, "Schwamb appeared cooperative although perhaps a bit demanding due to the royal reception offered him by everyone including his Long Beach employer. He was advised that he should continue his avowed intention of totally abstaining from the use of alcoholic beverages if he is to succeed in free society."

Whether he really meant to or not, Blackie also said that he intended to channel any publicity releases about his baseball comeback through his parole officer. The parole office had already received a call from the *San Francisco Examiner* trying to sniff out Blackie's home address, which he had asked the office to keep private. The office had also received a request from Paul Coates, a local TV personality, who wanted to do a half-hour show about Blackie. He wasn't interested.

After agreeing to show up for work the next day Ralph went to his mother's house in Hawthorne, not far from where he had grown up. He was going to stay with his mother until he could afford a place of his own.

Besides the invitation to try out for the Portland team, he also had high hopes for a job with Frank Kneilly and his sporting goods company in the Bay Area. He called Kneilly when he got back to his mom's house and according to Blackie Frank told him that he'd get back to him in a couple of days. Ralph figured that meant with a solid offer.

Early in the evening he called his friend Jimmy, who still ran Oliveri's, the bar that he had been in on the night that Ted and Joyce had shown up with Dr. Buge. "He said, 'Are you coming over?' I said, yes, much against my Mother's wishes. So I went over to Jimmy's and he'd got a hold of some five-hundred-a-night hooker from Hollywood. He had her waiting over in a motel on Crenshaw Blvd. I went there. There was a bottle of VO, ice, mix, and just a note, 'See you when you get here.'

"I got a good night's sleep. I was so keyed up I didn't do a goddamn thing. I romanced her a little, had two or three drinks, and just drifted off."

The Los Angeles Blackie woke up in the next day was very different than the city he'd left. He borrowed his mom's car to get to work. She gave him directions using the freeways that hadn't been there ten years before, but wanting to cruise by some familiar places, he took surface streets. He could still have taken the train, but not for long. The downtown to Long Beach Red Car was the last remaining trolley line in the city. It was rickety, slow, broke down a lot, and hardly anyone who didn't absolutely have to bothered to take it. By the next year it would stop running.

Almost no one took the train anywhere anymore. Boeing's 707 and Douglas's DC-8 jet planes were rapidly killing off passenger rail travel. According to an ad in the L.A. *Times* on January 6, 1960, American Airlines had four nonstops daily between L.A. and New York. The trip took just four hours and forty-five minutes and cost less than the train.

The *Times*'s headline story was about the end of the longest steel strike in U.S. history. It had been settled largely thanks to mediation by Vice President Nixon, who was also running for the Republican presidential nomination that year against New York's governor, Nelson Rockefeller.

Los Angeles was still construction crazy. In 1959, more than $650 million was spent on new buildings in the city, $90 million more than the previous year. And prices were going up. A small house in Ted and Joyce Gardner's old neighborhood cost somewhere around fifteen thousand to twenty thousand dollars. Apartments like the one that Blackie had left on that October night in 1949, were renting for about $150 per month and the neighborhood was now mostly black and increasingly poor.

The previous year the stock market had been more active than it had been since 1930 and electronics was where most of the action was. IBM stock had closed out 1959 at $437 per share.

Most people had TVs by then and only listened to the radio when they had no other choice, like in the car or for locally played ball games. The paper had a large section of TV listings. It was hard to find much of anything listed for the radio.

The sports pages gave him further hope of getting back into base-ball. Branch Rickey was one of the greatest, and most admired, men in the history of the game. In the 1920s and '30s with the St. Louis Car-dinals, he had revolutionized the minor leagues, creating a farm-team system to raise players for the major leagues. In the 1940s, then with the Brooklyn Dodgers, he had broken the game's racial barrier by hir-ing Jackie Robinson. At the end of 1959 he had decided to launch a third major league, the Continental League. It was a highly controver-sial move and organized baseball was fighting it tooth and nail. On the day Ralph walked out of prison, New York's powerful senator Kenneth Keating announced his support of Rickey's new league.

The new league was scheduled to start play in 1961. It would mean eight new teams with roster positions for 320 big league players and a lot more in the minors.[9]

Blackie, who always read the paper thoroughly, was no doubt amused to see the headline on the front page of section two of the *Times:* "Psychologist Finds 60% of Americans Normal—Introverts and Extroverts Balanced, But Most Don't Dare Be Themselves." The shrinks were everywhere it seemed, there was no escaping them. Dr.

---

[9] The Continental League never played a game. It was disbanded in August 1960. Rickey had threatened court action to overturn organized baseball's congressionally granted monopoly of the sport. The major leagues settled the matter by agreeing to accept four Continental League franchises into the American and National Leagues. The major league Los Angeles Angels and a new team of Washington Senators (the old team moved to Minneapolis-St. Paul in 1961) joined the American League for the 1961 season. The New York Mets and the Houston Colt .45s (now the Astros) joined the National League in 1962.

Klopfer at UCLA had discovered, according to the article, that "as many as half of all Americans suppress their natural urges."

"When I left, the only freeway in Los Angeles was the Pasadena," Ralph said. "When I came back there was the Harbor and the Hollywood and they were building some others. My dad told me to come over to dinner the second night I was out. He says, 'Here's what you do, you take the Harbor to the Hollywood, when you get down to the interchange be careful because you got to get over to get on the Hollywood side . . . ' Jesus Christ, I drove around like crazy. I should have parked and walked, should have called the cops and asked them to drive me over there. But I finally saw his off-ramp."

He spent his first week out catching up with his family. Nell had remarried, and her new husband had formally adopted Rich, but they were still in touch. "I was happy for it," Blackie said. "He was a fine man and I didn't want to cause any problems."

The Sunday after he got out, the annual football Pro Bowl game was in the Los Angeles Coliseum. Hunter got him a couple of good seats for the game and he took Rich. They went for pizza afterward. It was one of the very few times that he would see his son. Nell was happy. Rich was happy. There had been too much neglect and pain in the past. They didn't need or want Ralph back in their lives.

His mother, Janet, was delighted to have him out and back in her life. A month after his release she bought him a green 1953 Plymouth and he was given permission to drive by his parole officer.

The job went well for a little while. It was boring work but it was so good to be out of prison that anything was fine. Besides, he thought, it was only for a short time until some of these other things came through. "I got along fine," Blackie said. "Everybody just accepted me right off. I was going great, but if you wanted a bottle you just took it, put it on breakage."

He drank moderately at first. After all those years with just a bit of home brew to tide him over, Blackie couldn't hold his liquor like he used to. Not that he ever had it under control, but he didn't used to get so drunk, so fast. Then he got a letter from Frank Kneilly. The sporting goods company wouldn't hire him. "That didn't help my psyche," he said. "I wasn't the most stable person. Before long I found myself going home with a quart of vodka one night, a quart of whiskey the next. I never did get fired. I saw I couldn't handle it and those people were so good to me. So I went and talked to the general manager, and told him it just wasn't working out."

He was still planning to join the Portland team in March and thought that he'd go up to Sacramento before that. He knew a lot of people around the state capital from his time at Folsom. He figured he could pick up some money and get in shape playing semipro ball, he had a standing offer from at least one team, and it shouldn't be too tough to find a job.

His parole officer was not happy. He had quit his job without permission, or even giving notice. A parolee has almost no rights and must get permission from his agent to do almost anything other than the basics of day-to-day life. Chew told him to sit tight and wait to hear from Hunter, who was trying to get Blackie set up to pitch batting practice for the Los Angeles Dodgers.

The Portland team changed its schedule and now wasn't planning to be in L.A. until April, but they were still expecting Blackie to try out and make the team. In the meantime Hunter and Chew were arranging for him to work part-time for Young's Markets, and the Dodgers had accepted him as a batting practice pitcher. He'd agreed to that, then he got some bad news.

Blackie's reinstatement to professional baseball had been vetoed by George Trautman, the president of the National Association of Professional Baseball Leagues, the group in charge of all minor leagues. Trautman insisted that Blackie serve at least one year's probation in something less than fully professional baseball.

According to Blackie, Ford Frick, the commissioner of baseball, gave him the bad news personally. "He says, 'You're all set to go to Portland in the Coast League?' I said, 'Yeah I'm really excited about it.' He says, 'Well here's what I'm gonna do, I'm gonna put you on suspension for a year. We just want to make sure you're ready for baseball.'"

Blackie was despondent. He told Chew that he didn't want to pitch batting practice because the money was lousy and it might also peg him as a has-been.

Chew was more understanding than a lot of parole officers might have been. He called Frick and they talked the matter over. They came to the conclusion that Blackie would be better off playing semipro ball for the year, so that he could remain active and also be seen by scouts for the professional teams. Frick put that in writing to Chew for Blackie's case file.

With his parole officer's permission, Blackie went to Sacramento the first two weekends of April to pitch for a semipro team managed by Allen Simis. He won all his games and Simis also helped him get a job offer from Ted's Fire Equipment Supply Company. On April 26 his request to move to Sacramento was accepted and Chew told him to move up there to start his job and residence as soon as possible.

Despite his efforts to help him, Chew did feel it necessary to warn the Sacramento parole office in a report about its new charge. In his transfer report the Los Angeles parole officer wrote that Blackie seemed to think he was a special case who didn't need to conform to the parole requirements, that he was continuing to drink to excess, and that he was not above lying to his parole agent. He recommended that he be kept under close observation.

Blackie had already got off on the wrong foot with his Sacramento parole officer by missing meetings and showing up a day late from a trip back to L.A. At the end of May he disappeared. His new parole officer, Wilmer Leon, sent a teletype to Chew saying that Blackie had violated parole.

Chew found Blackie getting into his car in front of his girlfriend Irene's house. He said he was planning to drive back to Sacramento. He hadn't asked for permission to visit L.A. because he had been afraid Leon might refuse to let him go this time.

He ended up in the Los Angeles County Jail. Parolees need permission to leave the area of their parole. Leon, saying he didn't know what to do with him in Sacramento, asked Chew to keep him in L.A.

While Blackie sat in jail, Chew looked into his prospects in Los Angeles. Allen Simis had called to say that he very much wanted Blackie to continue pitching on weekends for his semipro team and that he could also provide a full-time job during the week. Chew spoke with several baseball people, and they all said that if Blackie didn't keep pitching in Sacramento it would destroy his chances for a comeback in the pros the following year.

The L.A. parole officer was also concerned about Ralph's social life. He'd been hanging out with several other ex-convicts as well as several of his old gangster buddies. To top it all off, his girlfriend, Irene, was married. Her husband was away in the military.

After three weeks in the L.A. county lockup, Blackie was sent packing back to Sacramento.

He failed to land any of the jobs that his parole officer had been told he was going to start and ended up working as a cleanup man and janitor at the Bob-Les Bar, which also had a semipro baseball team. Leon, the parole officer, was not at all pleased with his being employed in a bar and suspected that Blackie's baseball friends were more interested in the welfare of their teams than in the parolee's well-being.

Blackie also kept moving around and failing to get permission for the moves or even to inform his parole officer. Leon finally tracked him down where he was shacking up with his latest girlfriend, Nancy Black, and her seventeen-year-old daughter in a one-bedroom apartment. Leon made him move out to a residence hotel near downtown.

He felt like he was being hounded by his parole officer and that he didn't deserve it. At first he figured he was getting along just fine.

There'd been about six companies up there who wanted to take me when I got out, to play for their baseball teams. So I had no trouble. Almost all the teams were owned by bars in north Sacramento. It was nothing to see $2,500 to $3,500 bet on a ball game. I was making $600 a week, pitching Wednesdays and Sundays. I just kept drinking and playing ball. I was working a little construction, because the parole office made me do that. I had to have some kind of job. So I was working for a cement company, sittin' in the warehouse and playing cards all day.

I got out of prison the thing you're supposed to get out of it, that you're not going back. But I retained my temper for years. I had a hair-trigger temper. I didn't get into any [legal] trouble up there, but there were those kind of things where you walk into a beer joint and have a beer, a guy comes in, sits next to you and has a beer and sets his can down a little too loud for you or something, so whack. Or you look down the bar and a couple of guys are talking and one of them happens to look at you, so you go down there and say, "You have something you want to say to me."

He was a minor sports celebrity in the area. Not long after he had arrived in Sacramento, Bob McCarty, the sports editor of the *Sacramento Union,* wrote a column about him. Under the heading "Schwamb Facing Big League Test," the column's lead paragraph read, "You have to root for a guy like Ralph (Blackie) Schwamb. Victim of a bad rap, he took his lumps—10 years in prison—and now is trying to hurl his way back into society."

Blackie had pitched well in a county league game the day before, and McCarty interviewed him for his column. Attempting to rehabilitate his image, the interview wasn't strictly factual. According to Ralph he had stayed in the backseat of the car the night of Dr. Buge's murder and had only been sentenced to prison because he was along for the ride. Ignoring his other robbery conviction as well, he claimed to have never stolen anything. He sprinkled inaccurate statistics from his time with the Browns' organization, told a story about how he had voluntarily retired from Little Rock to play in Canada, and apparently he got the name "Blackie" because he reminded other players of Ewell Blackwell.

The column ended, "Primarily, Ralph Schwamb wants to be accepted by society and spend the rest of his days as a law-abiding citizen. He has a lot of well wishers—the rest is up to Ralph Schwamb."

But despite the well-wishers and his success on the semipro ball circuit, Ralph wasn't happy. "I couldn't get any good jobs or anything. I just felt sorry for myself." Whenever he tried to go straight, it seemed like circumstances always got in his way.

He wasn't drunk for a change at about eleven thirty on the night of July 18, 1960, when he passed through the bar of the Travelers Hotel on his way up to his room. At about midnight he called downstairs to ask the bartender to drop by his room after he got off work to pick up some letters to mail for him. The bartender, an ex-con named Jack Hapgood, thought his voice sounded odd on the phone. He asked a regular customer to go up and look in on him.

Al Cruz walked in on Blackie lying in bed, covered in blood, in a semiconscious state. Hapgood called an ambulance, which took him to Sacramento County Hospital, where they patched him up. The doctor's report read: "superficial lacerations on both wrists—mental depression—suicidal tendencies." The attending psychiatrist, however, didn't think he was likely to try it again. Blackie was enough of a local celebrity that the newspapers reported the incident.

Leon went to visit him in the hospital. Blackie admitted that it had been "a very foolish act" and said that he was sorry over the entire matter. In his report on the suicide attempt Leon wrote, "There is little doubt that subject was despondent, however, he did not do a very good job of cutting his wrists."

Blackie was released from the hospital just a day after he was admitted. He found a new apartment, in the same building as his girlfriend, Nancy, and he also landed a job with a local construction company through a friend of his father.

By mid-August Leon was becoming optimistic about Blackie's progress, noting in a report, that since his attempted suicide he was becoming more honest with himself and his parole agent and that he was beginning to make a good adjustment to his life on parole. They also had a "frank discussion" about Ralph wanting to live with Nancy. They did live down the hall from each other and the only thing maintaining the fiction that they weren't already living together was the fact that they paid rent on two apartments. The parole officer, however, said that he wouldn't allow a "common-law relationship" under any circumstances, but he would be willing to consider their request to get married.

Two months later Ralph and Nancy did request permission to get married and Leon gave it his blessing.

Originally from Idaho, Nancy was four years older than Ralph and twice divorced. They were married on November 12, 1960, at the Christ Unity Church just a few blocks from his apartment.

Meanwhile, it wasn't at all clear that Blackie really would be reinstated by professional baseball for the next season. There were apparently some indications that Frick was having second thoughts and that some of the minor-league team owners were dead set against it as well. Bob Hunter and Blackie started scheming over how to ensure his return to pro baseball.

Down in L.A., the new major-league Los Angeles Angels were getting ready for their first season. They were going to play in the old Wrigley Field, the longtime home of the Pacific Coast League Angels. The team wasn't getting a lot of good players from the other major-league teams, so it was holding open tryouts at parks around the city.

Ralph got permission to go to L.A. and on February 6, 1961, he and Hunter went to the Angel's tryout being held at Sawtelle Field, near UCLA. Bill Rigney was the manager of the Angels and they knew that Rigney knew Blackie and how good he was.

They were turned away. "They were nice enough," said Hunter, "but basically they said Ralph couldn't try out because he was an ex-con."

That made Hunter mad, madder even than Blackie who stayed calm because he had half expected it to happen. Hunter went back to his office and wrote Frick, who responded in a way that sounded like he had returned to his old hard line that ex-cons wouldn't be allowed to play ball.

Then Hunter remembered Ed Bouchee, who had played with both the Phillies and the Chicago Cubs the previous year and had been signed again by the Cubs for the coming season. While it was common knowledge that Bouchee had spent a few months in jail at the beginning of the 1958 season, what wasn't widely known was that he had been convicted on a morals charge involving underage girls.

"Baseball made a big effort to cover the whole thing up," said Hunter. "But of course all the sportswriters knew the true story. So I threw that up to Frick and Frick agreed that Ralph could play, if anybody wanted him."

A deal had been struck. Hunter continued to keep the Bouchee story quiet, and Frick reinstated Blackie.

Out in Ontario, California, about thirty-seven miles due east of downtown L.A., Hawaii's first professional baseball team, the Islanders, were just beginning to get ready for their first season in the Pacific Coast League. Tommy Heath, who had wanted to sign Blackie to Portland the year before, was their manager. Hunter and Ralph called up Heath who immediately invited Blackie to try out for the team.

After nearly twelve years, it looked like he was back in the game.

CHAPTER 24

I N 1960 THE SACRAMENTO SOLONS WERE SOLD to a businessman from Salt Lake City who got permission from the Pacific Coast League to move the team to Honolulu. Jet planes had made it possible, but it was still a long and expensive way to go for minor-league baseball teams. The other league teams would come to Honolulu to play only twice during the season. The first trip would be for the normal three, maybe four, games. The second time around they would stay for a much longer series.

If the other teams came to Hawaii the usual number of times a team would visit another city, the Islanders wouldn't have been able to afford to play. The only way that the league had agreed to a franchise in Hawaii was that the Islanders paid for the price difference in transportation between Sacramento and the islands. It was estimated that the team was going to have an airline bill of about $100,000 for the season, compared with an average $62,000 bill for major league clubs.

It cost the players too. It was a popular trip. Players' wives, who had seldom been enthusiastic about taking trips with the teams to Vancouver or Sacramento or San Diego, were happy to join their husbands for a series against the Islanders. But the teams didn't pay for the wives' tickets.

Spring training started for the Islanders on Tuesday, March 14 at John Galvin Park in Ontario, California. Ontario is a pleasant, small city at the western edge of San Bernardino County, just to the east of

Los Angeles. Like San Bernardino it is another railhead and shipping point for agricultural, and in more recent years, industrial products.

The team stayed at the Orange Hotel in the middle of downtown. Besides the players' rooms, the team kept a three-room suite on the second floor overlooking the entrance. With free drinks and smokes, it was by invitation only for the players. Players had to be in their rooms by midnight and got wake-up calls at seven thirty, but no one bothered to enforce the curfew all that much. There wasn't any nightlife around to keep anyone out much later than that anyhow.

"There really wasn't much in Ontario for a guy to do," said Jim Bryant, sports editor of the *Ontario Daily Report*, who covered the Islanders that spring, "other than look up the honeys. There were always girls flocking around at spring training."

Blackie arrived the night before the first practice. Nancy had stayed home in Sacramento and with all the available women around he took full advantage of being back in professional baseball.

When he wasn't with the latest girl, he was across the street from the hotel at the pool hall and beer bar. Blackie and the other players spent a lot of their off hours there. He'd always been something of a pool shark. Before long word got around and it became tough for him to find a game of eight ball with any of his teammates.

The Islanders were the top minor league club for the Kansas City Athletics. Since moving from Philadelphia in 1955, the As seemed to have taken on the old Browns' role as the perennial losers in the American League. (The Browns, having moved to Baltimore in 1954 and changed their name to the Orioles, were beginning to play very good baseball.) The first-year prospects for the As' top farm team weren't much better than they were for the parent club.

Roger Bowman, who was a year younger than Blackie and had pitched for five seasons in the major leagues, was the pitching coach for the team.

The owner wanted to get all the former major leaguers he possibly could so as to make Hawaii a gate-attraction. He didn't stop to think that the guys he was getting were all over the hill, and most of them weren't any good in the first place. So, we had a bad team. A terrible team. And to make matters worse, our major league working agreement was with the Kansas City Athletics, who at that time were the absolute worst team in the major leagues. At some point in the season the A's general manager wires our general manager and asks, "Who do you have who can help us?" And our guy wires back, "Help you? We can't even help ourselves." We had broken-down warhorses, a bunch of guys with a one-way ticket to nowhere.

As Blackie put it, "That was a riot. Every broke dick sucker in history came out of retirement to play in Hawaii. Guys that you hadn't heard of for ten years. I was a comparative youngster."

He worked hard to make the team. He'd been signed, but unless he performed well he could always be cut. The first intrasquad game, the thirty players in camp being divided into two teams, was scheduled for the first Sunday of training. Ralph was picked as the starting pitcher for "Hopkins Hulas," named for Tom Hopkins, sports editor of the *Honolulu Star-Bulletin,* who was covering spring training. The opposing team was called the "Borsch Alohas," and was named after Ferd Borsch, a sportswriter for the competing *Honolulu Advertiser,* who was also covering the training camp for his paper.

An article in the *Daily Report,* under the subheading "Tropical Talk," included the short item: "Those on the inside are pulling for Schwamb to make the grade."

"Everybody was cheering that he would do well," recalled Dave Thies, who was to become one of the Islanders best pitchers. "He had a demeanor about him that was very likable, no pretense. Once in a while I'd talk with him about some of the prison things and he'd tell me a little about this, that, and the other. He was trying to outrun his past though, so it wasn't nearly as interesting to him as it was to me."

Thies was one of the younger players on the team and for the most part the younger and older players didn't mix socially. Some of his younger teammates were leery of him; they'd heard stories, not just of his being in prison, but also of his wild days before that. Blackie spent most of his time with the older guys, the coaches, and the sportswriters.

"He and I got along great," said Bowman. "He was one funny man. I still laugh when I think of him in hotel lobbies, 'sizing up' people as they walked by or doing his impressions of Jimmy Cagney or Edward G. Robinson. [It was] very profane stuff, but very funny. He had worked up like a nightclub act. It was a baseball game in prison, with these famous actors as the players.

"He wasn't the least bit ashamed of his background. He found out that I had gone to Colgate [University], and told me he also had a degree, from 'the Big Q,' meaning San Quentin. He said if I would wear my 'C' letterman's sweater he would wear his 'Q' letterman's sweater."

Jim Bryant of the *Daily Report* had gone to junior high school with Blackie and Jim Muhe. They hadn't been friends when they were kids, but they enjoyed each other's company in Ontario.

Ralph was a very jolly fellow, a lot different than what I was expecting. We hit it off. So I invited Ralph to dinner and mentioned something about bringing my wife. He said that was fine, but he would feel more comfortable if I brought along a date for him.

No problem. There was a young lady who worked at the paper and she loved baseball. So Betty and I took her along, went to the hotel where the Islander's were staying, and then went to Vince's for a spaghetti dinner since Ralph said he loved Italian food.

Ralph and our young lady are hitting it off, and we had a very nice dinner and a lot of laughs. Ralph was a very funny fellow. He had these priceless stories about life in prison and all these goofy inmates he had known. A lot of fun. Ralph says that he'll pick up the tab. That was nice too since sportswriters don't make much money.

We were just winding it up and Ralph got up and said he had to use the men's room. Then this young lady gets up and says she has to use the ladies' room. Never thought anything about it.

The check comes, we are finishing up, all of a sudden Betty and I realize it's been ten or fifteen minutes. We wait about five more minutes, no sign of either Ralph or my coworker. So I go out to the cashier and she says, "Oh yeah. A tall guy? He left a few minutes ago with some dame."

I didn't see my coworker for about three days. [Then she comes back and] announces in the newsroom that the two of them are getting married. This is a big scandal by 1961 standards. Anyway, you kind of know the rest. Ralph is supposed to write her and send her a ticket to Hawaii and all that, and of course she never heard from him again.

Blackie pitched an okay four innings in his first outing. Nobody expected much of the pitchers that early in the spring. He struck out two batters and had pretty good control. He pitched again the following Friday, and again did merely okay, but none of the team's pitchers were doing all that well so it wasn't a big deal.

In his third outing, his first professional start against another team since 1949, Blackie pitched very well. In an exhibition game against the PCL San Diego Padres, he got out the first nine batters he faced. He only struck out one, but his control was excellent and the Padres never got a ball out of the infield. He pitched six very solid innings, giving up only one earned run. The umpire behind home plate for the game was Emmett Ashford, who had also umpired the very first semipro game Ralph had ever pitched.

Roger Bowman was impressed with what he saw. "Ralph was very much a competitor," he said. "And he really knew how to pitch. I don't know if they would have let him, but he was the only veteran guy on our staff I thought had a shot of going back up to the bigs."

The Islanders had been working out in the old Sacramento Solons' uniforms. On the Tuesday after Easter they put on their new colors for a team picture. "Gold socks, green pants, green cuffs, and gold long-sleeve sweat shirts," recalled Ralph, whose sense of aesthetics was violated. "You ought to have heard the ribbing we took."

That same day he pitched six innings against Dallas-Fort Worth, the tough triple-A farm team of the newly created Los Angeles Angels. It was a slugfest, in which all the pitchers on both teams were clobbered by the batters, but none more than Blackie. He maintained his cool under fire, but it was a bad performance. His previous appearance, as a relief pitcher, hadn't been much better. He needed to pitch a good game if he was going to stay with the team.

He started the game on Tuesday night, April 11 against the PCL Vancouver Mounties, who were considered one of the best teams in the league that year. Knowing that it might be his last chance, he came through. He pitched a complete game and was the winning pitcher, giving up just six hits and two earned runs. He walked two batters and struck out six. It wasn't the best game he'd ever pitched, but it was good enough that the next day the team offered him a contract at eight hundred dollars a month, plus his expenses during the season.

Nancy called Leon, Blackie's parole officer, to let him know the good news and to get his go-ahead for Blackie to sign a legal contract, something he couldn't do without permission, and then to accompany the team to Hawaii.

In a report written the next day, Leon stated, "Baseball has been his life and Subject has an insatiable desire to prove to himself whether or not he still can play in an organized baseball league. Whether or not he is successful, the most important factor is that he proves to himself his potential in baseball."

When the team's Pan Am flight left Los Angeles airport on Tuesday morning, April 18 bound for Honolulu, Ralph was on it. Nancy was with him.

Hawaii had become the fiftieth state less than two years before. It had long been a welcome stopover for sports teams and entertainers on their way to and from Asia, but it had never had a professional team of its own. There was a press conference at the airport when the team arrived. Nick Morgan, the owner, hiding a glass of bourbon and a smoldering cigarette under the table in front of him, answered questions, and then introduced Tommy Heath.

Heath just said, "It's the greatest spring roster I've ever seen," quickly introduced the team, then they all got out of there fast, anxious to start living the good life in a tropical paradise. "You should have seen the treatment we got," recalled Ralph. "[We were] on TV every day, we could eat anywhere we wanted to eat, do anything we wanted. Soon everybody's got a beautiful tan, we'd go to the clubhouse wearing shorts, loafers, colored T-shirts; everybody looks like they were born in Hawaii."

The Islanders played at Honolulu Stadium, just about a mile and a half from the beach. The rickety wood stadium had been built in 1926. *Honolulu Star-Bulletin* writer Tim Ryan, in a story about the stadium, quoted Larry Price, a local radio personality, as saying, "It creaked, actually creaked, like it was alive; [it was] kinda spooky." The stadium seated about twenty-five thousand people and had played host to high school football games, rodeos, polo matches, and hula festivals, as well as to Babe Ruth, Jesse Owens, Irving Berlin, Elvis, and evangelist Billy Graham.

The season opened against visiting Vancouver on April 20. Hula dancers in grass skirts and native drummers livened things up along the edges of the stands. Cece Carlucci, who had umpired games that Ralph had played in both Mexico and Folsom prison, was behind home plate and yelled out, "Play ball!" to get the game started.

Carlucci talked with Blackie a few times on the field during the first few weeks the team was in Hawaii. "He seemed kind of reserved," the umpire recalled. "He kept to himself. He remembered me from Folsom, so I wished him luck. He still had pretty good control, but not too much of anything else."

The Islanders won their first game in front of a crowd of 6,041. Ralph didn't play.

In Hawaii he was trying to live quietly. He spent most of his spare time with Nancy and was drinking moderately. "He was very quiet, kept to himself," recalls Ferd Borsch. "He was still trying to adjust I think. He didn't bring any spotlights on himself, trying to turn the corner. He kept his nose pretty clean with the Islanders, but he'd just been away from the game too long to pitch at that level."

Borsch, a careful writer with tremendous respect for the spoken and written word, was impressed with Blackie's manner. "He talked pretty well. He had a way with words. He could be a slick character, like a Ring Lardner type. He wrote well and could express himself very well. He had a good command of the language and could use it properly."

Ralph pitched his first regular season game for the Islanders on April 22. In four innings against Vancouver he was the losing pitcher, giving up six earned runs, walking two batters, hitting another, throwing one wild pitch, and striking out only two. After that disastrous start he pitched two good innings of relief in two successive games against Seattle and got back some of his confidence.

It was still early in the season, but with six wins and four losses the Islanders were off to a better start than anyone would have guessed. On April 29 Blackie started the game against the Portland Beavers. He pitched six innings, giving up no runs and only two hits and two walks. It was the first regular season, professional game that he had won since he was with Little Rock. The win moved the Islanders, at least temporarily, into first place in the league.

On May 1 the team played Seattle and he came within two outs of winning his second game. It was a lovely night in Honolulu—seventy-eight degrees, a light breeze—but only a small crowd of 1,423 fans came out to watch the game. He'd pitched a very solid eight innings, striking out six batters and not allowing any earned runs. The Islanders were leading by a score of three to one over the Rainiers. Blackie got the first batter out in the ninth inning. Then he walked the second. Then the third hit a home run and the game was tied. Blackie was sent to the showers. He'd pitched an excellent game. He hadn't lost it, but he didn't win it either.

"He disappeared for a couple of days without telling me," recalled Bowman. "I had to cover for him, which wasn't something I enjoyed doing."

Blackie caught up with the team in Vancouver, Canada, for the game on May 6. "It must've been twenty-nine degrees that night," he recalled. "We had an ensemble of hula dancers and their drummers.

Those broads didn't even have to move a muscle, they were just standing there shivering and shaking. They couldn't even move their feet, they were frozen. The drummers couldn't move their hands."

Maybe it was the cold, maybe he'd slipped into his old habits and was either drunk or hungover, but Blackie had nothing going for him in the game against the Mounties. He was called in as a relief pitcher late in the game. In two innings he gave up four runs on five hits, a walk, and a wild pitch. He was the losing pitcher.

The next day Tommy Heath called Bowman into his office and told him that word had come down from the owner that the team was going to release Blackie. Bowman, who didn't think he was pitching all that badly, figured that "this nut we had for an owner kind of got cold feet on the idea of having a murderer pitching for his team."

More likely, it was just a youth movement. It was, after all, the minor leagues, and one of the primary functions of a farm team is to raise a healthy crop of ballplayers who will go on to long, fruitful careers in the major leagues. Not far from turning thirty-five, even if Ralph did make it back to the majors, it wouldn't be for long.

Bowman and Nick Morgan, the owner, weren't on the best of terms. Just a few weeks after Heath asked him to tell Blackie he was being let go, Bowman was fired. A reporter had asked him what he would consider a successful first season for the Islanders. Bowman quipped, "If all the planes make it." Morgan flew out to Hawaii on a plane that made it, and gave him his walking papers.

Ralph and Tommy Heath had often enjoyed more than just a few drinks together. They got along well and it bothered the manager to have to let him go. According to Blackie, Heath gave him an extra three weeks on the payroll as a form of severance pay, but he asked him a favor.

"We were playing Vancouver that night and George Bamberger was pitching [for them]. George had been nasty for years in the Coast League and his kind of wet ones [spit balls, an illegal pitch] sailed up and in [at batters]. Our pitcher was going pretty good, but Heath pulled the third baseman, put our pitcher at third base, and brought me in to pitch to Bamberger.

"First pitch, I knock him down [throw a ball at his head so that he falls down to avoid being hit]. I was going for him, for Tommy. He comes runnin' out to the mound. I told him, 'Come on sucker, you're older than I am [by one year and twenty-five days], I'll break your ass.' So he went back. The second pitch, at the last second he dropped and it was so close, six inches lower and I would have got him right in the ear. So he comes out to the mound again and we had a little tussle. That was the end of my [season with the Islanders]. Tommy had the tickets ready for me [to go back to Hawaii and then home] and says, 'Go out and finish your tan.'"

CHAPTER 25

THE ISLANDERS SENT FOR REEVE "BUD" WATKINS, a nine-year veteran of the Pacific Coast League, to replace Blackie. Watkins had severely burned his pitching hand and couldn't throw the ball very well, but the team didn't know that until he showed up. He met Blackie only in passing, but he liked him.

"He seemed very jocular," said Watkins, "kind of a swaggery type guy. He liked to make fun of his checkered past and never tried to hide anything. I felt a little guilty about replacing him because he was trying to rehabilitate himself and make a comeback."

After Ralph and Nancy packed up and moved back to Sacramento, Watkins and Bowman were talking. "We knew it was going to be tough on him, being an ex-con and all that," recalled Watkins. "We felt sorry for him. I had an offer to pitch for a semipro team [the Potters] in Lincoln, north of Sacramento. So I contacted Schwamb and offered him my spot. The league had a lot of good ballplayers, pro ballplayers, in it. I got him together with the team's manager. It was pretty good money. They played a couple times a week on Saturdays and Sundays, and if you started a game you got $200, which wasn't bad dough back in 1961. I felt kind of good about myself, doing poor Blackie Schwamb a favor."

By summer Ralph had settled back into life in Sacramento. Nancy, however, had moved to Reno, Nevada. With his parole officer's permission he went to Reno to find work. His request to take a job tending bar was turned down and so he returned to Sacramento where he worked on construction jobs with his father. At night he was spending most of his time in bars and pool halls, hanging out with fellow ex-cons and sinking back into a lot of old, comfortable bad habits. Besides the Lincoln Potters, he was also pitching from time to time for Industrial League teams around the city.

Bud Watkins, who wasn't having a good year in Hawaii, hadn't given a thought to Ralph since setting him up with the semipro team. Then he got an irate phone call from the Potters' manager. "Where the hell is Blackie Schwamb?" asked the caller.

"I told him I had no idea," said Watkins. "So he says, 'That big SOB pitched a game for us, got knocked out of the box in the second inning, went in, cleaned all the wallets out of our locker room, and we haven't seen him since.' I guess they eventually smoothed it all out, but for a time I was worried that I might have to make restitution."

Things must have been worked out because everyone knew where to find Blackie and it wasn't back in jail. He continued working construction, hanging out in bars and pool halls, and pitching some evenings and most weekends. He was making a living and for the most part his life was stable.

The next spring the Islanders went to training in San Bernardino. They'd finished their first season in sixth place, out of eight, which wasn't as bad as it might have been, but it was almost entirely due to hitting. The team desperately needed pitchers. There was a new manager, Irv Noren, who had played eleven seasons in the majors, and a new pitching coach.

Ralph had played ball almost continuously since being dumped by Hawaii and he thought he might be able to make it back onto the team. He showed up in San Bernardino and asked Noren for a chance.

"He was out there working hard, running and batting practice and all that," recalled Noren. "He was there for a while and I gave him some meal money, things like that. One day he came to me and said that his legs were giving him a lot of trouble and he couldn't run hard. But he offered to do whatever I wanted. He seemed pretty good. I didn't have any pitching anyway, so I figured what the heck, if he can pitch we'll give him a shot. He threw the ball good and looked like he had pretty good stuff. He tried real hard but he just couldn't make it. He couldn't get himself in good enough shape."

It was Blackie's last try at getting into professional baseball. He went back to Sacramento, back to working on construction jobs with his father, back to the bars and pool halls and weekend semipro baseball and back to his fast-deteriorating marriage with Nancy.

In September Blackie lost his job when the company he was working for was shut down, its owners charged with embezzlement and contract manipulations. He quickly found a job as a salesman, working for commissions only, for Hammond Industries. The company, of course, also had a semipro baseball team.

Nancy didn't think he was doing well enough and started nagging him. It wasn't just Ralph who thought so. In his report of October 10, 1962, Leon wrote, "Unfortunately Subject's wife has taken on the attitude that Subject deserves more prestigeful employment and has been pressuring Subject to seek to obtain that type of employment that would satisfy her wishes. The irony of the situation is that Subject is not trained for an executive type job. This agent is working with the wife to help her recognize this fact and help Subject accept his limitations."

On November 13, 1962, Ralph and Nancy separated. She filed for divorce a couple of weeks later. The grounds were "extreme cruelty" due to "grievous mental pain and suffering." That isn't actually as terrible as it sounds, at least not necessarily.

At the time, in California a couple couldn't just get a divorce for the asking, there had to be "grounds" and they had to be significant. The wife citing "extreme cruelty" and the husband not bothering to contest it was the quickest and most commonly used way to get a divorce. Since there were no children or community property involved and Ralph agreed to pay all the court costs as well as Nancy's legal fees, the divorce was quickly granted.

Ralph's father had new contracts down in Southern California, so he moved back south to work. "There was some temptation to get back into collecting [for gangsters] but they watched me too close," he said. "They had me on maximum parole for ten years. They'd come to my house or I had to go see them or they'd come to my job. Two parole officers tried to get me locked up for drinking. And then every six weeks there'd be homicide dicks at my house. Somebody got their lights put out, they were beat to death, 'It fits you perfect.'"

Despite, or maybe in some odd way because of his womanizing, Ralph was a marrying kind of guy. He met Judy Norris[10], a twenty-six-year-old divorcee with three small kids, in the late spring of 1964. She worked as an assembler in an electronics factory near his apartment in San Bernardino. They were married on August 22.

Ralph, Judy, and the kids moved back up to Sacramento in early 1965. He felt there were better job opportunities for him there, and he had more friends in the area than he did in Southern California. At first he got a job as a bartender, but then soon found construction work. Leon, who was once again his parole officer, thought he was dealing with a changed man.

"Schwamb's second [sic—actually his third] marriage has been a stabilizing factor," the parole officer wrote. "He is now more realistic about his future and now gives evidence of planning for the future education of his children and maintaining his household. This agent has known Schwamb and supervised him on and off for a number of years and has noticed a great change in his attitude and behavior since his second return to Sacramento. He is happy with his employment to date and earns enough money to satisfy his needs. There is no indication of any serious emotional problems and contacts with Schwamb now are usually of a routine nature."

"I just kind of floated through the 1960s," Ralph said. He continued working on construction jobs with his father and also held a great many other low-paying jobs. For a couple of years he continued to pitch baseball on the weekends. He liked to tell a story about a game

---

10 Her surname has been changed to protect her privacy.

he was pitching against a team from the local sheriff's department. Just before he was about to throw a pitch, Ron Lacey, his friend and catcher, said to the opposing team's best hitter, "You know, our pitcher was in prison." The batter was distracted and missed the pitch.

"What for?" the batter asked the catcher.

Lacey waited until Blackie was in his windup to throw the next pitch and said, "Killing a cop." The batter just watched the next pitch go by.

But pitching was getting more difficult. "I started fooling around with a knuckleball," he said. "I had a great one, but I didn't notice soon enough that it would give me a kind of tight shoulder because I threw it straight overhand. I could make it break down. I just didn't throw one and dream, like most knuckleballers.

"One cold Sunday I pitched a doubleheader. I threw a few of the knucklers and won the first game. I didn't like the guy who was pitchin' the second game, so I told the owner, 'Hell I'll start it, keep this jack-off warm, in case I can't handle it.' About the seventh inning I threw a couple of the knuckleballs and got out of the inning. In the eighth I went out there and couldn't even raise my arm. I finished the game just goosing the ball up to the plate. But I could never get up there again. I tried, but I couldn't get anybody out."

His baseball life was behind him, but Ralph still craved attention. He never felt that he'd been rehabilitated by the time in prison, but he did think that his story might help discourage young people from making his mistakes. He also didn't want to be forgotten. In December 1965, *Sport* magazine published an article by the former New York Giants third baseman Hank Thompson, who was in prison in Texas for armed robbery. Blackie wrote to the editor about Thompson's article. "I feel the article leaves much to be desired because it is actually little more than a plea for sympathy, and this is something the Hank Thompsons and Ralph Schwambs do not need."

Ralph asked if the editor would accept an article from him and he was given the assignment. He worked long and hard on what was essentially his life story and sent it in. The sportswriter, Arnold Hano, was asked by *Sport* to rewrite the piece in the form of an open letter from Blackie to Thompson. Blackie wasn't happy about that, he liked his version better, but the article, still almost entirely his own words, ran in the August 1966 issue.

Around the time the article hit the stands, Blackie saw his son for the last time. Rich came to visit, they got into a fight, Rich walked out, and that was the end of it. They never spoke with or saw each other again. Rich could scarcely recall his father from when he was a little kid, before Blackie went to prison, but he had plenty of memories of how hurt and upset his mother had been. Losing the relationship to a scary ex-con whom he'd never really known wasn't much of a loss.

On November 10, 1966, Blackie lost his father. Chester Sr. had been living with his second wife, Edith, in Burbank for the past eighteen years. At the time of his death he was a construction superintendent for Union Bank. He died in the hospital of pneumonia, the end result of three years of emphysema, in large part brought on by smoking.

By the beginning of 1967, Blackie's new parole agent, Dan O'Leary, was impressed enough with his progress to recommend reducing his supervision from regular to "conditional." In his letter to the adult authority requesting the change, O'Leary wrote, "He now seems to have arrived at an understanding of himself and the world around him. He lives a rather quiet life, with wife and her two [sic] children with no evidence of any problems he cannot handle. He seems free of any criminal orientation, in fact this old ball player has joined the pot-belly-stove league."

But maybe he just had O'Leary snowed. Blackie had always been charming and likable when he wasn't drunk and he never drank before meeting his parole agent. He could come across as reasonably stable when he wanted to.

He was, at least to some extent, still up to his old tricks. "I've always been the kind of guy who could just pick up a buck," he said. "Not cheatin' or anything, just work at a bar here for some cash, win fifty bucks there shooting pool. If you wanted me you never called my house, you called the pool hall. I was a very good pool hustler, very good. I got a beer joint in Sacramento doin' it, two beer joints in fact.

I was a good enough pool player to pay the rent. They were never in my name; they were in my wife's name. You can't even tend bar when you're on parole, without their permission."

Leon, who was still involved with Blackie's case, was on vacation in August 1968 when another parole agent, W. H. Chapman, wrote an unflattering report that said, "Schwamb is a 'has been' who cannot accept his position in life of being an 'ex-con' with no saleable skills. A few offers of employment as an umpire in local sports have seemingly been beneath his dignity. These underlying feelings are thought to represent the crux of his problem with alcohol. Schwamb also has frequently associated with women of loose morals to which his wife objects strenuously. This action has caused considerable family disruption."

Back from holiday, in his next report Leon tried to correct the impression that Chapman had given, but by then there really were severe problems between Ralph and Judy.

One night in the late summer of 1968, Judy and he were having some drinks in a bar not too far from their small house. "And this guy comes in dragging Pat Bertelsman [from Aberdeen, South Dakota] with him. I hadn't seen her since they'd run me out of town. I just said, 'Hi Patty.' She wasn't quite that restrained."

Ralph and Pat reignited their affair and once again they weren't too discreet about it. Judy and Pat's husband were none too pleased. It didn't last all that long before Judy insisted, just after New Year's, that he move with her and the kids back to L.A.

They did, but in April 1969 Blackie was taken into custody for public drunkenness and Judy had had enough. She left him and in early October she filed for divorce. The complaint she filed asked for all the household furniture, furnishings, and appliances, the 1959 Oldsmobile (Blackie got to keep the 1959 Dodge pickup truck), all court costs and legal fees, and a restraining order to keep Blackie from "harming, molesting or annoying the plaintiff."

In November Blackie moved in with a new girlfriend, Jean Becker, who lived in Monterey Park, just to the east of downtown Los Angeles. Late in the month he cashed some checks at a bar then drove in Jean's

1963 Oldsmobile to San Diego with a friend. They got drunk, very drunk. He claimed to have woken up in El Paso, Texas. They continued east until they smashed up the car in Lake Charles, Louisiana. He returned to L.A. and was arrested on December 29 for leaving the state without permission and for having bounced the checks he had cashed.

They kept him in the county jail for a month then decided to let him out. Somebody paid the checks for him and he was given a severe reprimand. It was recommended that he be sent to a short term rehabilitation unit (STRU), but nothing ever came of it. He just walked back out onto the streets of Los Angeles. Jean even forgave him for wrecking her car.

"I just casually eased back into Los Angeles and was working for a concrete cutting company," Ralph said. "I had a nice little apartment, no ties, just sit by the pool, drink beer, and laugh and giggle."

It wasn't all giggles though. On February 6, 1970, he was drunk as usual and got into a horrible, screaming fight with Jean. He slashed both of his wrists again. Once more he didn't do a very good job of it. He was treated at a local hospital as an outpatient.

He spent most of the rest of the year avoiding trouble in L.A., working for the concrete company, hustling a little pool, seeing Jean sometimes, and picking up the occasional woman in any one of three neighborhood bars he spent time in. Then in the fall he heard from Pat.

> I'll never know how she got my address but I got a letter; her husband was beatin' her up. So I called her a couple of times and suggested that she leave him. Anyhow, what could I do?
>
> I had to go up and do a job in Oakland, so I decided to drive through Sacramento. I called Pat and met her at her house. I asked her what she wanted me to do and she told me, "I want him out of here, this house is mine, not his." So I gave him about a half hour to pack his clothes and take it down the freeway.
>
> I ended up staying there four days. I was supposed to have been in Oakland three days before, so I was fired. I moved in with her.

> She was three years younger than me, but she'd had bypass surgery a year before. One morning in early December she woke up and said, "I hurt, I hurt." I held her and she was ice cold and she just died there in my arms. I really went to pieces.

Yet again life had belted him right in the kisser just about the time he was figuring he might be happy.

Pat's oldest son was a marine. He had a gun collection that he kept at her house. About a week after Pat died Blackie took a 9 mm Luger, the same type of pistol that he had tried to sell to Ted Gardner twenty years before, got in his truck and drove to Los Angeles.

"I just drove around and sat in the car at night in parks and drank," he said. "I thought 'Bullshit, I ain't goin' anywhere, do myself in.'"

At 5 P.M. on December 30 Blackie showed up at his ex-girlfriend Jean's job as she was getting off work. He told her that he wanted to talk. They got into her car and as she was driving them to her house he pulled out his gun and said that he was planning to kill himself.

Jean drove around in circles for about a half hour, then pulled into the parking lot at Kim's Liquor in Monterey Park. They sat in the car and talked for an hour or two but they weren't getting anywhere.

Finally, frustrated, confused, not sure what he wanted to do, Blackie pointed the gun at her and told her to drive. After a while he had her pull over and let him out at Poncy's Bar, one of his old haunts. Jean drove away.

"So I went to this beer joint I hung out in," Blackie said. "I had the gun in my belt and a sweater on. When I walked in the door and unbuttoned the sweater, here's this big gun. I ordered a beer and three people headed for the phone. I just drank my beer and the police came and threw the net over me."

The police showed up at about 8 P.M. and arrested him for kidnapping, suspicion of robbery, and possession of a firearm by a convicted felon.

It was a very serious parole violation. He could have been sent back to prison to complete his life sentence.

For once he was lucky. He had an understanding parole officer who listened to his story and convinced the district attorney to file lesser charges. On February 10, 1971, he pleaded guilty to the one charge of possessing a firearm and was sentenced to four months in the county jail.

At the recommendation, however, of his Los Angeles parole agent, Donald Risner, and also of Franklin Drucker, M.D., a staff psychiatrist with the Parole Outpatient Clinic, his parole was revoked and he was sent to the STRU program at the minimum-security prison at Chino.

Risner summed up the reasons for his recommendation as "to interrupt his obvious pattern of self-destruction. Confinement in STRU would afford Schwamb as well as the parole agent time to formulate an adequate release program and time for Schwamb to resolve some of the interpersonal problems which seem to have beset him recently."

Drucker, who came to the same conclusion, noted that "Schwamb blames his problems on alcohol and women. He has been married three times. He has been with his most recent girlfriend [Jean] for approximately twenty months but their relationship has been a stormy one, as have other relationships with other women in his life. He plans now to end the relationship with this woman; as to future relationships, he says, 'I'll find one, I don't like to be alone.'"

Describing Blackie's demeanor during his examination, Drucker said, "Schwamb was alert, oriented and cooperative. Speech was relevant and goal-directed. No bizarre behavior was observed. He was quite dependent, self-deprecatory and self-uncertain but did not appear suicidally depressed, agitated or unduly pessimistic. He showed little insight. Judgment marked by an impulsive pattern of self-destructive and self-defeating behaviors."

Chino is not far from Ontario and San Bernardino, where Blackie had been to spring training. He was only forty-four, but in bad shape when he got there on March 12, 1971. He was sick, malnourished, his joints aching constantly, and not at all completely dried out from booze.

There were group-counseling sessions every day in which, according to Blackie, "all the liars got to tell their stories."

Once his health improved a little, he was assigned a job as assistant to Lieutenant Joe Pagano, the recreation director. "He was a very skilled con man," recalled Pagano. "I just sat back and let him order our athletic equipment. The stuff he could promote, at little or no cost, was pretty amazing. A very glib, outgoing guy. He was fun to work with, fun to be with as long as he wasn't drinking."

He'd also become a snitch. Though he'd had more than his fair share of battles with authority, Ralph had always been politically conservative. "A Goldwater Republican if there ever was one," said Bob Hunter. The 1970s were a very tough time in California's prisons. There had been a lot of significant changes since Blackie had last served time. Chino, like most other prisons, was being taken over by gangs, many of which were financing themselves with drug trafficking. Blackie had always hated gangs and dope.

"The administration [at Chino] used him as a fink," said Pagano, "to help get the drugs under control. Ralph helped us find the ringleaders. I think the guards would slip him a bottle [of booze] now and again [in payment] and get him a safe place to drink and sleep it off."

At Chino Ralph also took night classes. In particular he enjoyed writing and helped convince L. T. Rogers, a journalist from Ontario who taught English at the prison for several years, to start up a creative writing course. "Ralph was far and away the most talented guy I ran across while teaching at Chino," said Rogers. "He was very serious about it, wanted to get published.

"He wrote some short stories, kind of cops and robbers stuff. He wrote interesting characters. His plots were right out of the old pulp magazines, but he definitely had ability."

Chino also had a softball team, but with his shoulders and knees in almost constant pain, Blackie didn't play. Pagano felt a little bad about the only time that he managed to talk him into playing. "He trudged slowly out to right field and stood there looking awkward and uncomfortable. When the inning was over he walked slowly back in with his head down and just kept walking, away from the field."

He got out on October 6, 1971. Once again his mother picked him up at the prison gate. She helped him find a small apartment. It was in Inglewood, near his old haunts, but by then in what was considered a bad neighborhood. His landlady told him about a possible opening with a freight forwarding company that worked out of a warehouse at the airport, which was just a couple of miles to the west.

"I got all cleaned up, put on a suit, and went down there. I was dressed better than the general manager. I didn't know what kind of job it was, I thought it was sales or something. But it was driving. So I said, 'When can I start?' It was about noon. I started an hour later."

Bea Franklin was the operations manager, Ralph's boss, and they became friendly. Eventually she told him that she was going through a bad divorce and was getting worried for herself and her young daughter, Denise, because her husband was making threats.

"I'd never even taken her out to lunch, nothin'," said Ralph. "She was my boss, that's all. But she treated me so great. So I went home with her one night just to talk with this turkey. It was a hilarious situation. I had on a suit and a tie and he had on a pair of jeans and a short-sleeve shirt. I said to him, 'How come you're hassling Bea, making her all nervous around this baby and everything?'

"He's maybe five feet ten inches, a hundred and seventy or something like that. He says, 'It's none of your business, what are you doing around here?'

"I said, 'Well, I happen to like Bea, and she's a nervous wreck around work, not getting her job done. She puts a lot of pressure on all of us; five or six of us guys rely on her for their assignments.'

"He says, 'Tough shit,' pulls up his shirt sleeves and says, 'you'd better not fool around.' He had a small tattoo. He said, 'I was in the joint.'

"So I said, 'Oh a tattoo, Jesus.' I went to the kitchen and made myself a drink. I took off my coat, put it over a chair, took off my tie and I unbuttoned my shirtsleeves and rolled them up and his mouth just dropped. It should have been on the stage. Then the whole thing started working and I looked at him and said, 'You think you're going to pull that shit on me.' I didn't lay a hand on him. I just told him, 'Get your shit out of this house and stay away from her and that baby.' And he did."

Blackie's arms were totally covered with tattoos, most of them hideous, misshapen black blotches that had been done more to kill time in the cell than for any reasonable aesthetic purpose. They were instantly recognizable to anyone who'd spent time in prison.

"I was on this Dudley Do-Right kick. I probably would have lost her if I'd beat him up, or hurt him."

Instead, he won her over and they moved in together. Ralph wanted to get married, but Bea wouldn't go for it. She thought it was easier for her to remain independent if they just lived together. He loved her daughter and was a good, even attentive, father. Bea said that she thinks he fell in love with Denise before he did with her.

For the first time since he'd been a child he was settled and happy. He was drinking too much, as always, but doing it mostly at home other than when he'd take Bea out for the evening. With Bea and Denise he felt like he had at long last found peace, happiness, and acceptance. They had a calming influence on him that no one in his past had ever managed.

Life was good. He was in his mid-forties, healthy, happy, and the future was looking bright. But it couldn't stay that way. It never had. He wondered why it was that every time things seemed like they were starting to go his way, something would happen to cause him pain.

He hurt his back, badly, offloading a shipment at the airport. He couldn't get up or down the short flight of stairs at the house. One of Denise's earliest memories is of him on his hands and knees, in pain that brought tears to his eyes, trying to get down the stairs.

At first he got into a medical group that emphasized physical therapy, anything short of the operating table. He endured terrible suffering for nearly two years. Eventually surgery was the only option and it made things better, but his back would continue to give him trouble the rest of his life.

Workman's compensation paid off for the injury and when he was feeling better, Ralph took Bea to Jamaica with the money. It was a week that she remembers as the best time they ever had together. The last night they had a room-service dinner on the balcony of their hotel room, overlooking the ocean. Bea ordered duck à l'orange and everything felt just perfect. "Here I was, just a country girl from Oklahoma, the only fowl I knew was fried chicken."

When they came back they both found work with another freight forwarding company, but then Ralph tripped on a loose step and fell at their apartment house. He'd broken his knee, but at first it was misdiagnosed and wrongly treated. He sued the owners of the apartment building and the doctors he had first seen. It took about a year and a half, until April 1977, before the suits were settled.

That same year, on September 13, having caused no problems since leaving Chino, he was formally discharged from his parole. At long last he was totally free from the system.

With seven thousand dollars from the settlements, Bea, Denise, and Ralph moved to the far northeast reaches of Los Angeles County, to the high desert town of Palmdale. For a time he worked for the state, doing grounds maintenance work at Lake Castaic and parks in the area. But his back deteriorated and then he mostly stayed home while Bea supported the family. Every so often, when he felt better, he'd work a few shifts across the street at Shamrock Liquors, but the money from that didn't even pay his tab.

His mother, Janet, died in 1983. She was seventy-nine and died in bed at her own home in Hawthorne where she had lived most of the years after Ralph went to prison. On her death certificate, in box number eighteen, "Kind of Industry or Business," it says "Homemaking." She had fought hard for many years, mostly against the ravages of alcohol, to keep her family together. She hadn't been successful, but when she died every far-flung member of the Schwamb family, including all of Blackie's ex-wives, felt a deep sense of loss.

Ralph got work as a dispatcher with a cement company, but that didn't last long. The weekend after the company went broke, he and Bea went out on a boat with some friends to the Channel Islands. He slipped on the deck and blew a disk in his back. That required another surgery.

Stuck at home he'd drink and read until he was too drunk to read, then he'd find sports to watch on TV. He could still get around enough to be sociable and do housework. "It totally broke his spirit when he injured his back," says Denise. "His disability took away his manhood. He played Mr. Mom while my mom worked." Ralph was surprisingly good, and even cheerful some of the time about his role as homemaker. He liked to cook and taught Denise how.

Every Friday night he'd take the family out and as always he would overtip and flirt shamelessly with the waitresses no matter who was around. "We'd go out and he'd have the waitresses falling all over him," Bea recalled. "A friend once asked me if it bothered me, and no, it didn't. He just always tried to make every woman feel special. He had a lot of class. Not a lot of men take the time to cultivate that side of themselves. He'd order a huge amount of expensive food. Then, by the time the food came he had drunk so much that he never wanted to eat much of it. He always had expensive taste."

At least his tastes had modified a little. A few years after they had gotten together, Janet, Ralph's mother, told Bea, "Thanks for getting him out of those five-hundred-dollar suits and bringing him down to earth."

He no longer lived anything even approximating the high life, but apparently his old fast-lane friends hadn't completely forgotten him. "Sometimes, when we needed money," recalled Bea, "he would make a call and in a day or two money would just show up in our mailbox. He said it was because he kept quiet. His favorite saying was, 'Do your own time.'"

He had a terrible, debilitating cough from smoking but he didn't even try to stop. And drinking was a constant, from the first Budweiser of the morning to the last whiskey and 7-Up at night.

"He was always happiest when he was drinking," said Denise. "When he was drinking he was generous, fun, and kind. When he was sober he was volatile and angry, you had to walk on eggshells around him."

Denise loved him as the only father she knew and he reciprocated. "He taught me how to drive," she said. "We had five acres of undeveloped land behind the house and we'd go out there and drive around the trees. One time I hit a bump and ended up going into a ditch. He had a high-ball in his hand and didn't even spill a drop. Sometimes he would just show up at school and take me out to breakfast. No special reason, he just always tried to find ways to make things special.

"As a dad he mostly tried to steer me certain ways, not boss me around. He was strict about curfew and who I hung out with. But I could always sit down with him and tell him everything."

It's not easy for Bea to talk about her last year with Ralph. "His disability didn't cause any stress between me and him, but it did finish him personally. The last year, his equilibrium was shot; he would just fall down a lot. He was a night owl and you could hear him falling down in the middle of the night. He also developed paperthin skin, you could just touch him and he would start bleeding. He would get so frustrated he would just break down crying."

Toward the end, like many people do, Blackie became reflective. At the end of the *Sport* magazine article back in 1966, he'd written, "easy time is the hardest time of all. It looks like a gas—lots of drinks and goodtime pals and sweet women—but it's not a gas. It's the gas pipe."

Twenty years later, three years before he died, he said, "It wasn't all tears, my life, the whole thing. And it certainly wasn't all laughs. I like to feel there were a lot more laughs. I always felt that something good would be right around the corner. Usually it's worked out that way. I chose my own path, I always have."

On December 15, 1989, he went into the hospital in Lancaster, California. Everyone thought it was for pneumonia but the next day the doctor told him that he was in the end stages of lung cancer. It had been diagnosed six months before, but he hadn't told anybody.

In the hospital he told Bea and Denise that he didn't want a funeral or a grave. He wanted to be cremated and wanted a big party where everyone would get roaring drunk. He wanted his ashes to be scattered on the pitcher's mound at a baseball stadium. Or if that couldn't be arranged, he wanted them put in empty Budweiser cans on top of the TV so that his friends and family could watch sports events with him.

Six days later, at seven forty in the evening, his heart stopped beating and Blackie Schwamb died. It was four days before Christmas. Bea returned all the gifts that were waiting for him to open. Denise had bought him a big *Time-Life* coffee table book about baseball. She gave it to her grandfather instead. He was cremated just after the holiday and Bea took the box of ashes home to her mother's house, where to this day they sit in a closet.

"He always hated that house," said Denise.

Jim Muhe, Blackie's oldest pal, remembered the last time he saw him. Muhe was the clubhouse manager at Dodger Stadium and Blackie would show up for several games a year.

> I never shunned Ralph. I would always say hello when I saw him at the stadium. I knew him, but I didn't know him. I don't think anybody ever really knew what made him tick. An odd guy, with a sad life.
>
> I guess the last time I saw him was around 1980. I was working before a game at the stadium and an usher came up to me and told me that there was some big old guy out in the hall who wanted to see me. I went out and there was Ralph. Cripes, he was fifty-four, but he looked ninety-five.
>
> Houston was in town and I knew that Les Moss, their coach, had mentioned Ralph so I took Ralph in [to the clubhouse] and he and Les had a nice little chat about the good old days. Then Al Rosen came over, he was the general manager of the [Houston] Astros, and stuck his head in and raved about what a great pitcher Ralph was. Just three old-time ballplayers talking about the good old days.
>
> Anyway, it got to be the time where all visitors had to be out of the clubhouse, so I led Ralph back out to the hall. And I looked up and he had tears in his eyes. And he said, "You know Jim, I really could have been something."
>
> I guess I got a little misty-eyed myself. What could you say to the guy? He had ruined his life, and a few others along the

way. You have to live with yourself, and sometimes that's punishment enough.

So the game is about to start and I stick my head out of the
dugout and look for Ralph, he told me his seat number. And he's
way up there in those cheap blue seats behind the right field foul
pole. Just sitting there, all by himself, puffing on a cigarette. Who
knows what he was thinking?

APPENDIX

RALPH "BLACKIE" SCHWAMB'S PITCHING STATISTICS

YEAR	TEAM	LEAGUE	G	IP	H	R	ER	SO	BB	W	L	ERA
1947	Aberdeen	Northern	6	50	32	13	9	31	19	5	0	1.62
1947	Globe-Miami	Ariz-Tex	10	65	55	34	30	66	34	3	3	4.15
1947	Ciudad Obregón[1]	Northern Mexico	n/a	n/a	n/a	n/a	n/a	n/a	n/a	3	1	n/a
1948	Toledo	American Assoc.	25	77	79	54	44	45	52	1	9	5.14
1948	St. Louis Browns	American	12	32	44	34	30	7	21	1	1	8.53
1949	Little Rock	Southern Assoc.	3	19	21	5	5	4	4	2	0	2.37
1949	Sherbrooke	Quebec Province	12	44	36	28	28	22	32	4	4	5.73
1950– 1958	S. Quentin Folsom[2]	CA semi- pro	n/a	1,494 (Est.)	n/a	n/a	299	1,565	240	131	35	1.80
1961	Hawaii	Pacific Coast	6	21	27	16	12	9	0	1	2	5.14

[1] Pitched and played infield, mostly shortstop. The local newspapers didn't cover all the games and his team, the Ciudad Obregón Yaquis, though it still exists, doesn't have records dating back to 1947. Newspaper accounts make it clear that he was the team's top pitcher, both as starter and then in relief, and was also an excellent hitter.

[2] These are Schwamb's own statistics for his prison pitching career. They seem reasonable projecting from the incomplete reporting in the prison newspapers—

CAREER COTALS[3]

	G	IP	H	R	ER	SO	BB	W	L	ERA
Minor Leagues	62	276	250	150	128	177	141	17	19	4.17
Major League	12	32	44	34	30	7	21	1	1	8.53
Total (incl. prison)	n/a	1,802	n/a	n/a	457	1,749	402	149	55	2.28

the *San Quentin News* and the *Folsom Observer.* He also played nearly one-third of his prison games at shortstop and led his league in batting three times.

   A Note on Prison Competition: His prison games were played against semipro teams, most of which included numerous major and triple-A minor-league players in the off-season. He was backed up by completely amateur teams and, most difficult of all for a pitcher, amateur catchers who were not even close to minor-league standards. The prison yards were easy "hitters fields."

3 Career totals are incomplete because of the lack of statistics for his play in Mexico, missing stats from prison and the Quebec Province League's only accounting for earned runs, not total runs, scored against a pitcher.

BIBLIOGRAPHY

BOOKS

Adair, Robert K. *The Physics of Baseball*. 3rd ed. New York: Perennial, 2002.

American Psychiatric Association. *Diagnostic and Statistical Manual of Mental Disorders*. 3rd ed. American Psychiatric Press, 1987.

Bojorquez, Alfonso Araújo, *Historia de la Liga de la Costa del Pacífico 1945–1958*. Ciudad Obregón, México (Collection Biblioteca Municipal Ciudad Obregón).

Borst, Bill. *Still Last in the American League: The St. Louis Browns Revisited*. West Bloomfield, MI: Altwerger and Mandel Publishing, 1992.

Bowman, Lynn. *Los Angeles: Epic of a City*. Berkeley, CA: Howell-North Books, 1974.

Braly, Malcolm. *False Starts: A Memoir of San Quentin and Other Prisons*. New York: Little Brown and Company, 1976.

Bryant, Clora, Buddy Collette, William Green, Steven Isoardi, Jack Kelson, Horace Tapscott, Gerald Wilson, and Marl Young, eds. *Central Avenue Sounds: Jazz in Los Angeles*. Berkeley, CA: University of California Press, 1998.

Bunker, Edward. *Education of a Felon: A Memoir*. New York: St. Martin's Press, 2000.

Caughey, John, and LaRee Caughey. *Los Angeles: Biography of a City*. Berkeley, CA: University of California Press, 1976.

Clifton, Merritt. *Disorganized Baseball: History of Quebec Provincial League, 1890–1976.* Samisdat Press, 1990.

Cohen, Michael Mickey, as told to John Peer Nugent. *Mickey Cohen, In My Own Words.* Englewood Cliffs, NJ: Prentice-Hall, 1975.

Dawes, Amy. *Sunset Boulevard: Cruising the Heart of Los Angeles.* Los Angeles: Los Angeles Times Books, 2002.

Duffy, Warden Clinton T., as told to Dean Jennings. *The San Quentin Story.* Garden City, New York: Doubleday, 1954.

Duren, Ryne, and Robert Drury. *The Comeback.* Dayton, OH: Lorenz Press, 1978.

Editors of Time-Life Books. *This Fabulous Century, Vol. IV, 1930–1940.* New York: Time-Life Books, 1969.

——. *This Fabulous Century, Vol. V, 1940–1950.* New York: Time-Life Books, 1969.

Gebhard, David, and Harriette Von Breton. *Los Angeles in the Thirties: 1931–1941.* Los Angeles: Hennessey & Ingalls. 1989.

Golenbock, Peter. *The Spirit of St. Louis: A History of the St. Louis Cardinals and Browns.* New York: Avon Books, 2000.

Hawkins, John C. *This Date in Baltimore Orioles & St. Louis Browns History: The Complete History of the Franchise in Text, Statistics, and Photos.* New York: Stein and Day, 1982.

Heimann, Jim. *Sins of the City: The Real Los Angeles Noir.* San Francisco: Chronicle Books, 1999.

Henstell, Bruce. *Los Angeles: An Illustrated History.* New York: Knopf, 1980.

Hetrick, J. Thomas. *Chris Von der Ahe and the St. Louis Browns.* Lanham, MD: Scarecrow Press, 1999.

Kaiser, David. *Epic Season: The 1948 American League Pennant Race.* Amherst: University of Massachusetts Press, 1998.

Kerrane, Kevin. *Dollar Sign on the Muscle.* New York: Beaufort Books, Inc. 1984.

Klein, Norman M., and Martin J. Schiesl, eds. *Twentieth-Century Los Angeles: Power, Promotion, and Social Conflict.* Claremont, CA: Regina Books, 1990.

Longstreet, Stephen. *All-Star Cast: An Anecdotal History of Los Angeles.* New York: Thomas Y. Crowell, 1977.

Mazon, Mauricio. *The Zoot Suit Riots: The Psychology of Symbolic Annihilation.* Austin: University of Texas Press, 1984.

Mead, William B. *Even the Browns: The Zany, True Story of Baseball in the Early Forties.* Chicago: Contemporary Books, 1978.

McCutcheon, Marc. *The Writer's Guide to Everyday Life from Prohibition through World War II.* Cincinnati, OH: Writer's Digest Books, 1995.

McWilliams, Carey. *Southern California: An Island on the Land.* Salt Lake City, UT: Gibbs Smith, 1973.

Munn, Michael. *The Hollywood Connection: The Mafia and the Movie Business—the Explosive Story.* London: Robson Books, 1993.

O'Neal, Bill. *The Pacific Coast League 1903–1988.* Austin, TX: Eakin Press, 1990.

Parrish, Michael. *For the People: Inside the Los Angeles County District Attorney's Office 1850–2000.* Santa Monica, CA: Angel City Press, 2001.

Pitt, Leonard, and Dale Pitt. *Los Angeles A to Z: An Encyclopedia of the City and County.* Berkeley, CA: University of California Press, 1997.

Porter, Tana Mosier. *Toledo Profile: A Sesquicentennial History.* Toledo, OH: Toledo Sesquicentennial Commission, 1987.

Seymour, Harold. *Baseball: The People's Game.* New York: Oxford University Press, 1990.

Note: The following four books are part of what is a seven-volume (and hopefully growing) history of the state of California written by Kevin Starr, the state's librarian. For anyone with an interest in California history, or for that matter anyone who just enjoys beautifully written, thoughtful, provocative, informative and extremely well-researched history, I highly recommend the entire series. They were invaluable to my research and most important, a joy to read.

Starr, Kevin. *Material Dreams: Southern California through the 1920s.* New York: Oxford University Press, 1990.

———. *Endangered Dreams: The Great Depression in California.* New York: Oxford University Press, 1996.

———. *The Dream Endures: California Enters the 1940s.* New York: Oxford University Press, 1997.

———. *Embattled Dreams: California in War and Peace 1940–1950.* New York: Oxford University Press, 2002.

Stoker, Charles. *Thicker 'n Thieves*. Santa Monica, CA: Sidereal Company, 1951.

Weigand, Glorianne. *Dusty Trails Again*. Klamath Falls, OR: Graphic Press, 1997.

Weinstock, Matt. *My L.A.* New York: Current Books, 1947.

Wolf, Marvin J., and Katherine Mader. *Fallen Angels: Chronicles of L.A. Crime and Mystery*. New York: Facts on File Publications, 1986.

Woody, Clara T., and Milton L. Schwartz. *Globe, Arizona*. Tucson: Arizona Historical Society, 1977.

Wright, David K. *Ohio*. Emeryville, CA: Avalon Travel Publications, 1999.

Writers' Program of the Work Projects Administration. *Los Angeles: A Guide to the City and Its Environs*. 2nd ed. New York: Hastings House, 1951.

MAGAZINE & NEWSPAPER ARTICLES

Boyle, Robert H. "Fight On, For Sing Sing U." *Sports Illustrated*, January 23, 1967, 29–37.

Braly, Malcolm. "Prison Games and Other Escapes." *Sports Illustrated*, August 10, 1970, 48–55.

McConnell, Jim. "Then and Now. Schwamb Squandered His Baseball Talents." *Pasadena Star-News*, May 5, 1997.

Schwamb, Ralph, with Arnold Hano. "An Open Letter to Hank Thompson." *Sport Magazine*, August 1966.

WEB SITES

www.Baseball-almanac.com

www.BaseballLibrary.com

www.Baseball-reference.com

www.Coastleague.com

www.Combinedfleet.com

www.erha.org (Electric Railway Historical Association of Southern California)

http://wiwi.essortment.com/toledowar_rzxq.htm (P. J. Gladnick, *Toledo War: battle between Michigan and Ohio*) www.vino.demon.co.uk/tarling/lois.html (Lois from Montana's page on Tarling Family history)

www.LosAngelesalmanac.com

www.geocities.com/~zybt/index.html (Paul R. Machula's Web site on Arizona history)

www.geocities.com/big_bunko/minor.html (Mike McCann's page of Minor League Baseball History)

www.minersadvice.co.uk/index.htm (Miner's Advice—U.K.)

www.history.navy.mil/index.html (Naval Historical Center)

www.Retrosheet.org

www.Streetswing.com

http://www.attic.utoledo.edu (Toledo's Attic, a Virtual Museum of Toledo, Ohio)

www.wikipedia.com

INDEX

ACKNOWLEDGMENTS

RESEARCH

JIM MCCONNELL of the *Pasadena Star-News* made a generous and significant contribution to this book. At one time he too had considered writing a biography of Ralph Schwamb and for a variety of reasons it didn't work out. Before he put his project to rest, he had interviewed a number of people for his book. Some of those people died before I had a chance to interview them myself and in some cases memories faded over the years between Jim's and my interview with the same person. Jim very graciously provided me with transcripts of his interviews and allowed me to use them in any way that I saw fit. Excerpts from his interviews are used throughout the text, in some cases on their own and in some cases in conjunction with quotes from my own interviews with the same person. In particular I want to thank Jim for providing me with the story from Jim Muhe—who died before I could interview him—that ends the book. It wasn't easy figuring out a way to end a book about a guy who simply smoked himself to death, but thanks to Jim I got it.

Specifically, Jim provided me with transcripts of his interviews with the following people, ten of whom (their names are in italics) I was unable to interview myself: *Hank Arft, Roger Bowman,* Jim Bryant, Cliff Dapper, Bob Dillinger, *Jack Fournier, Jack Graham, Bob Hunter,* Don

Lenhardt, Frank Mancuso, *Jim Muhe,* Joe Ostrowski, Joe Pagano, *Evo Pusich, Bill Rigney, L. T. Rogers,* Joe Schultz, Bud Watkins, and *Al Zarilla.*

The extended SCHWAMB FAMILY, including members of Nell's family, in particular Rich and Merry, whose interest in a story that at times has been personally painful to hear, led them to assisting me in obtaining certain research material that otherwise would have been unavailable. Bea and Denise, who were generous with their time and collection of family photographs. Deb and Mark, Paul, Laura, and Karen. Lois Kenczka for her fantastic genealogical research. And of course Ralph Schwamb himself, who spent the better part of a week putting up with my questions and who only threatened to slug me once during that time.

A number of other people were very helpful in my research. Rebecca Blinn, Nina Corbin, Diane Gagel, and Elizabeth Walsh tracked down and made photocopies of newspaper articles on my behalf (they were paid for their efforts) in cities that I didn't have the time or budget to travel to. Cheryl Baker, librarian for Modoc County, California, helped to answer a lot of my questions about her community. Dennis Carter, librarian at the Folsom Prison Museum, helped me to obtain access to materials that are normally off limits to the public. Dr. Julia Eilenberg and Dr. Kathleen Scanlan, who provided valuable professional insights.

I'd also like to thank Sheila Cole and Barbara Harris, both of whom helped me to finally crack through the bureaucratic malaise and obtain copies of Ralph Schwamb's military and prison records.

The following people were interviewed for the book and/or provided important pieces of the puzzle: Bea Franklin, Ferd Borsch, Jim Bryant, Edward Bunker, Cece Carlucci, Merritt Clifton, Cliff Dapper, Deb, Denise, Bob Dillinger, Ryne Duren, Owen Friend, Ned Garver, Woodie Held, Tom Jordan, Laura, Don Lenhardt, Don Lund, Gene Mauch, Frank Mancuso, Gil McDougald, Merry, Sgt. John Moore, Les Moss, Ray Nemec, Irv Noren, Joe Ostrowski, Joe Pagano, Rich, Arthur Richman, Joe Schultz, Roy Sievers, Roy Smalley, Chuck Stevens, Fred Stone, Martin Stone, Dave Thies, Bud Watkins, William Weiss, Bill Werle.

PERSONAL

Meredith and Win Blevins, who not only encouraged me through the whole process of writing, but who gave the first draft its first critical read and were then kind and sensitive yet firm with their suggestions on how to improve it.

Jonathan Friedland and Victoria Godfrey, who also read the first draft, praising it where it deserved praise and tearing it up where it needed that.

Charles Fleming, who helped me greatly with the original book proposal, something that was invaluable in helping me to focus on the theme and structure of the book.

Nat Sobel, my agent, whose faith in this book and persistence on its behalf despite an initial avalanche of rejections, is the reason it has seen print.

Eva Eilenberg, who lives with me and whom I love and who has patiently listened to a whole lot more than she ever wanted to hear about Blackie Schwamb.

My mother, Elaine Stone, and my father, Martin Stone, for both the nature and the nurture that created my love of baseball, economics, history, Los Angeles, politics, and storytelling.

ABOUT THE AUTHOR

Eric Stone is a longtime journalist, specializing in the economics and politics of Asia, rather than in sports. He is a native, current resident, and booster of Los Angeles and a lifelong Dodgers fan. He's also the author of *The Living Room of the Dead,* the first of the Ray Sharp series of detective novels.